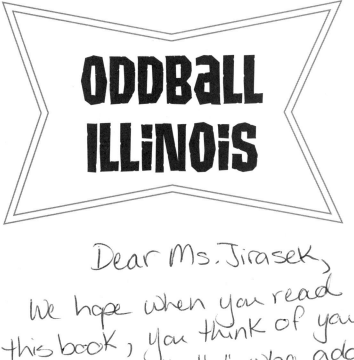

ODDBALL ILLINOIS

Dear Ms. Jirasek,

We hope when you read this book, you think of your two little "oddballs" who adore you, Max & Leo. I hope this helps inspire some local travels on your retirement.

Love, The Balingits

ODDBALL ILLINOIS

A Guide to 450 Really
STRANGE PLACES

2nd Edition

JEROME POHLEN

CHICAGO
REVIEW
PRESS

Published by Chicago Review Press, Incorporated
814 North Franklin Street
Chicago, Illinois 60610
ISBN 978-1-61374-032-3

The author has made every effort to secure permissions for all the material in this book.
If any acknowledgment has been inadvertently omitted, please contact the author.

Cover design: Mel Kupfer
Cover layout and interior design: Jonathan Hahn
Cover photograph: Jerome Pohlen
All interior images from the author's collection unless otherwise noted.

Library of Congress Cataloging-in-Publication Data
Pohlen, Jerome.
Oddball Illinois : a guide to 450 really strange places / Jerome Pohlen. — Second edition.
pages cm
Includes index.
ISBN 978-1-61374-032-3 (pbk.)
1. Illinois—Guidebooks. 2. Curiosities and wonders—Illinois—Guidebooks. 3. Illinois—
History, Local—Miscellanea. I. Title.

F539.3.P64 2012
977.3—dc23

2011049472

Printed in the United States of America
5 4 3 2 1

TO JiM FROST,
WHO talked Me iNto
MY FiRSt road trip

CONTENTS

INTRODUCTION

Whenthe first edition of *Oddball Illinois* was published a decade ago, I secretly worried that the state's weirdest days were behind it, that the forces of "good taste" and homogeneity were winning. Boy, was I wrong. Like a statewide game of Whack-a-Mole, every time a tacky tourist trap closed its doors, another popped up somewhere else. Berwyn's *Spindle*, eight cars impaled on a giant spike that appeared on the cover of my first book, is now gone, but say hello to Horrorbles, a garish ghouleteria in the same town. Arcola's Raggedy Ann and Andy Museum may be gone, but just down the highway you can now find a life-sized, coin-operated, fire-breathing dragon. That's right—put in Illinois terms, the bland Jim Edgars are being replaced by the cable-ready Rod Blagojeviches.

Better still, some of the strangest attractions from the first edition have been expanded and improved. Not long ago, the World's Biggest Abe Lincoln was given a new index finger and a fresh coat of paint. The good folks of Gays just built a charming park to surround their two-story outhouse, and Alton recently turned its Piasa petroglyph into a picnic pullout. The town of Chester had only a Popeye statue in 2000, but 10 years later you can find monuments to Olive Oyl, Swee' Pea, Castor Oyl, Bluto, Wimpy, the Sea Hag, and more around town.

None of this should suggest that you take these roadside gems for granted, that if you wait long enough there will be even more to see. Shortly after my first book was published, a new attraction, the Museum of Funeral Customs, opened in Springfield. But before I could include it in this edition, it met its own untimely demise. Nothing is certain, not even a museum of taxes or death. Besides, do you think gas is going to stay at the low, low price of four dollars per gallon forever? GO!

While I've made every attempt to give clear directions from major streets and landmarks, you could still become lost on your journey. Don't panic. Think of it as part of the adventure, and remember these tips:

1. **Stop and ask!** For a lot of communities, their Oddball attraction might be their only claim to fame. Locals are often thrilled that you'd drive out of your way to marvel at their underappreciated shrine. But choose your guides wisely; old cranks at the town café are good sources; pimply teenage clerks at the 7-Eleven are not.
2. **Call ahead.** Few Oddball sites keep regular hours, but most will gladly wait around if they know you're coming. This eliminates the infuriating possibility that you'll find yourself standing just outside the World's Largest Collection of Bottle Caps reading a "Gone Fishin'" sign on the door.
3. **Don't give up.** It often happens that your brain starts to shout, "This is stupid!" while you're driving down a country road looking for the World's Largest Bedbug. Perhaps it is stupid, but ask yourself, is it any stupider than waiting an hour for a table at Planet Hollywood?
4. **Don't trespass!** Once you get to where you're going, don't become a Terrible Tourist. Just because somebody built a sculpture garden in their front yard doesn't mean they're looking for drop-ins.

Do you have an Oddball site of your own? Have I missed anything? Do you know of an oddball site that should be included in an updated version? Please write and let me know: Jerome Pohlen, c/o Chicago Review Press, 814 N. Franklin St., Chicago, IL, 60610.

CHICAGO! CHICAGO!

Chicago has been called many things, so it's odd that it has adopted "The Windy City" and "The Second City" as its nicknames. Both were originally intended as put-downs.

Contrary to popular belief, Chicago is not exceptionally windy. The average wind speed is 10.4 mph, much calmer than in many towns. "The Windy City" is instead a nickname coined by Charles Dana of the *New York Sun*, who was criticizing city boosters as loudmouthed windbags. When Chicago and New York were bidding on the 1893 Columbian Exposition, he advised his readers to "pay no attention to the nonsensical claims of that Windy City. Its people could not hold a World's Fair, even if they won it." Well, Chicago did both, but still the name stuck.

"The Second City" was the title of a derisive piece about Chicago in *The New Yorker* in 1951. It was written by reporter A. J. Liebling, who accused Windy City folk of always wanting to be everything New York already was. Again, rather than taking it as an insult, Chicago's citizenry adopted it.

These nicknames are much better than titles like "Hog Butcher Capital of the World" or "Porkopolis" and much preferred to "The Stinky Onion." The word *Chicago* is a bastardization of *Checagou*, meaning "wild onion" or "stinky onion," a common plant in the swamps along the river. Early settlers spelled the Native American term Schuerkaigo, Shikkago, Ztschaggo, Stachango, and Psceshaggo, among others, according to Bill Bryson's *Made in America* (1994). Thank goodness they settled on Chicago.

WHO'S BADMOUTHING CHICAGO?

More than a few writers have weighed in on Chicago's merits, or lack of them:

Nelson Algren: "Loving Chicago is like loving a woman with a broken nose."

Saul Bellow: "You can say this about Chicago—there is no hypocrisy problem there. There's no need for hypocrisy. Everyone's proud of being a bastard."

Arnold Bennett: "Chicago: a mushroom and a filthy suburb of Warsaw."

Theodore Dreiser: "Chicago, a gaudy circus beginning with the two-bit whore in the alley crib."

E. M. Forster: "Chicago—a facade of skyscrapers facing a lake and behind the facade every type of dubiousness."

John Gunther: "Chicago is as full of crooks as a saw with teeth."

Rudyard Kipling: "Having seen [Chicago], I urgently desire never to see it again. It is inhabited by savages. Its water is the water of the Hughli, and its air is dirt."

D. H. Lawrence: "It rained and fogged in Chicago and muddy-flowing people oozed thick in the canyon-beds of the streets. Yet it seemed to me more alive and more real than New York."

Shane Leslie: "Chicago has all the possibilities of becoming the earth's final city, the Babylon of the Plains."

Ashley Montagu: "Hell has been described as a pocket edition of Chicago."

Louella Parsons: "There are two types of people in this country. There are the ones who love Chicago and the ones who think it is unmitigated hell."

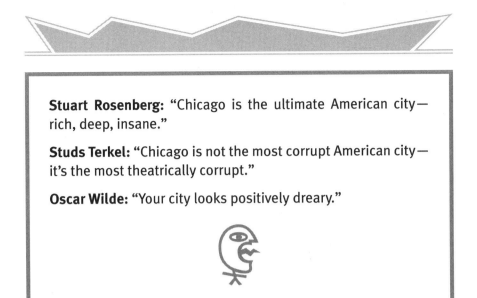

Stuart Rosenberg: "Chicago is the ultimate American city—rich, deep, insane."

Studs Terkel: "Chicago is not the most corrupt American city—it's the most theatrically corrupt."

Oscar Wilde: "Your city looks positively dreary."

What Goes Up
What They Rarely Tell You on the Architecture Tour

Chicago has a lot to be proud of when it comes to architecture. It invented the skyscraper. It has North America's tallest building. And when Frank Lloyd Wright designed a mile-tall, sunshine-blocking superscraper with atomic-powered elevators, did he propose it be built in New York? Absolutely not! It was Chicago where his massive ego felt at home.

There are some, however, who don't see tall buildings as architectural advancements. They block the light, diminish the humans who live and work in them, and invite a messy form of suicide. Well, the war's over, gang, and the skyscrapers won. Here are a few you should check out on any Chicago visit.

Site of the World's First Skyscraper

Most architectural historians now agree that the 10-story Home Insurance Building, designed in 1884 by William LeBaron Jenney and completed in 1885, was the world's first skyscraper. A skyscraper is defined as a tall building supported by an interior steel structure where the exterior walls bear no weight.

Jenney never lived to receive his due, nor did the Home Insurance Building. His groundbreaking accomplishment was not acknowledged

until the building was being torn down in 1931. Historians got a good look at the interior structure as the wrecking ball leveled the innovation floor by floor. Yep, they were demolishing a landmark. Now all there is to look at is a bank.

135 S. LaSalle St., Chicago, IL 60602

No phone

Hours: Torn down

Cost: Free

Directions: On the northeast corner of LaSalle and Adams Sts.

~~Sears~~ Willis Tower

When the Petronas Towers in Malaysia bested the ~~Sears~~ Willis Tower for World's Tallest Building in 1996, American architects had to look around for a new way to brag, and for a time the ~~Sears~~ Willis Tower could still claim it had the highest occupied floor and highest top roof, though those eventually were bested, too. Now it has to be satisfied being North America's Tallest Building. It all makes you wonder if Freud had a point.

Regardless, it is hard not to be impressed by this building. Built in 1973, it's 1,454 feet tall (1,707 if you count the antennas), weighs 222,500 tons, offers 4.5 million square feet of office space (that's 101 acres), and contains enough concrete to build a five-mile, eight-lane highway. When it was built, it even had its own zip code: 60606.

The view from the 103rd-floor Skydeck is impressive. You can see four states on a clear day: Illinois, Indiana, Michigan, and Wisconsin. On a foggy day you won't even see Illinois. And on a windy day, you might be able to feel it sway 6 to 10 inches back and forth, baaack and forrrth, baaaack and forrrrth. For daring souls, the observation deck added a Skydeck Ledge, four glass boxes that extend 4.3 feet out into nothingness. Step on in and look right past your feet to the pavement a quarter-mile below.

233 S. Wacker Dr., Chicago, IL 60606

Tower, (312) 875-0066; Skydeck, (312) 875-9447

Hours: April–September, daily 9 AM–10 PM; October–March, daily 9 AM–8 PM

Cost: Adults $15.95, Kids (3–11) $11

Websites: www.willistower.com, www.theskydeck.com

Directions: In the southwest Loop, bound by Adams St., Wacker Dr., Jackson Blvd., and Franklin St.

Tribune Tower

The *Chicago Tribune* Tower is both a modern gothic masterpiece and the city's greatest monument to institutionalized vandalism. Embedded into the exterior walls of this 1925 structure are hunks ripped from the world's most famous historic buildings, including the White House, Great Pyramid of Cheops, Independence Hall, Cologne Cathedral, Westminster Abbey, Fort Sumter, Lincoln's Springfield Home, Notre Dame de Paris, the Alamo, the Parthenon, the Great Wall of China, the Arc de Triomphe, the Kremlin, China's Forbidden City, the Berlin Wall, and the Taj Mahal. Every US state contributed a brick or rock, too. Most are within arm's length, so you can touch these pieces of history if you want.

The Tower also contains several unique architectural features. Gargoyles and grotesques on the fourth and fifth floors include an owl with a camera, a monkey, and a porcupine holding a horn. The Robin Hood and howling dog figures over the entryway are nods to its architects, Raymond Hood and John Mead Howells.

435 N. Michigan Ave., Chicago, IL 60611

No phone

Hours: Always visible

Cost: Free

Directions: On Michigan Ave. just north of the river.

DO NOT take your own samples.

The **311 S. Wacker Building**, aka the Giant White Castle, is the world's tallest reinforced concrete structure at 65 stories.

Daniel Goodwin climbed the outside of the ~~Sears~~ **Willis Tower** (233 S. Wacker Dr.) on May 25, 1981, wearing a Spiderman costume. The trip took seven and a half hours using suction cups.

The former **Conrad Hilton** (720 S. Michigan Ave.), site of the 1968 Democratic Convention riots, once had an 18-hole golf course atop its roof.

Warren G. Harding was nominated as the Republican candidate for president in the first "smoke-filled room" in American politics. It took place in Suite 804–805 of the **Blackstone Hotel** (636 S. Michigan Ave.) on June 11, 1920.

Maude Van Dusen jumped from the **McCormick Building** (332 S. Michigan Ave.) on November 25, 1912. A suicide note claimed the Falls City, Nebraska, native and her sister had been forced into prostitution. The tragedy led to the Mann Act, forbidding transport of individuals across state lines for "immoral purposes."
Grant Park was built with rubble from the Chicago Fire. Before the fire, Michigan Avenue bordered Lake Michigan.

After Donald Trump's "birther" rantings during his 2011 noncandidacy, Rosie O'Donnell backed out of her plans to move to the penthouse suite of the **Trump International Hotel and Tower** (401 N. Wabash Ave.).

The original marble facade on the **Amoco Building** (200 E. Randolph St.) was replaced with granite after the original panels began to buckle. The replacement is believed to have cost more than the building's original construction.

Feng shui experts have claimed the **Smirfit-Stone Building**'s angular, pointed roof (150 N. Michigan Ave.) brings bad energy to the city.

A 29-year-old lawyer took off his glasses when chasing a coworker through the **Prudential Building** (138 E. Randolph St.) in the 1980s. He missed a corner, flew through a window, and fell 39 floors to his death.

The Hancock Tower (870 N. Michigan Ave.) was supposedly built on the birthplace of Anton LaVey, founder of the Church of Satan. Daniel "Spider" Goodwin also scaled this building in November 1981, despite the fire department's attempts to wash him off with buckets and hoses.

MORE LOOP BUILDING FACTOIDS

➡ Most Loop buildings are in violation of an obscure 1898 Chicago ordinance that buildings cannot be more than 130 feet tall.

➡ One-third of the world's revolving doors are in Chicago.

➡ According to legend, a ghost's face can be seen peeking out the top windows of Chicago's **Water Tower** (806 N. Michigan Ave., (312) 742-0808), apparently of a man hung from the top in the 1800s. Some witnesses claim to have seen a body hanging on the outside. Oscar Wilde once criticized the building: "Your Water Tower is a castellated monstrosity with pepperboxes stuck all over it. . . . It should be torn down."

➡ The **James R. Thompson Center** (100 W. Randolph St.), designed by Helmut Jahn, uses more energy to cool itself in the winter than it takes to heat most buildings. In the summer, the offices near the top have reached temperatures around 115°F.

➡ The **Hancock Tower Observatory** (875 N. Michigan Ave., (888) 875-VIEW; http://jhochicago.com/en) has an 80-foot caged Skywalk deck on the 94th floor where you can experience the high winds without being blown off the roof.

➡ The former **Jewelers Building** (35 E. Wacker Dr.) once had a parking garage at its center for the first 22 floors. Cars were lifted to their spaces on an elevator.

➡ The netting on top of the 27-story **Metropolitan Correctional Center** (71 W. Van Buren St.) was installed to prevent helicopter escapes after an unsuccessful attempt was made.

- **Marina City** (300 N. State St., (312) 222-1111, www.marina -city.com) was originally commissioned by the International Union of Janitors to provide affordable housing downtown.

- Potter Palmer invited reporters to try and set his "fireproof" hotel rooms afire after the **Palmer House** (17 E. Monroe St., (312) 726-7500) was rebuilt in 1871.

- There are six different shades of white on the exterior of the **Wrigley Building** (400–410 N. Michigan Ave. (312) 923-8080, www.thewrigleybuilding.com), arranged so that it looks brighter near the top. The bridge between the original building and its annex was built to circumvent state branch banking regulations; there were banks in the ground floors of both buildings and the gangway made them nonbranches.

- The **Harold Washington Chicago Public Library** (400 S. State St., (312) 747-4300, www.chipublib.org) is the world's largest public library, with more than two million volumes.

- The **Chicago Cultural Center** (78 E. Washington St., (312) 744-6630, www.explorechicago.org/city/en.html) houses the world's largest dome made of Tiffany stained glass. It is 38 feet in diameter and made from 2,848 individual pieces of colored glass.

- The **First United Methodist Church** (77 W. Washington St., (312) 236-4548, http://chicagotemple.org) is the tallest church in the United States at 568 feet. It is topped by a Sky Chapel.

- The onion dome atop the **InterContinental Hotel** (505 N. Michigan Ave., (312) 944-4100, www.icchicagohotel.com) is a holdover from its founding as the Medinah Athletic Club, an offshoot of the Shriners.

- Ceres, the Roman goddess of grain, sits atop the **Board of Trade Building** (141 W. Jackson Blvd., (312) 435-7180, www.cbotbuilding.com). The 31 ½-foot aluminum statue does not have a face. This imposing building was used as the headquarters of Wayne Enterprises in 2005's *Batman Begins*.

- The **Merchandise Mart** (350 N. Wells St., (800) 677-6278, www.merchandisemart.com) was the nation's largest building until the Pentagon was constructed, and the largest commercial building until the Sears Tower went up. It was purchased by Joseph Kennedy in 1945 for its overdue real estate taxes. The Kennedy family unloaded it in 1998.

- Ludwig Mies van der Rohe's first glass-and-steel apartment skyscrapers (**860–880 N. Lake Shore Dr.**) were built in 1951.

- The Lindbergh Beacon on the **Palmolive Building** (919 N. Michigan Ave.) once guided pilots to Midway Airport from 300 miles away, but when it was reinstalled in 2001, residents of neighboring condos complained and it was extinguished.

- The **Chicago Theatre**'s facade (175 N. State St., (312) 462-6300, www.thechicagotheatre.com) was designed to resemble Paris's Arc de Triomphe.

Big Car

If you're headed to the Loop, you'll soon discover that most street-side parking is banned. So if you must pay for parking, you should at least support a lot with a sense of humor: the SelfPark on Lake Street.

You could pass it without noticing, so step back and take a good look. The building's facade was designed to look like the front of a 1930s touring car. The floors and railings form a grill and the awnings are two treaded tires. A large vanity license plate says GOLF, a statue on the roof serves as a hood ornament, and two "headlight" domes finish off the illusion.

SelfPark, 60 E. Lake St., Chicago, IL 60601

Phone: (773) 436-7275

Hours: Always visible; Parking Monday–Friday 6 AM–Midnight, Saturday 7 AM–Midnight

Cost: Free to view; parking $4–$35

Directions: One block east of the El tracks' turn at Lake St. and Wabash Ave.

Ship-Shaped Beach House

A daydreaming tourist driving down Lake Shore Drive might think a steamer ship has run aground near North Avenue. But it turns out to be nothing more than a ship-shaped concession stand, lifeguard station, and restroom facility.

The original North Avenue Beach House was constructed in 1938 by WPA workers. Though made of little more than plywood, it lasted until 1998–99, when another beach house was erected. The new structure is even more realistic than its predecessor and includes two smokestacks, a mast, and two fake air vents on the roof/deck.

North Avenue Beach House, 1600 N. Lake Shore Dr., Chicago, IL 60614

Phone: (312) 742-PLAY

Hours: Always visible

Cost: Free

Website: www.chicagoparkdistrict.com

Directions: At the North Ave. exit from Lake Shore Dr.

Reebie Storage and Moving

The discovery of King Tut's tomb in 1922 led to a surge in public interest surrounding ancient Egyptian culture; Egyptian Revival became an archi-

tectural fad. The Reebie Storage and Moving Company Building, built on North Clark Street in 1923, is an excellent example of this style.

Two pharaohs guard the entrance to the storage facility. Rumors say they resemble John and William Reebie, the two brothers who founded the business and commissioned the building. Hieroglyphics over the entrance translate as "I give protection to your furniture" and "Forever I work for all your regions in daylight and darkness." Now that's service! Where else can you get your sofa protected by an ancient curse?

2325–33 N. Clark St., Chicago, IL 60614

Phone: (847) 994-8000

Hours: Always visible

Cost: Free

Website: www.reebieallied.com

Directions: Just south of Fullerton Ave. on Clark St.

A curse on those who dare to scratch your dresser.

The *Raisin in the Sun* House

While not *architecturally* significant, this South Side brownstone has had a greater impact on the way people live in Chicago than any other building.

A *Raisin in the Sun* is a classic in American drama, and it is based upon events that happened to the family of its playwright, Lorraine Hansberry. Central to the plot is the story of an African American family that plans a move to a new home in a restricted white community.

When Hansberry was just eight years old, her father, real estate broker Carl Hansberry, bought a home in west Hyde Park, and the family moved in on May 26, 1937. The neighborhood reacted violently, harassing the children as they played outside and throwing a brick through their home's front window. Anna M. Lee, on behalf of the Woodlawn Property Association, filed suit against the Hansberrys, saying they were in violation of a local covenant.

The Circuit Court of Cook County and the Illinois Supreme Court sided with Lee, but the US Supreme Court overturned the lower courts' decisions in 1941. While *Hansberry v. Lee* did not universally abolish real estate restrictions based upon race, it dealt a major blow to the practice.

A *Raisin in the Sun* was published in 1959 to critical acclaim. Whether by coincidence or design, the family's name in the play was Lee, the surname of those who had challenged the Hansberrys in court two decades earlier. The Hansberrys' former home still stands, though there is no official recognition given this historic piece of property.

6140 S. Rhodes Ave., Chicago, IL 60637
No phone
Hours: Always visible
Cost: Free
Directions: Three blocks east of Martin Luther King Dr., two blocks north of 63rd St.

Playboy Mansion (Midwest)

Si Non Oscillas, Noli Tininnare (If you don't swing, don't ring). This was the Latin motto at the Gold Coast's Playboy Mansion for more than 20 years, and did it ever live up to it. No discussion of funky Chicago buildings would be complete without mentioning this place.

Hugh Hefner, former student council president of Steinmetz High School, class of '44, founded *Playboy* magazine (first called *Stag Party*)

on December 10, 1953, with a $600 bank loan and $8,000 from investors, including $1,000 from his mother. At the time he was living in a first-floor apartment at 6052 South Harper Street.

The magazine was an instant success, and before long Hef had purchased the ultimate groovy bachelor pad, the Playboy Mansion, a mere two blocks from the Archbishop's residence. The mansion had four bedrooms, five fireplaces, an indoor pool, a game room, and a single-lane bowling alley. A fire pole dropped visitors into the Underwater Bar, a cozy joint with a window that looked into the swimming pool from below. Bunnies were allowed to stay in the mansion for $50 a month, though they had to bunk four to a room and share the bathroom facilities.

Hef felt quite comfortable here, lounging around in silk pajamas, smoking his pipe, and guzzling up to 36 bottles of Pepsi a day. He left the building only nine times during one three-year stretch. When questioned why, he confessed, "Why should I? I've got more right here now inside this house than most people ever find in a lifetime." But a case and a half of Pepsi a day? Maybe he couldn't stray too far from a bathroom.

Eventually, the lure of the West Coast became too great, and Hefner took up permanent residence in his Los Angeles digs. He donated the mansion to the Art Institute in 1989, and for a while it was used as a dorm, though not with the old Bunny accommodations. Later it was divided into two private residences, which is what it is today.

If you're into *Playboy* history, take a quick stroll over to the former flagship Playboy Club on the Magnificent Mile (919 N. Michigan Ave.) The former Palmolive Building was converted to the members-only club in 1960, and it hung on until 1988, when Christine Hefner shut its doors. The northwest corner of Walton Street and Michigan Avenue has since been given the honorary designation of Hugh M. Hefner Way.

Playboy Mansion, 1340 N. State Pkwy., Chicago, IL 60610

No phone

Hours: Private residence; always visible

Cost: Free

Directions: Two blocks south of North Ave.

Chicago Public Art
Little-Known Masterpieces in Fiberglass, Concrete, and Bronze

Formal public art in Chicago is confusing. There's a statue of Abraham Lincoln in Grant Park, and a statue of Ulysses S. Grant in Lincoln Park. Were their work orders mixed up? And who knows what that Picasso is in Daley Plaza (50 W. Washington St.)? A baboon? A woman? A lion? It recently has been upstaged by an even more enigmatic sculpture, Millennium Park's Cloud Gate (201 E. Randolph St.), which looks like neither a cloud nor a gate. Perhaps that's why most folks just call it *The Bean*.

While everyone's deeply confused about the highbrow subsidized art of the city, nobody's paying any attention to Chicago's tacky and wacky masterpieces, the downright odd and misplaced public artworks of the city. Nobody, that is, but this travel guide.

Note: What follows are hard-to-categorize artworks. Sculptural themes can be found later in this book—Big Men (see pages 152–54), Big Weenies (pages 45–49), Big Indians (pages 120–21), and Big Cows (pages 161–62).

Crappy Sculpture

If you're like sculptor Jerzy Kenar, you're no fan of dog crap. If you're like sculptor Jerzy Kenar, you want to draw attention to the issue. And if you're like sculptor Jerzy Kenar, you'd do this by making a bigger-than-life, dog-crap-shaped fountain in your front yard. Chances are, you're nothing like sculptor Jerzy Kenar.

Back in 2005, Kenar had had enough of dog owners who wouldn't clean up after their pets, so he created *Shit Fountain*, a brown bronze monument to man's inhumanity to man's shoes. Neighbors were both amused and appalled. Either way, he'd made his point. And before you dog lovers assume that Kenar is a dog hater, you should know that the artist has a pooch of his own . . . he just doesn't let it use the city sidewalks as a toilet.

1003 N. Wolcott Ave., Chicago, IL 60622

Private phone

Hours: Always visible

Cost: Free

Website: www.religiouskenar.com

Directions: Two blocks east of Damen Ave. at Augusta Blvd.

Slushy Sculpture

So maybe you're no more a fan of the Windy City's winters than you are of its sidewalk dog poo. As it happens, just a couple blocks from *Shit Fountain* you'll find Tony Tasset's *Snow Sculpture for Chicago*. This 2004 work can be found in the only remaining display window of the old Goldblatt Brothers Building on Chicago Avenue. It isn't a quaint *Currier and Ives* wonderland or a sparkling snowscape; instead it's a more realistic version of January in Chicago: an enormous grime-covered pile of slush littered with cigarette butts, coffee cups, and other garbage.

When asked to explain himself, Tasset stated, "These piles of snow are sublime, both ugly and beautiful, like life." Well that may be true of life, but a Chicago slush pile? Does anyone see an oversized, never-melting, black sidewalk iceberg as a *beautiful* thing . . . other than a mayoral challenger?

1637 W. Chicago Ave., Chicago, IL 60622

No phone

Hours: Always visible

Cost: Free

Directions: One block west of Ashland Ave.

Big Ball and Bat

The only thing worse than Chicago's dog poo and bone-chilling winters has to be its two professional baseball franchises—just ask Cubs fans about the White Sox or vice versa. So, as long as canine crap and crusty crud have their monuments, so should this city's favorite sport.

The big baseball outside Thillens Stadium draws visitors to the park district's North Side Little League stadium. It's about ten feet in diameter, which in theory both Sox and Cubs players could actually hit.

Thillens Stadium, 6404 N. Kedzie Ave., Chicago, IL 60645

Phone: (847) 329-7102

Hours: Always visible

Cost: Free

Website: www.chicagoparkdistrict.com

Directions: Where Devon Ave. crosses the Chicago River.

However, it would be a lot easier to hit a ball of this size if you had a bat to match. Back in 1976 the city erected a 101-foot slugger outside what

is today known as the Harold Washington Social Security Center. It is the work of Claes Oldenburg, titled *Batcolumn*, but given its mesh construction could just as easily be titled *Whifflebat*.

Harold Washington Social Security Center, 600 W. Madison St., Chicago, IL 60661

Phone: (312) 353-8277

Hours: Always visible

Cost: Free

Directions: West of Jefferson St.

A mighty big ball.

Big Ball and Pin

Maybe baseball isn't your thing. Bowling, perhaps? The Woodmac Lanes may be out of business, but their giant bowling ball and pin still loom over Western Avenue, ready to pick up that 7–10 split. The pin once had BOWL outlined in neon, and the ball urged passersby to stop by their Snack Bar for cocktails. It must have been a classy joint.

Woodmac Lanes, 7601 S. Western Ave., Chicago, IL 60620

No phone

Hours: Always visible

Cost: Free

Directions: Near the intersection of Western Ave. and 76th St.

The Wizard of Oz Statues

There's no place like Oz Park!

There's a place in Chicago that is nothing like the Midwest, a place where you'll find a yellow brick road, a brainless Scarecrow, a heartless Tin Man, a Cowardly Lion, and a young girl with a little dog looking to find her way home. No, not the Greyhound station—Oz Park!

Local kids named this park long before *Wicked* ever came to town. In it you'll find statues of your favorite characters, though not if you're a fan of the Wicked Witch of the West or flying monkeys. Talking trees won't grab at you, either, nor is there a field of poppies that will put you to sleeeeeep. The statues are the works of John Kearney and are more faithful to the book than to the movie.

2021 N. Burling St., Chicago, IL 60614

Phone: (312) 742-7898

Hours: Always visible

Cost: Free

Website: www.chicagoparkdistrict.com

Directions: Southwest of the intersection of Webster and Lincoln Aves.

Miniature Wrigley Field and Maxi Harry Caray

As pro ballparks go, Wrigley Field is one of the smallest, but there's an even tinier version of the Friendly Confines across the street from the stadium. Perhaps "tiny" isn't the right word—the 1':⅛" scale model in the back bar at Murphy's Bleachers isn't that small at 6½ feet on each side. Bar owner Jim Murphy commissioned the puny park from model maker Steve Wolf back in 1999. It took Wolf a year to build; Murphy paid him $21,000 for it. Fans can only see it during Cubs home games.

Murphy's Bleachers, 3655 N. Sheffield Ave., Chicago, IL 60613

Phone: (773) 281-5356

Hours: Back room open only on game days

Cost: Free

Website: www.murphysbleachers.com, www.majorleaguemodelsbystevewolf.com
Directions: Across the street from the northwest corner of Wrigley Field.

Just across the street from Murphy's Bleachers you'll find a statue of Harry Caray, this one larger than the original subject, who died in 1988 at the age of 84. The seven-foot sculpture is the work of Omri Amrany and Lou Cella and depicts Caray with a mic in his hand leading a drunken rendition of "Take Me Out to the Ball Game." His other hand is open and outstretched, though it sometimes grasps an empty beer can that has been jammed between its fingers by a besotted fan. This was an endemic problem before the bronze Caray was mounted on a pedestal. Now you have to be sober to get it up there.

Waveland and Sheffield Aves., Chicago, IL 60613

No phone

Hours: Always visible

Cost: Free

Directions: At the northeast corner of Wrigley Field.

Painted Testicles

It has been a tradition for years, even if it is a misdemeanor. Whenever the Chicago Cubs play a home game against the San Francisco Giants or the Cincinnati Reds, the testicles on General Sheridan's horse change colors. This is not some sort of sports miracle, but the work of out-of-town vandals. Rowdy baseball hooligans, under cover of darkness, paint the low-hanging *huevos* of the general's trusted steed whenever the cops turn their backs. For Giants games, they're orange, and for Reds games, they're red.

This oft-abused statue was erected to honor the Civil War hero who dynamited many city blocks in a desperate and unsuccessful attempt to stop the advance of the Great Chicago Fire. It was sculpted by Gutzon Borglum in 1923. Borglum went on to carve Mount Rushmore, which has four presidents and no testicles. Now you know why.

400 W. Belmont Ave., Chicago, IL 60657

No phone

Hours: Always visible; check the Cubs schedule

Cost: Free

Directions: Devon Ave. at Lake Shore Dr.

Go, baby, go!

Banksy's Buggy

There's nobody in the street art movement as simultaneously well-known and unknown as Banksy. He emerged from the Bristol underground scene in the 1990s, where he developed a style of humorous stenciled graffiti with a strong social message critical of corporate and state power. Each work is unique and site specific, from a crucified Jesus carrying Christmas shopping bags in his outstretched arms to a dove of peace wearing a flak jacket.

Banksy's true identity has never been revealed, though he has been captured on a few security cameras. Because he is so mysterious, it can sometimes be difficult to authenticate whether a work attributed to him is really his. One piece in Chicago, however, is most definitely a Banksy, for he has posted a photograph of it on his website. In a nod to *The Untouchables*, which gave a nod to *The Battleship Potempkin*, Banksy spray-painted a runaway baby buggy careening down the shadow of an old staircase on the outside of a West Loop restaurant.

844 W. Randolph St., Chicago, IL 60607

Phone: (312) 491-0844

Hours: Always visible

Cost: Free

Website: www.banksy.co.uk

Directions: Two blocks west of Halsted St. at Peoria St.

Mussolini's Pillar

You might think it insensitive to have a public monument, donated by a Fascist dictator who cost thousands of American soldiers their lives, sitting in the shadow of Soldier Field . . . and you'd be right . . . but there it sits: the Balbo Monument, aka Mussolini's Pillar.

The Balbo Monument was dedicated in 1934 following the Century of Progress Exposition. The 2,000-year-old Roman column sits on top of a pedestal that explains why: "Fascist Italy, with the sponsorship of Benito Mussolini, presents to Chicago a symbol and memorial in honor of the Atlantic Squadron led by Balbo, which with Roman daring, flew across the ocean in the 11th year of the Fascist Era." Whether by pollution or vandalism, it is difficult to read the inscription today.

Italo Balbo was accidentally shot down by his own troops during World War II, and Mussolini was hung by his heels by his countrymen, but the pillar remains, as does the Grant Park boulevard named for the Italian flying ace.

Burnam Park, 1400 S. Museum Campus Dr., Chicago, IL 60605

No phone

Hours: Always visible

Cost: Free

Directions: East of Soldier Field and north of McCormick Place, along the Burnham Harbor
bike path.

Mr. Imagination's Grotto

Until he moved away, Greg Warmack was one of Chicago's best-known intuitive artists, but few people knew him by his real name. Instead, they called him Mr. Imagination. He is famous for using bottle caps to build thrones, crowns, and walking sticks, but he turned his talents to concrete at a South Side youth center. Embedded in this 14-foot grotto are rocks, shells, and other found objects. Warmack enlisted the help of local kids to embellish the structure, and buried beneath it is a time capsule with letters to the children of the future.

Elliott Donnelley Youth Center, 3947 S. Michigan Ave., Chicago, IL 60653

Phone: (773) 268-3815

Hours: Monday–Friday 9 AM–8 PM, Saturday–Sunday 11 AM–5 PM

Cost: Free

Website: www.chicagoyouthcenters.org

Directions: One block south of Pershing Rd., two blocks east of State St.

Intuit

Not every artist is classically trained. In fact, throughout history, most haven't been. But there is a subset of untrained artists referred to as intuitive or outsider artists whose work has gained considerable attention in the last few decades. They are self-taught and often driven by an inner desire to express themselves whether anyone takes notice or not.

Well, the nonprofit organization Intuit: The Center for Intuitive and Outsider Art has definitely taken notice. Intuit was established in 1991 and has amassed an impressive permanent collection from around the United States, with works from such well-known artists as Lee Godie, Wesley Willis, Minnie Evans, Reverend Howard Finster, William Dawson, Martin Ramirez, and dozens more.

The best-known outsider artist in its collection, however, is Henry Darger. This recluse slaved away for 40 years on a 15,415-page illuminated manuscript in his Lincoln Park apartment (851 Webster St.) but never

Darger's den.
© The Henry Darger Room Collection of Intuit: The Center for Intuitive and Outsider Art, a gift of Kiyoko Lerner

showed it to anyone. His landlords found it after he died in 1973. *The Story of the Vivian Girls, in What Is Known as the Realms of the Unreal, of the Glandeco-Angelinnian War Storm, Caused by the Child Slave Rebellion* isn't exactly light reading, but the accompanying art is fascinating—Darger clipped images from comic books and magazines and glued them together with line drawings, tracings, and watercolors to show the plight of the Vivian Girls, many of whom meet very nasty ends. The story, as well as Darger's, is captured in the brilliant documentary *In the Realms of the Unreal*. Intuit has reproduced his cluttered room with original artifacts in the back corner of its museum.

756 N. Milwaukee Ave., Chicago, IL 60642

Phone: (312) 243-9088

Hours: Tuesday–Wednesday and Friday–Saturday 11 AM–5 PM, Thursday 11 AM–7:30 PM

Cost: Adults $5, kids (12 and under) free

Website: www.art.org

Directions: One block southeast of Ogden Ave.

Radium Gals

It happened at a factory along the Illinois & Michigan Canal years ago. Women painting glow-in-the-dark clock faces were told to lick their brushes between applications to keep the tips pointy. Unfortunately, the glowing paint contained radium, and most of the women came down with oral cancer.

The whole sordid affair is commemorated as part of the large mosaic bench at Gateway Park at Navy Pier. Scenes from the canal's history are laid out in tile, and the Radium Gals' poisoning is just one panel. Look for the woman painting an alarm clock.

Navy Pier, 600 E. Grand Ave., Chicago, IL 60611

Phone: (800) 595-PIER or (312) 595-PIER

Hours: Daily 8 AM–10 PM

Cost: Free

Website: www.navypier.com

Directions: East of North Pier, on the first bench facing away from the pier.

Museums Big and Small
Crazy Collections and Funky Artifacts

If museums are your thing, then you've come to the right city. Chicago has plenty of well-known institutions—they're easier to find than afford—but there are many mini-museums as well, and with admission prices in the single digits or free. Are you interested in professional cleaning products? Stained glass? Italian sports memorabilia? S&M? All of the above? No problem!

Even the big museums have something to offer connoisseurs of kook, from stuffed man-eating lions to skin from the serpent at the Garden of Eden. If you can avoid being distracted by the world-class exhibits and focus on the truly weird items in their collections—the telescope used to find Uranus!—you've got the makings of a truly funky field trip.

Note: A few Chicago museums appear elsewhere in this guidebook. Be sure to check out entries on the Museum of Science and Industry (pages 72–74), the National Museum of Mexican Art (page 94), Intuit (pages 24–25), and Jane Addams Hull House (pages 268–70) as well.

How many beaver buttons could the Busy Beaver Button Company buy if the Busy Beaver Button Company could buy beaver buttons? Apparently seven.
Photo by author, courtesy Busy Beaver Button Company

Busy Beaver Button Museum

The folks at the Busy Beaver Button Company sure are busy beavers. Not only have they created more than 18,000 unique buttons designs since their founding in 1995, they've also amassed a large collection of historic buttons they now display on the walls of their West Side Chicago office. (To be clear, these are the types of buttons that you put on your lapel or backpack, not the kind that holds your shirt closed, though they could.)

The Button Museum's collection is displayed by theme, from political to humorous to commercial and more. This is a working office, so you'll have to step around the graphic artists as you view the displays, but fear not—though they all have large buckteeth, they only use them to fell trees.

3279 W. Armitage Ave., Chicago, IL 60647

Phone: (773) 645-3359

Hours: By appointment

Cost: Free

Website: www.busybeaver.net

Directions: Two blocks west of Kedzie Ave.

Chicago History Museum

The Chicago History Museum is a prime example of a museum that seems to have a wealth of exhibits that belong somewhere else. You'd expect melted silverware from the Chicago Fire, but why is George Washington's inaugural suit here? Thankfully, the museum isn't shy about mixing these incongruous items in among its genuine Chicago stuff, nor do they avoid displaying less pleasant aspects of the city's past, such as a stuffed ballot box or a foot-long cleaver used to kill cattle at the Union Stock Yards before electric saws were invented.

Artifacts in the museum's collection rotate, so some of their goodies might be in storage when you visit. Its Chicago artifacts include two unexploded pipe bombs reportedly found near Haymarket Square after the riot in 1886, Michael Jordan's 1989 uniform and Nike shoes, Jane Byrne's inaugural pantsuit, Chief Black Hawk's death mask, Al Capone's official 1931 mug shot, and Hugh Hefner's pajamas and smoking pipe. Abraham Lincoln is well represented with the Emancipation Proclamation table from the White House, John Brown's Bible with all the fire and brimstone passages underlined, Robert E. Lee's Appomattox surrender table, Mary Todd Lincoln's bloody Ford's Theater cape, and Lincoln's death bed—he had to be laid out diagonally because he was too long. The museum's incongruous artifacts include George Washington's spyglass and compass, stripper Sally Rand's seven-pound fans, and the "Skin of the Serpent that Tempted Eve in the Garden of Eden" in a shadow box.

Some of the things you won't see include an early draft of the Emancipation Proclamation (which was destroyed along with the first Chicago Historical Society building during the Chicago Fire) and bone chips from the twelve Apostles (which the museum auctioned off).

Finally, you may be wondering what that big chain is doing in the hedge on the plaza behind the museum. Back in the 1880s, junk dealer John Abbey sold the massive 114-pound links to benefactors of the Chicago Historical Society, claiming they were part of the Great Chain that George Washington strung across the Hudson River in 1778 to stop British warships. The museum displayed them for years until they were discovered to be fake, at which point it dumped them outside.

1601 N. Clark St., Chicago, IL 60614

Phone: (312) 642-4600

Hours: Monday–Saturday 9:30 AM–4:30 PM, Sunday Noon–5 PM

Cost: Adults $14, seniors (65+) $13, teens (13–22) $12, kids (12 and under) free

Website: www.chicagohs.org

Directions: At the south end of Lincoln Park at Clark St. and North Ave.

DEAD IN LINCOLN PARK

Chicago's Lincoln Park is a peaceful place, but at one time it was a rest-in-peace place—it was Chicago City Cemetery! The graveyard extended from North Avenue to Armitage Avenue, and from Clark Street to Lake Michigan. But from 1866 to 1870, worried that it was polluting the drinking water drawn from the lake, the city moved its bodies to newer, outlying cemeteries like Graceland and Rosehill. Crews didn't get all the bodies, however, and you can still find graves there today.

For example, the family tomb of hotelier Ira Couch still stands just behind the Chicago Historical Society. Neither the funds nor the permission were ever available to move the 100-ton mausoleum. Nobody is quite sure how many bodies are inside the lonely structure.

Early Chicago native David Kennison is also buried in Lincoln Park, closer to the zoo. Kennison claimed to have participated in the Boston Tea Party, the Battle of Bunker Hill, and the Fort Dearborn Massacre. For his stories to have been accurate, he would have had to have been 115 years old when he died in 1852, hardly believable to anyone but the DAR. The organization erected an engraved boulder to Kennison near the Academy of Sciences building.

There are many unmarked bodies still left in the park, too. Fifteen bodies were unearthed in 1986 during construction near the Chicago Historical Society, and fragments of six more were discovered while excavating the museum's new parking garage in 1998. So if your dog retrieves a bone during a walk through the park, take a good look—it might be older than you think.

Culinary Curiosity Exhibition

Anyone who's ever visited a high-end kitchen store or sat through a night of TV infomercials knows that there are almost as many tools and utensils for cooking food as there are types of food to be cooked. Mel and Janet Mickevic had a lifelong fascination with these items—Mel was a professional food scientist and Janet's father was a candy technologist—and over the years they amassed an impressive collection. More than 300 of their most unique finds can be seen in a dozen display cases scattered through the building that houses Kendall College.

Foodies will no doubt be familiar with many of these items, such as sausage stuffers, flavor injectors, fireless cookers, corn shellers, and induction burners, but there are plenty of items that fall into the category of who-would-think-there-needed-to-be-a-tool-for-that: asparagus bunchers, coconut shredders, sugar nippers, ash rakes, lard presses, and Davis swinging churns.

Kendall College, 900 N. Branch St., Chicago, IL 60642

Phone: (866) 667-3344

Hours: Monday–Friday 9 AM–5 PM

Cost: Free

Website: www.culinarycuriosity.org

Directions: One block north of Chicago Ave., west of Halsted St.

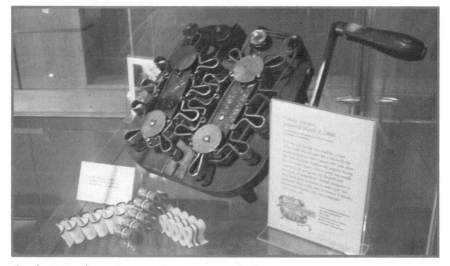

Candy contortions. Photo by author, courtesy Kendall College

Field Museum

The stuffed critters at the Field Museum are a sordid lot. If you look into their glassy eyes today they appear docile and lovable, but things were different when human-hating blood flowed through their veins.

Take Ziggy the elephant. He started life with Singer's Midget Circus, smoking cigarettes and playing the harmonica to everyone's delight. But in 1941 he killed a marine band trombonist in San Diego's Balboa Park. This landed him in solitary at the Brookfield Zoo, where he nearly gored his trainer, George "Slim" Lewis, and tossed turds at unsuspecting schoolchildren. Ziggy died in his cage in 1975, and his bones were boiled down for the Field to display.

And then there's Bushman, the much-loved gorilla from the Lincoln Park Zoo. He arrived in Chicago in 1930 and over the next 20 years chucked his fair share of excrement. He also assaulted a few visitors who got too close to his cage. Bushman died on January 1, 1951, and while Chicago mourned, he was stuffed for Field patrons.

Sue, the most famous T. rex fossil ever unearthed, never killed a human, but she (or perhaps he) did cost sponsors Walt Disney and McDonald's $8.36 million—that's a lot of Happy Meals and *Lion King* videos, so believe me, somebody suffered. Sue was named for Sue Hendrickson, the South Dakota paleontologist who discovered her in 1990. In the main display, Sue's skull is a casting, but the rest of the fossilized bones you'll see are real; Sue's actual skull is on the second floor balcony—it was too heavy to mount on the full skeleton.

But the hands-down winners in the Field's human-hurting collection are the Lions of Tsavo, two big cats believed to have devoured more than 35 railway workers (or 72 or 135, depending on who you ask) in East Africa in 1898. Their story, and the story of the man who shot them, was made into the movie *The Ghost and the Darkness*. The lions were felled by John Patterson, a civil engineer on the railroad, who made them into two rugs. The pelts were purchased by the Field Museum in 1924 and made back into what now resembles two very hungry cats.

Field Museum of Natural History, 1400 S. Lake Shore Dr., Chicago, IL 60605

Phone: (312) 922-9410

Hours: Daily 9 AM–5 PM

Cost: Adults $15, seniors (65+) $12, students $12, kids (3–11) $10, check website for free days

Website: http://fieldmuseum.org

Directions: On the south end of Grant Park at Roosevelt Rd.

GEMS OF THE OTHER BIG MUSEUMS

There are other big-name museums like the Field in Chicago, and should you visit the others, be sure to seek out these items among all the other stuff.

American Gothic by Grant Wood

Art Institute of Chicago, 111 S. Michigan Ave., Chicago, (312) 443-3600, www.artic.edu

The painting provides a great opportunity for a gag photo, but it's very difficult to sneak a pitchfork past the Art Institute guards.

Atlantic Saltwater

Shedd Aquarium, 1200 S. Lake Shore Dr., Chicago, (312) 939-2438, www.sheddaquarium.org

That's not just any old saltwater in those tanks! The first five million gallons was shipped in 160 boxcars from Key West in 1930.

The Uranus Telescope

Adler Planetarium, 1300 S. Lake Shore Dr., Chicago, (312) 922-STAR, www.adlerplanetarium.org

Housed in the world's first planetarium, this Uranus Telescope was used by William Herschel to spot the distant planet in 1781.

Imperial Hardware

Joe Swiatek is part of that vanishing breed of (mostly) men who grew up tinkering with Erector sets and soapbox derby cars, and through it developed an appreciation for all things mechanical. No surprise that he now runs a neighborhood hardware store, though it will surprise you to see what he's jammed in amongst the shelves: hundreds of model steam

engines, toy trains, antique locks, animated banks, mementos from both Chicago World Fairs, and gizmos of all sorts.

Many of the items are on the high shelves and hard to see, the easy-to-reach space reserved for actual merchandise, but there is an impressive display case of Swiatek's best finds at eye level in the adjoining storefront. Bring your dad for a trip down memory lane.

1208 W. Grand Ave., Chicago, IL 60642

Phone: (312) 421-0475

Hours: Monday–Friday 10 AM–5:45 PM, Saturday 10 AM–5 PM

Cost: Free

Directions: One block east of Grand Ave.

International Museum of Surgical Sciences and Hall of Immortals

Everybody's a collector, even surgeons, especially Dr. Max Thorek. The instruments and artifacts he amassed served as the seed for this museum's galleries. Over the years, other surgeons also sent their most prized finds to this place, expanding it to a 7,000-piece exhibit, including a copy of Napoleon's death mask, Florence Nightingale's nurse's cap, a working iron lung from the 1920s, a bronze speculum found in Pompeii, trepanned (drilled) Peruvian skulls, and a plaster bust of the Angel, a Neanderthalic French wrestler who suffered from acromegaly.

Yet the most surprising part of this collection is not the instruments; it's the art. You can find a rendering of the first ovariectomy with doctors removing a basketball-sized tumor, Dr. Dorry Pasha operating on a case of elephantiasis of the scrotum, a geisha having her arm removed by Dr. Pompe V. Meerdervoort, and Xavier Cugat's painting of an operating room where a surgeon reads *Playboy* and a dog waits for scraps. And they've got dozens of busts of famous surgeons, many carved by other doctors, demonstrating that you can be handy with a scalpel and not with a chisel.

1524 N. Lake Shore Dr., Chicago, IL 60610

Phone: (312) 642-6502

Hours: Tuesday–Thursday and Sunday 10 AM–4 PM, Friday–Saturday 10 AM–9 PM

Cost: Adults $10, seniors (65+) $6, kids (4–13) $4

Website: www.imss.org

Directions: One block south of North Ave. on Inner Lake Shore Dr.

Leather Archives and Museum

You won't find this institution in most guidebooks to the Windy City, which is not to say that it's uninteresting or unsubstantial. Quite the contrary, though it is the only museum where you're given a content warning before entering. When they say leather, they're not talking about the wallet you made at Camp Weemaway. The belt? Perhaps . . .

The LA&M is the nation's largest repository of material chronicling the "alternative sex culture," from fetishism to sadomasochism to, well, you name it . . . as long as it's kinky, safe, and consensual. Founded in 1991, it is today housed in a two-story former synagogue. It contains eight galleries and a large research library with thousands of back issues of dirty magazines, all meticulously archived in protective, acid-free sleeves. Check out the elaborate, anatomically disproportionate murals in the Etienne Auditorium, Tom of Finland–esque paintings done by Dom Orejudos, lover of the LA&M's founder, Chuck Renslow. Stop by the re-created Leather Bar under the stairs or the Dungeon in the basement's back corner. Follow the Leather History Time Line and see memorabilia from every International Mr. Leather and International Ms. Leather competition, as well as colors, pins, vests, and uniforms from clubs and bars around the nation. And visit the Oral History Lounge (not what you think) where you'll hear taped interviews with the pioneers, purveyors, and practitioners of kink.

6418 N. Greenview Ave., Chicago, IL 60626

Phone: (773) 761-9200

Hours: Thursday–Friday 11 AM–7 PM, Saturday–Sunday 11 AM–5 PM

Cost: Adults $10, seniors $5

Website: www.leatherarchives.org

Directions: Just north of Devon Ave., two blocks east of Ashland Ave.

Money Museum

Though it might not be on the itinerary for you Ron Paul supporters, the Chicago Federal Reserve's Money Museum is a must see for all the rest of you capitalists. Admission is free—taxpayers have already paid plenty— but because of antigovernment nuts the security is insane, enough to rival any airport.

Once x-rayed, wanded, and probed, you're allowed to enter a wondrous room filled with millions of dollars. Think Willy Wonka meets

Scrooge McDuck. The first million is a large plexiglass cube neatly packed with $1 bills. A smaller million-dollar pile of bundled $20s can be found around the corner, followed by a briefcase of $100s. It's small enough to carry out the door if you could unbolt it from its stand, which you can't—Ben Bernanke knows I tried. Maybe you should just have your photo taken with it like everybody else. The museum does give you a baggie containing roughly $350 in shredded currency on your way out. If you enjoy jigsaw puzzles and aren't prone to sneezing, your visit could pay for itself.

The Money Museum isn't just about the paper currency the Fed prints willy-nilly. You can also see exhibits on counterfeit bills, rare American currency, and the Rube Goldberg contraption Alan Greenspan used for years to determine monetary policy.

Federal Reserve of Chicago, 230 S. La Salle St., Chicago, IL 60604

Phone: (312) 322-2400

Hours: Monday–Friday 8:30 AM–5 PM (closed bank holidays)

Cost: Free

Website: www.chicagofed.org/webpages/education/money_museum/index.cfm

Directions: Downtown at the corner of Jackson Blvd. and La Salle St.

$1 million with drool guard. Photo by author, courtesy Federal Reserve, Chicago

A SPOTLESS RECORD ON A TECHNICALITY

Chicago's Federal Reserve has never been robbed . . . technically. But on September 22, 1933, Alvin "Creepy" Karpis and the Barker gang got away with a handcart being wheeled out to the sidewalk in front of the building. They were chased by officers and crashed at Adams and Halsted Streets, but they escaped in another hijacked car after shooting a policeman. Their stash turned out to be mail.

National Italian-American Sports Hall of Fame Museum

The National Italian-American Sports Hall of Fame Museum has had a tough life. It used to be located in Arlington Heights, and although thousands of drivers saw it from the toll road each day, few got off the highway to check it out. So it closed its doors and started looking for another home. Where better than in Chicago's Little Italy? The museum started by erecting a statue of Joe DiMaggio, but after the statue was unveiled, locals started having second thoughts. Did they want their through street turned into a cul-de-sac? Would the museum bring in the riffraff, assuming it brought in anyone at all?

Well, not to worry—the $1.7 million complex finally opened in 2003, and was it ever worth it. Today you'll find hundreds of Italian American sports artifacts displayed over several floors: Rocky Marciano's heavyweight belt, Tommy Lasorda's baseball cap, Joe DiMaggio's baseball glove, Jennifer Capriati's tennis racket, Joe Montana's 49ers jersey, Jake Lamotta's leopard-skin warm-up robe, Mario Andretti's 1970 Indy car, Phil Esposito's hockey skates, Matt Biondi's 11 Olympic medals, Mary Lou Retton's Olympic podium jumpsuit, Randy "Macho Man" Savage's sequined *Wrestlemania II* cape, Lou Ferrigno's muscle shirt, and Tony Danza's boxing cape. Abbondanza!!

1431 W. Taylor St., Chicago, IL 60607

Phone: (312) 226-5566

Hours: Monday–Friday 9 AM–5 PM, Saturday–Sunday 11 AM–4 PM

Cost: Adults $5, seniors $4, kids (12 and under) $3

Website: www.niashf.org

Directions: Two blocks east of Ashland Ave.

The Oriental Institute

The Oriental Institute is a brave institution. Ignoring the possible consequences of ancient curses, they've dragged out a huge collection of Egyptian mummies for all to see. And not just human mummies (they've got seven), but preserved hawks, crocodiles, rodents, and ibises. You name it, those Egyptians wrapped it.

The mummies are just a small part of the 25,000-plus artifacts in the institute's collection. They've got hundreds of statues, jugs, scarabs, and dioramas of the pyramids for scholars and Indiana Jones wannabes alike. The institute sponsors research projects and digs throughout the Middle and Near East, and once they find the Ark of the Covenant they'll use its supernatural powers to rule the world.

1155 E. 58th St., Chicago, IL 60637

Phone: (773) 702-9514

Hours: Tuesday and Thursday–Saturday 10 AM–6 PM, Wednesday 10 AM–8:30 PM, Sunday
   noon–6 PM

Cost: Suggested donation—adults $7, kids (under 12) $4

Website: http://oi.uchicago.edu

Directions: Just west of Woodlawn Ave. on 58th St., one block north of the Midway Plaisance.

MORE MUMMIES

As many human mummies as the Oriental Museum has, another Chicago institution has far more—the **Field Museum** (see page 31) has 23! The **Seabury-Western Seminary** in Evanston (2122 Sheridan Rd., (847) 328-9300, www.seabury.edu) has a wrapped Egyptian, too. Another mummy, this one of an eight-year-old boy, can be found in a display case at **Naperville Central High School** (440 W. Aurora Ave., (630) 420-6320, http://schools.naperville203.org/central); it's been in the Humanities Department offices since the 1940s. And a Loop antiquities dealer, **Harlan J. Berk Galleries** (31 N. Clark St., (312) 609-1309, www.harlanjberk.com), occasionally has a mummy for sale if you're interested in taking one home with you.

A wall of washing wonders. Photo by author, courtesy Pert Cleaners

Pert's Antique Fabricare Museum

What better place to house a museum of fabric-care history than in a working dry cleaner? Tony Lupo, owner of Pert Cleaners, has turned the front foyer of his West Side establishment into a minimuseum to the professional cleaning industry. Here you'll see antique irons and ironing boards, dress forms and scissors, sewing machines and bobbins, wringers and washboards, and old boxes and cans of soap flakes, Lux and Duz detergents, and more. It'll all make you glad that you don't have to do your laundry the old-fashioned way, which, considering that you're in a dry cleaner, you probably don't like doing it the new-fashioned way, either.

Pert Cleaners, 4213 W. Irving Park Rd., Chicago, IL 60641

Phone: (773) 282-6216

Hours: Monday, Wednesday, and Friday–Saturday 7 AM–7 PM, Tuesday and Thursday 7 AM–6 PM

Cost: Free

Directions: One block west of the Kennedy Expy.

Smith Museum of Stained Glass Windows

You don't have to go to church to see beautiful stained glass—head out to Navy Pier, where you'll find the Smith Museum of Stained Glass Windows, the nation's only museum dedicated to this spectacular art form. The museum's 150-plus exhibits are found behind bulletproof glass in the darkened lower pedway, each backlit for full effect. They are divided into subgroupings of Victorian, Prairie, Modern, and Contemporary styles, with both religious and sectarian subjects represented, from Biblical scenes to stunning gardens to sparkling portraits of Michael Jordan. You'll also see a wide variety of techniques and materials, including traditional Tiffany leaded glass, broken bottles, and chunks of glass reminiscent of *Land of the Lost* pylons.

Navy Pier, 600 E. Grand Ave., Chicago, IL 60611

Phone: (800) 595-PIER or (312) 595-PIER

Hours: Always visible

Cost: Free

Website: www.navypier.com/things2do/rides_attract/smith_museum.html

Directions: On the lower hallway near the center of the Navy Pier complex.

Uncle Fun

While technically not a museum, Uncle Fun sure feels like it, and the best part about it is you can buy the artifacts! They've got spider rings and Scooby Doo magnets, snow globes and windup toys, rubber rats and 1950s postcards, costume jewelry and 3-D Jesus portraits . . . thousands of pop-culture doodads tucked in old card catalogs, crammed in bins, or piled on the counter. If you don't know what you're looking for, you'll still find it at Uncle Fun's.

Ted Frankel, aka Uncle Fun, has been in the ephemera business for more than three decades in what he describes as "a habit that got out of control." He insists that his clientele is strictly kids, though he admits that some come in older bodies. Ted scours the country looking for toy closeouts and mass market knickknacks, always keeping three criteria in mind: (1) the item must be visually exciting, (2) it must be cheap, and (3) it must be fun. Talk about a dream job!

Three times a year, Uncle Fun holds fabulous garage sales. Get the dates and mark them on your calendar; they are not to be missed. Closeouts and

overstocks, slightly dented and in mint condition, it's spring cleaning at the coolest toy chest in town.

1338 W. Belmont Ave., Chicago, IL 60657

Phone: (773) 477-8223

Hours: Monday–Saturday noon–7 PM, Sunday noon–6 PM

Cost: Free; toys extra, but not much

Website: www.unclefunchicago.com

Directions: Two blocks east of Ashland Ave.

They call him Uncle Fun for a reason.

Willie Dixon's Blues Heaven Foundation

Chess Records had been in Chicago since 1950, first at 4750 Cottage Grove Avenue, but it wasn't until Leonard and Phil Chess moved the operation to the South Loop in 1957 that things really started taking off. It was here on February 29, 1958, that Chuck Berry recorded "Johnny B. Goode," one of Chess's biggest hits. The studio also produced records for Muddy Waters, Aretha Franklin, Bo Diddley, Etta James, Koko Taylor, Jimmie Rogers, Howlin' Wolf, the Yardbirds, the Dells, the Rolling Stones, and Willie Dixon.

Today it is Willie Dixon's foundation that keeps the legacy of Chess Records alive, and rightfully so. Dixon was not only an accomplished musician and songwriter, but as an arranger and producer he helped craft almost every recording made at the studio.

Chess Records closed its doors in 1967, and the building sat unrecognized until being purchased by Dixon's widow, Marie Dixon, in 1993. It is currently being restored and contains a small museum of gold records, instruments, playbills, and costumes from the studio's heyday.

Willie Dixon's Blues Heaven Foundation, 2120 S. Michigan Ave., Chicago, IL 60616

Phone: (312) 808-1286

Hours: Monday–Friday 11 AM–4 PM, Saturday noon–2 PM

Cost: $10 per person

Website: www.bluesheaven.com

Directions: Just north of Cermak Rd.

Eccentric Eateries
Brats, Burgers, Weenies, and More

Chicago has its fair share of overpriced, fancy restaurants, but most visitors are looking for deep-dish pizza, cheeseburgers, and Italian beef— blue-collar food for the City That Works. Paris may have given the world vichyssoise and rude waiters, but Chicago has given humankind Twinkies, Cracker Jack, and Crock-Pots. Would summer barbecues be the same without Chicago-area innovations such as beer cans, screw-cap bottles, and the Weber Grill? And did you know that the Kraft General Foods plant (7400 S. Rockwell) makes all the nation's Kool-Aid?

So chuck that Zagat's! Try these eateries with personality.

The Jungle

No discussion of this city's hamburgers and hot dogs would be complete without a little background on Chicago's infamous slaughterhouses.

Hurray for hot dogs!

Chicago's Union Stock Yards opened on Christmas Day 1865. Business expanded until the pens, slaughterhouses, and packing plants covered a square mile bounded roughly by 39th Street, 47th Street, Halsted Street, and Ashland Avenue. The stockyards' operations went relatively unchecked until Upton Sinclair wrote a muckraking exposé in 1906. Though it was a novel, *The Jungle*'s description of life in the yards was nauseatingly accurate. Sinclair hoped it would inspire workers to organize, but its immediate effect was to gross out the reading public, who then demanded food and drug reforms. "I aimed at the public's heart, and by accident I hit it in the stomach," he later observed.

Listen to Sinclair's description of the Chicago River branch that ran through the stockyards: "Bubbles of carbolic acid will rise to the surface and burst, and make rings two or three feet wide. Here and there the grease and filth have caked solid, and the creek looks like a bed of lava." Locals called it Bubbly Creek; Gustavus Swift was known to inspect the putrid water to make sure his sausage makers weren't throwing out anything usable. And when it comes to sausage, what isn't? It was Swift who first observed, "In Chicago, meatpackers use everything from the pig except the squeal."

The Jungle led to the Pure Food and Drug Act of 1906, but it didn't slow down the yards' operations. An outbreak of hoof-and-mouth disease closed the plants in November 1913, but they quickly reopened. The Union Stock Yards reached their operational peak in 1920 when they employed more than 30,000 workers. In that year 300,000 hogs, 75,000 cows, 50,000 sheep, and 5,000 horses were "processed." That's a lot of weenies.

The Union Stock Yards finally closed on July 30, 1971. All that remains is its 1875 stone entryway, topped by a bull's head (prizewinner "Sherman"), straddling Exchange Avenue. In its 106 years of operation, more than a billion critters met their maker just beyond this gate.

850 W. Exchange Ave., Chicago, IL 60609

No phone

Hours: Always visible

Cost: Free

Directions: Just west of Halsted St. (at about 4150 S.) on Exchange Ave.

EAT UP!

Sometimes it isn't just four-legged animals that end up in sausage casings. On May 1, 1897, Louise Leutgert disappeared. Her husband, Adolph, one of the city's sausage barons, had a violent temper and a full-time mistress. Police searched Leutgert's factory and found suspicious evidence in one of the large vats: teeth, a bone from a big toe, and Mrs. Leutgert's wedding ring engraved with "L.L."

Adolph was charged with Louisa's murder and eventually convicted after a second trial. Though the vat was supposedly being "cleaned" with potash at the time of the murder, wiener sales plummeted that summer. Louisa's ghost was said to haunt Adolph the rest of his days. The sausage factory, located at Hermitage Avenue and Diversey Parkway, burned down in 1902.

Rosario's Italian Sausage and Carnitas Uruapan

If you're more of a visual learner, *The Jungle* might not give you the clearest picture of how the whole sausage-making process works. If that is the case, stop on by Rosario's Italian Sausage, where you can see whole pigs ground into sausage before your very eyes. No, not real pigs, but nine neon likenesses marching into a meat grinder on the sign over the front window. This classic advertisement was created in 1969, and, after falling into disrepair, was restored to its grisly glory in 2009. The good folk at Rosario's

would like you to know, however, that in reality their sausage meat is made from only the finest cuts, not the whole hog from snout to tail.

8611 S. Pulaski Rd., Chicago, IL 60652

Phone: (773) 585-0660

Hours: Always visible; store, Monday and Wednesday–Friday 9 AM–5 PM, Saturday–Sunday 9:30 AM–12:45 PM

Cost: Free

Directions: One block north of 87th St. and Columbus Ave.

Carnitas Uruapan, in Chicago's Pilsen neighborhood, takes a similar advertising approach, only its porkers are killed by psychotic knife-wielding butchers. At least that's what the mural along its front counter shows. Also, the front awning depicts one little piggie boiling another in a large cauldron, cannibal-and-missionary style. Adorable!

1725 W. 18th St., Chicago, IL 60608

Phone: (312) 226-2654

Hours: Daily 8 AM–5 PM

Cost: Free

Directions: One block west of Ashland Ave.

The truth hurts . . . them more than you.

It's SUPERDAWG!!

Superdawg

In a town that loves its hot dogs, Maurie and Flaurie reign as king and queen. The eight-foot-tall pair has stood atop the northwest side's Superdawg Drive-In since 1948. Maurie, named for Superdawg's owner Maurie Berman, is dressed in a leopard-skin Tarzan singlet and strikes a muscleman pose; Flaurie, a topless Jane in a miniskirt, looks on adoringly. Both have glowing red eyes that are best appreciated after dark.

Superdawg is one of the Chicago's few remaining drive-ins where you never have to leave your car—just place your order through a call box and the carhop will bring your food right to your car. The burgers are awesome, the service is better, and the weenies are enormous.

Superdawg Drive-In, 6363 N. Milwaukee Ave., Chicago, IL 60646

Phone: (773) 763-0660

Hours: Always visible; store, Sunday–Thursday 11 AM–1 PM, Friday–Saturday 11 AM–2 PM

Cost: Meals $5–8

Website: www.superdawg.com

Directions: At the intersection of Milwaukee, Devon, and Nagle Aves.

Even more enormous are Superdawg's next-generation Maurie and Flaurie, upsized reproductions that grace the roof of Superdawg's new, second store. It opened in Wheeling in 2010 and can handle even larger crowds than the original.

333 S. Milwaukee Ave., Wheeling, IL 60090

Phone: (847) 459-1900

Hours: Always visible; store, Sunday–Thursday 11 AM–11 PM, Friday–Saturday 11 AM–midnight

Cost: Meals $5–$8

Directions: Two blocks south of Dundee Rd.

MORE BIG WEENIES

Don't let anyone tell you otherwise—size does matter. With so many hot dog joints in Chicagoland, one surefire way to grab customers' attention is to stick out a big wiener for all to see. Here are just a few of the area's standup standouts.

Don's Original Hot Dogs

7748 Kedzie Ave., Chicago, (773) 476-9392

The condiment-covered smiling dog atop this South Side establishment is splattered in ketchup from a bottle he's squirting on his head. The only other protection this tan guy wears is a pair of tube socks, while a compact bun barely wraps his engorged body. While there, be sure to check out the big hamburger guarding the picnic table out back.

Hot Dog and Hamburger Man

Elston Ave. and Division St., Chicago

The happy-faced hot dog and hamburger at this intersection once stood above Pig Outs Hot Dogs on Milwaukee Avenue across from Schurz High School. When that place went out of business, the pair were given a fresh coat of paint and mounted on the roof of a now-abandoned restaurant by the river.

Henry's Drive-In

6031 W. Ogden Ave., Cicero, (708) 656-9344

There's no smile on the Italian sausage over the entryway to this Old Route 66 eatery, but no frown either—it's just a big encased meat log with a pile of fries on top.

Wolfy's

2734 W. Peterson Ave., Chicago, (773) 743-0207

This poor weenie wouldn't smile if it could—somebody has jammed it onto a two-pronged fork!

Chubby Wieners

4652 N. Western Ave., Chicago, (773) 769-1394

In most cases, if you spotted a chubby wiener while riding on the Brown Line El you should probably call the CTA cops, but if you look out the north side of the train while passing over the Western stop, you'll see one monstrous wiener that nobody but a vegetarian could object to. The cutout wooden mascot atop this hot dog stand wears nothing but a neckerchief, a chef's hat, and a smile.

Hot Doug's

3324 N. California Ave., Chicago, (773) 279-9550, www.hotdougs.com

Though they're not physically large, the wieners at Hot Doug's have made a big impression in a town that loves its dogs. Yes, they have the standard cow-based products, but they also sell other critters ground up and crammed into sausage casings for your pleasure—elk and duck, wild boar and alligator, rattlesnake and panda. OK, maybe not panda. Not yet. Hot Doug's motto: "There are no two finer words in the English language than Encased Meats, my friend." So true.

Felony Franks

229 S. Western Ave., Chicago, (312) 243-0505, http://felonyfranks.com

The huge hot dogs at Felony Franks are just paintings, but they're still attention getters. You see, these wieners have been bad and are now behind bars wearing striped prison uniforms. They've drawn the ire of the city's Second Ward alderman and the homeowners of West Town Home, none of whom appreciate the take-out restaurant's marketing strategy and corporate mission. You see, Felony Franks is a job placement program for ex-cons, people who often have a difficult time getting back into the job market after being released. Owner Jimmie Andrews gives them that chance serving up Misdemeanor Wieners, Cell Mate Dogs, Probation Burgers, and Chain Gang Chili Dogs—"Food so good, it's criminal!"

Oscar Meyer Wienermobile

Always on the road, http://hotdoggerblog.com

Oscar Meyer's first Wienermobile was built by the General Body Company of Chicago in 1936. The original is in the Henry Ford Museum in Dearborn, Michigan, but there are plenty of the later models on the road today. Drivers over the years have included onetime Munchkin coroner Meinhardt Raabe and congressional überweenie Paul Ryan, who would go on to represent Wisconsin in Washington. Today's Wienermobile fleet can be seen at street fairs and grocery store openings from coast to coast. If you want to see one in person, follow the schedule on its blog.

Jimi Hendrix's Penis Cast

Hilton Hotel, 720 S. Michigan Ave., Room 1628, Chicago, (312) 922-4400, www.cynthiaplastercaster.com

Cynthia Plaster Caster wasn't just any rock 'n' roll groupie — she was a historian (of sorts). Over the years she convinced dozens of singers, musicians, and roadies to have their male members molded for posterity. Her first subject was her most famous, none other than Jimi Hendrix. The guitarist made the impression in his hotel bathroom on February 25, 1968, and Plaster Caster later made it into a statuette. Those who have seen it say it has a distinct curvature, though it's not clear whether that's an issue of physiology or casting.

Cheezborger! Cheezborger!

"Cheezborger! Cheezborger! No Pepsi. Coke! No fries. Cheeps!" The menu and atmosphere of the Billy Goat Tavern were faithfully spoofed on *Saturday Night Live* by John Belushi and Dan Akroyd in the 1970s, but you'll see not much has changed in 30 years, except that Mike Royko doesn't come around as often.

The Billy Goat Tavern did not just make an impression on *SNL* cast members and local reporters. It reportedly holds the key to the Cubs' dismal postseason record. The bar's owner, Billy "Goat" Sianis brought his faithful pet, Billy Goat III, to Wrigley Field during the 1945 World Series. When the pair was ejected, in part because the goat stunk, Sianis put a Greek hex on the Cubs. They quickly blew the series, and Sianis sent the owners a note, "Who stinks now???"

Many years passed before the team returned to postseason play. On July 4, 1983, Sam Sianis tried to get Billy Goat IX into Wrigley Field, but he too was rejected by the ushers. Guess what happened to the Cubs? Don't mess with the goat.

Billy Goat Tavern and Grill, 430 N. Lower Michigan Ave., Chicago, IL 60611

Phone: (312) 222-1525

Hours: Monday–Thursday 7 AM–2 AM, Friday 7 AM–3 AM, Saturday 10 AM–3 AM, Sunday
   11 AM–2 AM

Cost: Meals $3–6

Website: www.billygoattavern.com

Directions: Underneath the Wrigley Building, just north of the river.

The Meatloaf Bakery

If you prefer your ground meat without the casing, might we suggest the Meatloaf Bakery? Don't be confused by those cupcakes in the display case—they're actually miniature meatloaves topped with mashed potato icing.

The Meatloaf Bakery is the creation of Cynthia Kallile, who is always coming up with ideas to run through her grinder. Kallile's recipes are an improvement over the standard hamburger-with-ketchup entrée mom used to make. The Wing and a Prayer Loaf is ground chicken with bleu cheese and celery; the No Buns About It Burger Loaf contains bacon, cheddar, and pickles; and the Omega-3 Loaf has salmon spiced with parsley, lemon, and dill. For you vegetarians, try the Yentyl Lentil Loaf—no critters were harmed for this one.

2464 N. Clark St., Chicago, IL 60614

Phone: (773) 698-6667

Hours: Tuesday–Friday, noon–8 PM, Saturday 11 AM–8 PM, Sunday 1–5:30 PM

Cost: Cupcakes, $8–$10; meatloaf, $35–$45

Website: www.themeatloafbakery.com

Directions: Two blocks north of Fullerton Ave.

Gulliver's Pizza

Imagine Snooki exploded in a lighting showroom and somebody catered the event—that's Gulliver's Pizza. Three hundred or so dimly burning chandeliers choke the ceiling; every wall, booth, and crevice is encrusted with gilded mirrors and art nouveau bric-a-brac; and Sinatra music wafts from the shadowy back corners. Each and every item they've decorated with has a large white sticker with a number on it—for "insurance purposes," you are told. All that's missing is vinyl slipcovers on the chairs.

The food here is all right—Applebee's fare, maybe better. Yet somehow it tastes a little blander given the visual overload your eyeballs are experiencing. This looks like a perfect place for a prom date, though if you wear a powder blue tux you might walk out stickered and catalogued by mistake.

(Note: There are three Gulliver's locations, but only the Chicago establishment is this special.)

2727 W. Howard St., Chicago, IL 60645

Phone: (773) 388-2166

Hours: Monday–Thursday 11 AM–11 PM, Friday–Saturday 11 AM–midnight, Sunday noon–11 PM

Cost: Meals $8–$16

Website: www.gulliverspizza.com

Directions: One block east of Dodge/California Ave.

The Matchbox

If you want any elbow room at the Matchbox you should apply for a job, because there is more space behind this bar than there is in front of it. This sliver of a drinking establishment is widest at the front door, about two stools' worth, and tapers to a point at the rear. When you sit at the bar your back is nearly resting on the front window. This makes for cozy drinking, but be sure you're sitting next to the person you want to speak to, because you'll be beside them all evening.

The Matchbox, open since 1995, is best known for its vodka gimlet: lime juice, egg whites, and vodka served in a martini glass, its rim ringed with powdered sugar. High in Vitamin C, low in cholesterol, and it almost glows in the dark. What could be better for you?

770 N. Milwaukee Ave., Chicago, IL 60642

Phone: (312) 666-9292

Hours: Roughly 4 PM–2 AM

Cost: Gimlets $4

Website: http://thesilverpalmrestaurant.com/TheMachBox.php

Directions: At the corner of Ogden Blvd. and Milwaukee Ave.

CHICAGO CULINARY CREATIONS

Is your idea of eating out parking after the drive-thru? Well then, Chicago is your kind of place. Fast food, fattening food, all created right here in the City of Big Shoulders and Bigger Stomachs.

→ **Beer Cans:** In 1935, **Chicago's American Can Company** introduced its post-Prohibition sensation to a thirsty nation.

→ **Cracker Jack:** F. W. Rueckheim first sold Cracker Jack at the 1893 Chicago World's Fair; prizes weren't included until 1912. Cracker Jack, the boy, was fashioned after his grandson, Robert, who died at age seven (and is buried at **St. Henry Cemetery**, 6346 N. Ridge Ave.).

→ **Crock-Pot:** The 1970s sensation was invented by Rogers Park engineer Irving Naxon; the Crock-Pot was originally named the Naxon Beanery.

→ **Deep-Dish Pizza:** Known around the world as Chicago-style pizza, the first deep dish was served at **Pizzeria Uno** (29 E. Ohio St., (312) 943-1995, www.unos.com) in 1943. It was the invention of Ric Riccardo and Ike Sewell.

→ **Dove Bars:** The first Dove Bars were produced in 1952 by Leo Stefanos at his South Side confectionery (61st St. and Pulaski Rd.).

→ **Foot-Long Hotdogs: Riverview Amusement Park** (Belmont and Western Aves.) began selling foot-longs in the 1930s.

→ **Screw-Cap Bottles:** Edward Ravenscroft of **Abbott Laboratories** in North Chicago (Waukegan Rd.) patented the screw-cap bottle in 1936.

- **Sundaes:** Deacon Garwood invented the sundae after Evanston banned seltzer water on the Sabbath. Ice cream and syrup were still legal. The name's modified spelling reflects Evanston's blue laws.

- **Twinkies:** The manager of the **Continental Baking Company's Hostess Bakery** in Schiller Park, James Dewar, concocted the snack food in 1930. Dewar claimed he ate two Twinkies every day for the rest of his life, and lived into his 80s.

- **Weber Grills:** Mount Prospect metalworker George Stevens made the first Weber Grill (aka George's Bar-B-Q Kettle) in 1951 at the **Weber Brothers Metal Works of Palatine,** his employer.

Hooray for Chicagowood!

Summertime in the Windy City means location shoots for Hollywood studios. It is not uncommon to find blocks' worth of neighborhood parking gobbled up by film trailers, but the payoff is seeing Alec Baldwin or Meg Ryan eating in your favorite restaurant on the silver screen. Pinch me!

Yet Chicago's Hollywood connection is greater than just being a backdrop. It was once the home of the fledgling film industry and has been the artistic training ground of many movie and television stars.

Essanay Studios

Before there was Hollywood, there was Chicago. During the fledgling years of the film industry, the Windy City was home to several studios, the largest of which was Essanay.

Essanay was in business from 1907 to 1917. It was the collaboration of George Spoor and Gilbert "Bronco Billy" Anderson, the S and A of Essan-ay. Together they amassed an impressive talent pool of early silent stars, including Charlie Chaplin, Gloria Swanson, Ben Turpin, Wallace Beery, Tom Mix, Francis X. Bushman, and, of course, Bronco Billy. Chaplin (who

lived in the Brewster's penthouse at 2800 N. Pine Grove Ave.) worked at Essanay from 1915 to 1916 after leaving Keystone. Here he made 14 movies, including *The Tramp*, at the unheard-of salary of $1,250 a week. But because of creative differences with the owners, Chaplin didn't last long at Essanay.

Uptown was home to the stars and the site of many location shots. The nearby Chicago & North Western tracks along Ravenswood featured heavily in many *Perils of Pauline* cliffhangers. Castlewood Terrace became a one-block forerunner to Beverly Hills, and the Green Mill (4802 N. Broadway, (773) 878-5552, www.greenmilljazz.com) was a favorite star hangout. And Gloria Swanson and Wallace Beery were married on the Essanay lot in 1916.

It was the public's insatiable appetite for movies and the bitter winters that eventually closed the Chicago studios. Producers needed to film year-round, which was impossible given the climate, so they loaded up their trucks and moved to Beverly. Hills, that is. All that remains of Essanay is the Indian head insignia over the doorway to the old studio building.

1345 W. Argyle St., Chicago, IL 60640

No phone

Hours: Always visible

Cost: Free

Directions: Between Broadway and Clark St.

Hollywood before Hollywood.

The Music Box

Every movie theater should be this magnificent. One visit to the Music Box and you'll never want to go back to your Octoplex, unless you have a craving for something that doesn't have subtitles or a complicated plot.

The Music Box was built in 1929 and restored in 1983 by Chris Carlo and Bob Chaney. It still has its original Wurlitzer organ, twinkling stars, projected clouds floating across the ceiling, and Mediterranean facades. And if you come early on a Friday or Saturday, a live organist will entertain you before the show, including sing-alongs!

Gene Siskel once said that his favorite movie seat in Chicago was the first seat in the last row of the Music Box. It's on the left as you enter the right-side entrance, and he isn't using it anymore.

3733 N. Southport Ave., Chicago, IL 60613

Phone: (773) 871-6604

Hours: Call for show times

Cost: Monday, $5; first show (Monday–Thursday), $8.25; all other shows $9.25

Website: www.musicboxtheatre.com

Directions: Between Addison St. and Irving Park Rd. on Southport Ave., four blocks west of Clark St.

Blues Brothers Tour

You can argue the point, and be wrong, but *The Blues Brothers* is Chicago's best "location" movie. Other films have portrayed the city more realistically, but none have done it with such affection. When it comes to Blues Brothers sites, however, the Windy City has not returned the affection; most of the movie locations have been closed, bulldozed, or forgotten, though there are still a few sites left around to see.

The movie opens with Elwood picking up Joliet Jake as he's released from **Joliet Prison** (1125 N. Collins St., Joliet). On the way back to Chicago, Elwood jumps the half-open **East 95th Street Bridge** (95th St. and South Chicago Ave., Chicago) in the new Bluesmobile.

The pair end up at the fictitious St. Helen of the Blessed Shroud orphanage in Calumet City (fake building entrance built in an alley near 18th St. and Normal Ave., Chicago) where they learn from the Penguin that the city is about to shut the place down for back taxes. At the urging

Do you see the light?!

of Cab Calloway, the janitor, Jake and Elwood head over to the Triple Rock Church (**Pilgrim Baptist Church**, 3235 E. 91st St., Chicago) to "get wise." During a service led by James Brown, Jake sees the light and sets out to put the band back together. Heading back to Elwood's flophouse, their car is pulled over in Park Ridge (729 N. Cumberland Ave.) by Illinois state troopers. Elwood ditches the cops using an escape route through the now-demolished **Dixie Square Mall** (15201 S. Dixie Hwy., Harvey). They end up downtown at the **Plymouth Hotel** (22 W. Van Buren St., Chicago), where they are fired upon by Jake's ex-fiancée. The Plymouth was not blown up by Carrie Fisher's rocket launcher; it was torn down in 1991 to make way for Pritzker Park across from the Harold Washington Library.

The brothers rescue Murph and the Magic Tones from the Armada Room at a **Holiday Inn** (3801 Manheim Rd., Schiller Park; today a Quality Inn). Next they recruit Mr. Fabulous from his maitre d' gig at **Chez Paul** (660 N. Rush St., Chicago; closed) after harassing the restaurant's snooty guests. The following day, they run a band of Illinois Nazis into the **Jackson Park Lagoon** (6000 S. Lake Shore Dr., Chicago). The bridge in the movie is actually a walking path south of the Museum of Science and Industry. The Nazis get the license plate number from the Bluesmobile and join in the movie-long chase, diverted at first by showing up at Elwood's false address: 1060 W. Addison Street, **Wrigley Field**.

The final band members, Matt "Guitar" Murphy and Blue Lou, work at **Nate's Delicatessen** (807 W. Maxwell St., Chicago), next to the old Maxwell Street Market. Here, Aretha Franklin tells her husband Matt to "Think" about why he shouldn't leave her, but he does anyway. Nate's and the Maxwell Street Market were run off by the expansion of the University of Illinois at Chicago campus.

With the band back together, the Blue Brothers stop by Ray's Record Exchange (**Shelley's Loan and Jewelry**, 300 E. 47th St., Chicago; the mural painted for the film is still on the west side of the building), where they pick up musical equipment from Ray Charles, on an IOU, of course. After nearly being killed in the **Howard Johnson's** parking lot phone booth (Des Plaines Oasis, I-90) by Carrie Fisher and her flamethrower, they play their first gig at Bob's Country Bunker in Kokomo, Indiana, substituting for the Good Ol' Boys, unbeknownst to the management. They come across the same Illinois troopers (completely outside their jurisdiction!) who chased the pair through the mall. The troopers ram the Good Ol' Boys' Winnebago and the Blues Brothers escape.

Jake and Elwood hatch a plan to stage a benefit concert. Midway through the show at the Palace Hotel Ballroom (exterior, **South Shore Cultural Center**, 7059 S. Shore Dr., Chicago; interior, LA's Palladium), Jake and Elwood receive a lucrative recording contract and head off to Chicago, followed by police, Nazis, and rednecks.

During the Chicago Loop high-speed chase, the Blues Brothers break through a police barricade at **McCormick Place** (2300 S. Lake Shore Dr.), race along under the **Lake Street** and **Wells Street El** tracks, jump a police car near the **Lyric Opera** (Lower Wacker Dr. ramp to Upper Wacker at Monroe St.), drive through the lobby windows of the **Richard J. Daley Civic Center and Plaza** (50 W. Washington St.), and park outside the **Cook County Building** (118 N. Clark St.). They pay the taxes and the orphanage is saved, but the pair end up back in Joliet.

A replica of the Bluesmobile is sometimes parked outside Dan Akroyd's **House of Blues**. Statues of Jake and Elwood can be found dancing atop the **Rich and Creamy Ice Cream Shop** (920 N. Broadway St., (815) 740-2899) in Joliet. And if it's the music you like, you can also check out the Blooze Brothers (www.sweethomechicagoband.com), a Blues Brothers tribute band that plays Chicagoland venues.

House of Blues, 329 N. Dearborn St., Chicago, IL 60654
Phone: (312) 923-2000
Hours: Lunch, Monday–Saturday 11:30 AM–4 PM; dinner, Sunday–Thursday 4–10 PM,
    Friday–Saturday 4–11 PM
Cost: Lunch $7–$15; dinner $10–$25
Website: www.houseofblues.com
Directions: West of Clark St. on the north side of the river.

SOME CHICAGOLAND MOVIES

About Last Night
Backdraft
Barbershop
Batman Begins
The Breakfast Club
Candyman
Class
The Color of Money
Cooley High
The Dark Knight
Eight Men Out
Endless Love
Escape from New York
Ferris Bueller's Day Off
Flatliners
The Fugitive
Henry: Portrait of a Serial
   Killer
High Fidelity
Hoffa
Hoop Dreams
A League of Their Own
Little Fockers

Looking for Mr. Goodbar
Medium Cool
The Music Box
My Best Friend's
   Wedding
My Bodyguard
Native Son
Natural Born Killers
North by Northwest
Ordinary People
Planes, Trains, and
   Automobiles
Risky Business
Silver Streak
Sixteen Candles
Sleepless in Seattle
Soul Food
Spiderman II
Transformers: Dark of the
   Moon
The Untouchables
Wayne's World
When Harry Met Sally

Good Times

Good Times, a spinoff of *Maude*, which was a spinoff of *All in the Family*, was perhaps Norman Lear's most controversial 1970s sitcom, and that was just among the cast members. The show was set in Cabrini-Green and was intended to address issues of the African American underclass. It quickly degenerated into a three-syllable interjection: Dy-no-mite! Jimmy "J. J." Walker became an instant superstar, and the rest of the cast began to grumble. John Amos left the series, turning the TV family's dynamic in an

even more stereotypical direction, according to Esther Rolle, who played the matriarch.

The opening credits were shot outside Cabrini-Green, but nothing else was filmed there. Cabrini-Green was built on the site of Edwin G. Cooley Vocational High School (1225 N. Sedgwick St.) of *Cooley High* fame. The popular 1975 movie, based on the life of Eric Monte (who wrote for *Good Times*), was the inspiration for *What's Happening!*

Cabrini-Green was also the home to the urban legend of the Candyman. According to the story, a mob executed a man on this site by chopping off his hand, smearing him with honey, and allowing bees to sting him to death. The Candyman kills those who do not believe he exists with his hooked stump. The story was made into two horror movies.

The last of Cabrini-Green was torn down in the 2000s by crews with wrecking balls and, yes, dy-no-mite.

Division and Halsted Sts., Chicago, IL 60622

No phone

Hours: Torn down

Cost: Free

Directions: Northwest of downtown.

Hi, Bob!

The Bob Newhart Show, which ran from 1972 to 1978, was set in Chicago, though there is some debate as to exactly where. One thing's for sure: Bob Hartley's office was located on Michigan Avenue just north of the Wrigley Building. Don't try getting in—the security guard will stop you.

The location of the Hartleys' apartment, however, is a bit of a mystery. According to the script, they lived in the "Meridian Beach Apartments," number 523, in the zip code 60611. The show's exterior shots zoom in on the Buckingham Plaza apartments across the river (in zip code 60601), and focus on the seventh floor, not the fifth. Did the producers think nobody would count? Buckingham Plaza isn't open to the general public either.

Even though Hartley has long since retired his practice, the good folks at TV Land had him, his chair, and an empty couch cast in bronze and placed outside his Michigan Avenue office in 2004. It was later moved to Navy Pier, where you can recline and tell him all your kooky, only-on-television issues.

Robert Hartley's Office, 430 N. Michigan Ave., Suite 715, Chicago, IL 60611

The Hartleys' Apartment, Buckingham Plaza, 360 E. Randolph St., Chicago, IL 60601

Bob Newhart's Couch (Statue), Navy Pier, 600 E. Grand Ave., Chicago, IL 60611

No phone

Hours: Always visible

Cost: Free

Website: www.bobnewhart.com

Directions: In the park next to the cab dropoff.

The author unloads.

Hill Street Blues

Hill Street Blues was never officially set in any city, but most suspected it was Chicago. Part of the reason was that location shots were often filmed in the Windy City, and that the precinct shown was an actual Chicago police station. The television series ran from 1981 to 1987, but the old police station had a longer run. The Maxwell Street station was built in the late 1800s as a response to the Haymarket Riot (see pages 68–69). It had a notorious dungeon for holding and roughing up prisoners, and Al Capone was once briefly detained here, as were protesters picked up in the 1968 police riot at the Democratic National Convention.

The precinct was closed in the late 1990s, but it reopened as the head-quarters for the campus police of the University of Illinois at Chicago.

UIC Police Station, 943 W. Maxwell St., Chicago, IL 60608

Phone: (312) 996-2830

Hours: Always visible

Cost: Free

Directions: One block south of Roosevelt Rd., two blocks west of Halsted St.

Family Matters

We want an Urkel statue!!

When it comes to African American sitcoms based in Chicago, *Family Matters* was a step up from *Good Times*, but honestly, was there anywhere to go but up? And as with *Good Times*, the show that might have started with good intentions was unexpectedly hijacked by the popularity of its goofiest character—in this case Steve Urkel. The nerdy next-door neighbor of the Winslow family didn't show up until midway through the first season, but once he did he never left. Urkel was played by Jaleel White, who later expanded his repertoire by playing Stefan Urkquelle, Urkel's tempera-mental opposite, and Myrtle Urkel, his biological opposite.

The series was a spinoff of *Perfect Strangers* and premiered on ABC's fall 1989 lineup, and it lasted eight seasons. After it was canceled, it was picked up by CBS for another year. The home shown in the opening credits is a real home facing Chicago's Wrightwood Park, and no, TV Land has not erected a bronze statue to Urkel at the site. Yet.

1516 W. Wrightwood Ave., Chicago, IL 60614

Private phone

Hours: Always visible

Cost: Free

Directions: One block east of Ashland Ave. on the north side of Wrightwood Park.

Bundy Fountain Light Show

Though its history is refined, the Buckingham Memorial Fountain is best known as the opening shot on *Married with Children*. In fact, many European visitors are surprised to learn that its name isn't the Bundy Fountain.

The Buckingham Fountain, built in 1927, is based on the Latona Basin fountain at Versailles and is named in honor of Clarence Buckingham, late brother of Kate Buckingham, its patron. It pumps 14,100 gallons a minute, some of it 150 feet into the air. Every night during the summer there's a multicolored light show after dusk, on the hour. It's well worth the trip downtown, unless Grant Park is overrun by Taste of Chicago or Blues Fest revelers.

Grant Park, 250 S. Lake Shore Dr., Chicago, IL 60601

Phone: (312) 742-PLAY

Hours: Summers; light show 8–10 PM

Cost: Free

Website: www.chicagoparkdistrict.com

Directions: Where Congress Pkwy. meets Columbus Dr.

WHEN STARS ATTACK

Cabbies and limo drivers beware—sightseers, too! Celebrities from both coasts have been known to attack while in the Windy City.

Take **Dan Rather.** He refused to pay a $12.50 fare after his Chicago cabbie got lost in November 1980. The driver then took off down Lake Shore Drive with Dan still inside screaming, "I'm being kidnapped!" to any motorist who would listen. Nobody did.

Peter Fonda stole a limo from a downtown hotel in September 1988 after arguing with the chauffeur, then drove his friends to O'Hare Airport. Chicago police nabbed Fonda there, but the limo service never pressed charges.

Butch "Eddie Munster" Patrick actually beat up his limo driver in November 1990 after the chauffeur got lost. And if that wasn't enough, Patrick reportedly stole the man's wallet, a charge for which he was later acquitted. Patrick ended up paying the driver $850 in damages and a $200 fine. He also received two years' probation with 200 hours of community service.

Actor **Shia LaBeouf** was arrested on November 4, 2007, for being drunk and belligerent in a downtown Walgreens (757 N. Michigan Ave.). He was trying, not very successfully, to buy pimple cream and Gummi bears.

And finally, on August 8, 2004, sightseers on a Chicago River cruise were splattered with 800 pounds of human waste dumped from the Kinzie Street bridge by the driver of the **Dave Matthews Band** tour bus. The driver pled guilty to reckless conduct; the band paid a $200,000 fine and gave $100,000 to the Friends of the Chicago River (www.chicagoriver.org/home /index.php).

When Things Go Wrong
Fires, Floods, and Other Windy City Catastrophes

Chicago loves disasters. Why else would the city commemorate the Great Chicago Fire and the Fort Dearborn Massacre on its flag? That's right, two of the flag's four stars signify those tragedies; the other two stars are for the city's World Fairs.

So if Chicago doesn't have any difficulty bringing up these horrific events, why should you, the humble traveler, worry if visiting them is in poor taste? Lighten up. Enjoy the carnage!

The Great Chicago Fire

The most popular explanation for the Chicago Fire's origin has been all but debunked, but here it is anyway: Mrs. Catherine O'Leary's cow kicked over a lantern while she was milking it on October 8, 1871. It was 9:30 PM. During the next 27 hours, a conflagration leveled 3.5 square miles of the Midwest's largest city, killing 250, destroying 17,450 buildings, and leaving more than 94,000 homeless, one-third of the city's population. Ironically,

Don't blame the cow.

the O'Learys weren't among the victims; their home survived the fire. The flames kicked up a 60-mph draft inward as it gobbled 65 acres an hour. Heat from the flames could be felt 100 miles away, and the fire's glow was spotted from Lake Geneva, Wisconsin, to towns in Michigan.

Citizens fled the wall of flames, running out into Lake Michigan or into Lincoln Park, where they huddled in recently exhumed graves at the old City Cemetery. Buildings were blown up along Congress Street by General Sheridan to stop the fire, but that didn't halt its advance. A small fraction of the male population used the opportunity to raid abandoned saloons, putting themselves in no position to fight or outrun the approaching flames. The fire didn't burn itself out until it reached Fullerton Avenue on the North Side.

So how did the fire really start? Several theories have been presented. Everyone agrees today that O'Leary was not in the barn when it ignited. At the time, some pointed the finger not at the cow but at a group of Irish youths who had gone to O'Leary's barn to get some milk to make their alcoholic "punch" and started the fire by mistake. Today, some accuse O'Leary's neighbor, Daniel "Peg Leg" Sullivan, who was all too eager to accuse poor old Kate. Sullivan apparently was lying when he told an inquiry board that he saw the fire start in O'Leary's barn, a barn that was actually blocked from his view by a two-story home.

The most interesting theory presented blames a heavenly body: a comet! Author Mel Waskin, in the book *Mrs. O'Leary's Comet*, claims Biela's Comet broke into two pieces in 1845, one of which crashed to earth when it circled back around in 1871. Interestingly enough, more than 20 towns around the Midwest were leveled by three major fires that all started at about the same moment, including Peshtigo, Wisconsin, and Manistee, Michigan. Many witnesses claim to have heard a thunderous roar before the fires began, and a mysterious rain of sand during the fire. It sounds wacky, but the book is quite convincing.

A bronze, flame-shaped monument to the victims, titled *Pillar of Fire*, now stands at the former site of O'Leary's barn. It is also the location of the fire department's training center. Just around the corner you'll find the CFD's Survive Alive House, should you want to avoid a similar tragedy of your own.

Chicago Fire Academy, 558 W. DeKoven St. (137 before renumbering), Chicago, IL 60607
Phone: (312) 747-7238
Hours: Always visible
Cost: Free
Website: www.cpfta.com, www.survivealivehouse.com
Directions: One block north of Roosevelt Rd., two blocks east of the Dan Ryan Expy.

DEBUNKING A MYTH

One of the buildings to survive the fire, **Holy Family Catholic Church** (1080 W. Roosevelt Rd., (312) 492-8442, www .holyfamilychicago.org), still commemorates its survival. Seven candles—today, lightbulbs—are kept lit in front of a statue of the Virgin Mary, Our Lady of Perpetual Help. The candles fulfill a solemn oath made by the church's pastor, Father Arnold Damen. He was in New York City at the time, but he had gotten the news by telegraph and prayed to the Virgin Mary as the fire headed for Holy Family. Parishioners claimed the flames miraculously turned, but any student of the fire knows they were bearing false witness. From the beginning, the flames burned toward Lake Michigan, not inland toward Holy Family. In other words, the church was never in any danger. Still, the lightbulbs remain illuminated, just in case.

Other Chicago Fires

While the Great Chicago Fire was disastrous, it was not the most deadly fire in Chicago history. Both a 1903 fire at the Iroquois Theater and a 1995 heat wave racked up more casualties. So if you're a firebug, check out these other Chicago sites, or consider taking one of O'Leary's Chicago Fire Truck Tours (www.olearysfiretours.com).

- The **Iroquois Theater**'s (24 W. Randolph St., today the site of the Oriental Theatre) backdrop caught fire during a performance of *Mr. Bluebeard* on December 30, 1903. More than 600 theatergoers were burned or trampled, most of them women and children. The Iroquois had been dubbed "absolutely fireproof" during its grand opening only 27 days earlier. The asbestos safety curtain jammed as it was being dropped. The fire led to the first red EXIT signs, fireproofed scenery, and the practice of having exit doors opening outward with "panic bars." A monument to the victims is located in Montrose Cemetery (5400 N. Pulaski Rd., (773) 478-5400, www.montrosecemetery.com).

- Goodyear's first dirigible, the *Wingfoot*, crashed through the skylight of the **Illinois Trust and Savings Bank** (231 S. LaSalle St., today the site of the Bank of America building) on July 21, 1919, after an engine set the hydrogen-filled balloon on fire. It was on its maiden voyage. Twelve died, nine of them in the bank, and many more were injured.

- The **La Salle Hotel** (LaSalle and Madison Sts.) caught fire on June 6, 1946. Sixty-one people died after burning, asphyxiating, or jumping to their deaths. Owners had billed the hotel as "the largest, safest, and most modern hotel west of New York." The structure was repaired and used as a hotel until it was razed in 1976.

- Three nuns and 92 children perished on December 1, 1958, when **Our Lady of the Angels Parochial School** (909 N. Avers Ave.) caught fire. All public and private schools were ordered to install sprinklers after the tragedy; none could be "grand-fathered" to avoid compliance as Our Lady of the Angels had been. Twenty-five of the victims were buried near a memorial at Queen of Heaven Cemetery in Hillside (1400 S. Wolf Rd.). A new school has been built near the site (3820 W. Iowa St.).

- The **Haber Corporation plant** in Chicago (908 W. North Ave.) burned following an explosion on April 16, 1953. It was in the process of being remodeled and the front entrances were blocked. Thirty-five workers perished.

- The **Paxton Hotel** (1432 N. LaSalle St.) caught fire on March 16, 1993, killing 19 residents. The SRO hotel was not required to install sprinklers in order to keep the rents reasonable for its low-income residents.

- More than 700 Chicago residents died during a July **1995 heat wave**. Though not a fire, it sure felt like Hell.

- It wasn't the 12th-floor fire at the **Cook County Administration Building** (69 W. Washington St.) that killed six on October 17, 2003, but the smoke. Employees evacuating down the east stairwell were told to head back up, but all the doors were locked until they reached the 27th floor. The victims died on the 22nd floor before they ever reached safety.

Haymarket Riot

On May 4, 1886, a group of workers and anarchists gathered in Haymarket Square to protest working conditions at the McCormick Farm Machinery Works (Blue Island and Western Aves.) where two protesters had been shot the day before. Central to their grievances was the call for an eight-hour workday. By all accounts, the gathering was peaceful—even Chicago Mayor Carter Harrison stopped by for a look. Then the police arrived.

A battalion of 176 police officers approached the workers near the corner of Randolph and Des Plaines Streets. Without warning, a bomb was thrown at the police. One policeman was killed immediately. Pandemonium erupted, and before it was over, six other cops and four civilians (probably more) were either dead or mortally wounded. An investigation later suggested that most of the police casualties were shot in the back by other trigger-happy cops during the fracas.

Each side blamed the other for the explosion, though it was never determined who was responsible. That didn't mean, however, that nobody was indicted for the crime. Eight men, all anarchists and/or labor organizers, were tried and convicted, even though six of them had not even been there that night. Four were eventually hanged on Black Friday, November 11, 1887: August Spies, Albert Parsons, Adolph Fischer, and George Engel. A fifth, Louis Lingg, was scheduled for the gallows but committed suicide in his cell the day before; Lingg bit down on a dynamite cap smuggled into his cell. Before the trap door opened, August Spies shouted, "The day will come when our silence will be more powerful than the voices you are throttling today." George Engel was less prophetic but more upbeat, shouting, "Hurrah for anarchy! This is the happiest moment of my life!"

Three men who received prison sentences, Michael Schwab, Samuel Fielden, and Oscar Neebe, were pardoned in 1893 by Illinois governor John Peter Altgeld. Though scorned and soundly defeated in the next election, Altgeld proclaimed, "No man's ambition has the right to stand in the way of performing a simple act of justice."

For many years, a monument stood at the site of the riot. It was dedicated not to the workers looking for a fair deal but to the police who shot one another in the backs. The statue of a policeman, arm outstretched, topped a pedestal that read, "In the name of the people of Illinois, I command peace!" the words supposedly uttered by police captain William Ward before the riot started.

Power to the people!

The monument had its critics and had to be shuffled around Chicago for years. At each new location it was threatened by vandals, workers, or Yippies. It was bombed in 1890, rammed by a proletarian streetcar driver in 1927, and blown up by the Weathermen in 1969 and by another unnamed bomber in 1970. It was then moved to the lobby of the Chicago Police Academy where it stands today. What remained of its base was jackhammered away before the 1996 Democratic National Convention.

Finally, in 2004, a proper memorial to the whole affair was erected. The sculpture by artist Mary Brogger depicts a rabble-rouser atop a flatbed cart. It was placed on the exact location of the speakers' platform that fateful evening.

600 W. Randolph St., Chicago, IL 60661

No phone

Hours: Always visible

Cost: Free

Website: www.illinoislaborhistory.org/haymarket-tragedy.html, http://dwardmac.pitzer.edu/
  Anarchist_Archives/haymarket/Haymarket.html

Directions: At Randolph and Des Plaines Sts. in the West Loop.

CHICAGO LAWS

Advocating for an eight-hour workday isn't the only thing that can get you in trouble with the cops. Here are a few more ways to run afoul of the law in the Windy City:

→ Wear pince-nez glasses while driving a car.

→ Bring a French poodle to an opera house.

→ Walk a hog through the city streets without a ring in its nose.

→ Fish off the breakwater in your pajamas.

→ Eat in a burning restaurant.

→ Install a pay toilet.

→ Go outside if you've been deformed, diseased, or maimed so that you are "an unsightly or disgusting object."

Murder Castle

It is in a strange way reassuring that mass murder is not a modern phenomenon. The case of Herman Mudgett ("Dr. H. H. Holmes") is an excellent case in point.

Mudgett built a three-story edifice across the street from his Chicago drugstore in 1892, just prior to the 1893 Columbian Exposition. Locals called it the Castle. By continually hiring and firing construction workers, he was able to keep his blueprints secret. The 60-room building contained a soundproof dungeon, trap doors, hidden staircases, false walls, a third-floor door that dropped to the alley, sealed rooms that could be locked from the outside and gassed from the inside, and more than one slippery body chute.

The Columbian Exposition and the lonely hearts papers provided Mudgett with plenty of victims. The smooth-talking murderer would convince visitors to sign over their savings accounts and insurance policies, people who would then "disappear." They would then "reappear" as skel-

etons that Mudgett fenced to medical schools, no questions asked. High estimates put the number of victims at 200.

This continued until Mudgett was arrested for bumping off his assistant, Benjamin Pitezel, and his three children in a fraud scam that started in Philadelphia. Word of Mudgett's arrest got back to Chicago, and police entered the Castle. Though no corpses were found, evidence of his sinister operation was damning. Mudgett was executed in Pennsylvania on May 7, 1896, and his corpse was sealed in cement before burial. Bad as he was, there is no truth to the legend that a lightning bolt struck Holmes in the neck just as the gallows' trapdoor opened.

The Castle became a tourist attraction during the murder trial; people gladly paid 25 cents to see Mudgett's chambers. But locals thought the place was bad for business and somebody burned it to the ground on August 19, 1896.

So the next time you hear someone lament, "What is this world coming to?" point out that it could be worse . . . and sometimes was.

701 W. 63rd St., Chicago, IL 60637

No phone

Hours: Torn down

Cost: Free

Directions: At 63rd St. and Wallace St., where the US Post Office stands today.

Eastland Death Site

Believe it or not, the United States' second most deadly inland marine tragedy occurred downtown only a few feet from the banks of the Chicago River. The *Eastland* was docked at the Clark Street bridge along Wacker Drive between LaSalle and Clark Streets on July 24, 1915. About 2,500 employees of the Western Electric Company squeezed onto the boat meant for half that number. The top-heavy ship tipped toward the dock, the passengers shifted to the other side at the same moment the crew flooded ballast tanks, and the craft capsized in the opposite direction. In all, 812 people died, including 22 entire families.

Interestingly enough, public reaction to the *Titanic* disaster three years earlier might have contributed to the tragedy. The *Eastland* was overloaded with lifeboats on its upper deck, retrofitted after the *Titanic* sunk, which made the craft unstable.

Some of the tragedy's victims were sent to the 2nd Regiment Armory (1054 W. Washington Blvd.), where a makeshift morgue had been opened. This same building houses Oprah's Harpo Studios today, and the talk show host has claimed she has felt the spirits' presence. One of those who didn't die in the wreck was George Halas, who would later become the Bears' football coach. He arrived at the dock too late because of a baseball game in Indiana. Lucky George!

180 W. Wacker Dr., Chicago, IL 60606

No phone

Hours: Always visible

Cost: Free

Directions: Along the Wacker Dr. walkway between the LaSalle Blvd. and Clark St. bridges.

ANOTHER CHICAGO WATER DISASTER

Returning from a campaign rally in Milwaukee, 297 Chicago Democrats died on September 8, 1860, when the *Lady Elgin* steamer collided with a schooner, the *Augusta of Oswego*, and sank in Lake Michigan. Only 98 people survived the 10-mile swim to shore. The tragedy spurred the construction of the Grosse Point Lighthouse in Evanston. In 1989 the wreckage was discovered, and plans are underway to either salvage the ship or make it an underwater museum (www.ship-wrecks.net /shipwreck/projects/elgin).

Three Submarines and Something Else

You wouldn't expect to hear a strange submarine story associated with Chicago, but there are actually four.

Salvage crews dredging the river following the *Eastland* tragedy snagged a small craft on the riverbed. It turned out to be a one-man submarine with two skeletons inside, one human and one dog. Investigators believed it to be the wreck of an experimental vessel made by Lodner Phillips from Indiana. He had sold the imperfect contraption to William Nis-

Will somebody please let me out?
Photo by author, courtesy the Museum of Science and Industry, Chicago

sen, most likely the victim found inside. The craft was dubbed the *Foolkiller* and put on display downtown, along with the two skeletons.

The *Eastland*, on the other hand, was righted and eventually rechristened the USS *Wilmette*. It served as a Navy gunboat in World War I and a trainer out of Navy Pier following the war. At the same time, a confiscated German UC-97 sub needed to be scuttled under terms of the Treaty of Versailles, and it was the USS *Wilmette* that sent it to the bottom of Lake Michigan, 20 miles off the Chicago shore.

Years later another sub, a Nazi U-505, was captured off the West African coast on June 4, 1944, along with two M4 Enigma machines and 900 pounds of Axis codebooks. The sub was donated to the Museum of Science and Industry in 1954, where it's on display today along with several fake crates of sauerkraut. In 2004 the submarine exhibit underwent extensive renovations.

The final underwater craft was found just inside the Chicago River locks in the ship-turning basin. The 31-foot-long object was shaped like a hotdog and had a square hatch in its side. It was made of wood, banded with iron straps, and had a pipe running from end to end. What was it? Some say it was a TymBarge, named after its inventor Michael Tym. This underwater barge was designed to secretly transport fuel during World War II, hidden from view beneath the water's surface. After a test run off Navy Pier, the US Navy passed on ordering a fleet, and the TymBarge was scuttled where it berthed. In 1999 divers towed it four miles offshore and sank it for good.

Museum of Science and Industry, 5700 S. Lake Shore Dr., Chicago, IL 60637

Phone: (773) 684-1414

Hours: June–August, daily 9:30 AM–5:30 PM; September–May, daily 9:30 AM–4 PM

Cost: Adults $15, seniors (65+) $14, kids (3–11) $10; check website for free days

Website: www.msichicago.org

Directions: At the north end of Jackson Park, off Lake Shore Dr. at 57th St.

Where Nothing Happened

Considering all the horrible disasters that have befallen the Windy City, isn't it nice to know that there's a place you can visit where people weren't drowned, immolated, or dropped from the sky? Check out the plaque outside the door of Chicago's oldest tavern, the Green Door: ON THIS SITE IN 1897 NOTHING HAPPENED.

But 1898? Well . . .

Green Door Tavern, 678 N. Orleans St., Chicago, IL 60654

Phone: (312) 664-5496

Hours: Always visible

Cost: Free

Website: http://greendoorchicago.com

Directions: One block south of Chicago Ave., three blocks west of LaSalle St.

God and the Devil Come to Town
Holy and Unholy Visitations

If given the choice to equate Chicago with Heaven or Hell, most people choose Hell. It is, after all, the birthplace of both Anton LaVey and the Devil Baby of Hull House (see pages 268–70). Ashley Montague once said, "Hell has been described as a pocket edition of Chicago," and Carl Sandburg concurred: "Here is the difference between Dante, Milton, and me. They wrote about Hell and never saw the place. I wrote about Chicago after looking over the place for years and years."

Still, Chicago has had its fair share of visitors from on high. Jake Blues saw the light in James Brown's South Side parish (see page 56). John Lennon apologized here for saying the Beatles were more popular than Jesus in a nationally televised news conference from Chicago's Astor Towers Hotel (1340 N. Astor St.) on August 11, 1966. In the 1980s a naked man claiming he was Jesus Christ jumped into a moving convertible on Lake Shore Drive, then hopped back out and ran into Lake Michigan. Another self-appointed messiah set fire to two cars in two days during rush hour on the Michigan Avenue bridge, screaming, "I come in the name of Jesus Christ, my father, to save America!"

There's no doubt that Chicagoans love their religion, however much they do or don't live up to their faiths' precepts. The following entries are for them.

Mother Cabrini Death Site

What's a saint gotta do to get a little respect around here? On December 22, 1917, Mother Frances Xavier Cabrini died while sitting in a wicker chair in a small room at Columbus Hospital, a facility she helped found in 1905. Three decades and a few confirmed miracles later, Cabrini was canonized on July 7, 1946, as the patron saint of immigrants.

For years her room was a shrine that contained her death chair, the habit she wore the day before she died, her eyeglasses, and a floor mat that caught a drop of her blood when her soul departed this earth. But then in 2001 Catholic Health Partners shuttered the hospital's doors and the site was redeveloped as—what else?—condominiums! No word yet as to whether Cabrini will also be named the patron saint of unobstructed views of Lincoln Park.

2520 N. Lakeview St., Chicago, IL 60614

No phone

Hours: Always visible

Cost: Free

Directions: Two blocks north of Fullerton Ave. on the west side of Lincoln Park.

Padre Pio Holy Relic

Padre Pio is perhaps one of the twentieth century's best-known stigmatics. He got the wounds during World War I, not by fighting but by offering his own life to God in exchange for the end of the war. Shortly after making the offer he developed a wound in his side . . . and the war ended. Coincidence, hmmmm? Later he developed wounds on his hands and feet, which he usually covered with bandages to discourage lookie-loos. He died in 1968.

Not everyone believed Padre Pio's story. In fact, the Vatican asked Agostino

Padre Pio's dirty laundry.

Gemelli of Milan's Catholic University of the Sacred Heart to investigate Padre Pio; Gemelli proclaimed the priest to be "an ignorant and self-mutilating psychopath who exploited people's credulity." Ouch! Nevertheless, Padre Pio had his supporters in the Church and he was canonized in 2002.

Which brings us to St. John Cantius Church on Chicago's Near West Side. The church has possession of one of Padre Pio's first-class relics, a small linen scrap daubed in the blood oozing from his torso. If the portable relic isn't on display when you arrive, they'll go and find it for you, giving you more time to look around this stunningly beautiful church.

St. John Cantius Church, 825 N. Carpenter St., Chicago, IL 60642

Phone: (312) 243-7373

Hours: Daily 8 AM–5 PM

Cost: Free

Website: www.cantius.org

Directions: Just north of the intersection of Ogden and Chicago Aves.

Salt stain or Mother of God?

Our Lady of the Underpass

File this one under "God Works in Mysterious Ways." In 2005 the Virgin Mary appeared in an unlikely Chicago location: the Fullerton Avenue underpass at the Kennedy Expressway. No, she wasn't a ghost or a glowing vision, but the stain caused by salty runoff dribbling through a crack in the cement.

Mary was first spotted in April, but soon hundreds of the faithful (and local TV news crews) began making a pilgrimage to check it out for them-

selves. A makeshift shrine was built around the stain and commuters complained about traffic jams at the busy intersection. A nonbeliever smeared BIG LIE across Mary in shoe polish, but followers were able to scrub it off. Then in 2006 somebody spray-painted a swastika over the shrine, and the city decided enough was enough and painted it over.

But Mary wasn't so easily deterred, nor were the people who believed in her. There's a new Mary stain and underpass shrine surrounded by plastic flowers, rosaries, and photos of the healed, though there aren't the crowds there used to be.

Fullerton Ave. and I-90/94, Chicago, IL 60647

No phone

Hours: Always visible

Cost: Free

Directions: On the north-side accident-pull-out lane; enter from Fullerton Ave. westbound.

WEEPING AND OOZING AROUND CHICAGOLAND

The Virgin Mary's recent appearance under the Kennedy Expressway is nothing new—weeping statues, icons, and just about everything else are commonplace in Chicago. Here are just a few of the best-known apparitions from recent years.

Bloody Saint

St. Adrian's Church, 7000 S. Fairfield Ave., Chicago, (773) 434-3223

Details are sketchy, but some parishioners at St. Adrian's Church on the South Side still remember when the 1,700-year-old remains of St. Maximina, a first-class relic, began oozing watery blood back in May 1970. Apparently it's easier to get blood from a saint than a turnip.

Mary Cries for Albania

St. Nicholas Albanian Orthodox Church, 2701 N. Narragansett Ave., Chicago, (773) 889-4282, http://stnicholasalbanianchicago.org

A painting of the Virgin Mary in St. Nicholas Albanian Ortho-dox Church began weeping from her eyes and between her fingers on December 6, 1986, "crying for Albania," the official story went. Not only did the painting cry, but the image of the Virgin seemed to be red-eyed and puffy as well. This went on for seven months, during which time her fingers dripped water and a cross appeared on her forehead. Due to ample parking at the adjacent Brickyard Mall, attendance was heavy. The icon stopped weeping in July 1987, then did brief return engage-ments in September 1988 and July 1995. At that time, the tears she produced were used to anoint 19 other icons in Pennsylva-nia, and they all began crying, too.

Weeping Icons

Apanacio and St. John Church, 1416 W. Waveland Ave., Chicago

Several icons at Apanacio and St. John on the North Side began weeping in the early 1990s. The temptation to possess a chan-nel to heaven was too much for one sticky-fingered individ-ual—somebody stole the icons. They were later returned, their tears no longer flowing. The church has since been disbanded and the building torn down.

Mary, Queen of Heaven

Queen of Heaven Cemetery, 1400 S. Wolf Rd., Hillside, (708) 449-8300

A fiberglass crucifix in Hillside's Queen of Heaven Cemetery still bleeds on occasion and turns colors, according to pilgrims. You can find it in the southeast Military Section of the cemetery; it's usually surrounded by the kneeling faithful. Some visitors claim to have seen the Virgin hovering by the cross, some have seen the sun "spin," and others have had their silver rosaries turned to gold. If you visit this site, be sure to talk to some of the gathered. Many have albums of miracle photos show-ing angels in the clouds, light beams shooting out from Jesus's wounds, blood dripping from the statue, and the occasional fingers over their lenses.

The apparitions began after local resident Joseph Reinholtz returned from Medjugorje in 1987. The Virgin appeared to him and restored his eyesight. She then showed up every day as he prayed at the Queen of Heaven crucifix. Word got around and soon hundreds visited the cross each day . . . except Tuesday. Mary did not appear on Tuesday at the request of the Archdiocese; it wanted Reinholtz to give the cemetery a day of rest and the Virgin complied. The Archdiocese also issued a statement on July 26, 1991, that stated its policy on the apparitions: "The Church does not readily accept as authentic any claims made by an individual."

Our Lady of Cicero, the Oily, Oozing Icon

St. George Antiochan Orthodox Church, 1220 S. 60th Ct., Cicero, (708) 656-2927, www.stgeorgecicero.org

An icon panel of the Virgin Mary began weeping oil at the beginning of Holy Week in suburban Cicero on April 22, 1994. Eight Orthodox bishops examined the tears and declared, unanimously, that it was a miracle. Just to be sure they weren't being fooled by the Devil, they performed an exorcism on the icon. Mary continued to cry, so she had to be the real thing. The icon has since been renamed Our Lady of Cicero. Her tears were not enough, however, to prevent a recent fire.

Bowing Plastic Marys

Angel Kisses of St. Charles, 504 E. Main St., St. Charles, (630) 377-0588, www.angelkissesofstcharles.com

In what some cynics might suggest was a crass publicity stunt, the owner of the Angel Kisses religious supply store claimed in November 1994 that six plastic Mary statuettes bowed their heads after rosaries were placed around their necks. Or maybe they just melted in the heat.

Mary of the Parking Lot

2420 Glendale Terrace, Hanover Park

The Virgin of Guadalupe also made a visit to a Hanover Park apartment complex in July 1997. Her image appeared out of the shadows as a security light shined on the side of a building. When the light was turned off, Mary took off, too. But the people remained. A tent was erected in the far southwest end of the building's parking lot, and inside were hundreds of votive candles surrounding a statue of the Virgin of Guadalupe.

Mary of Joliet

611 Abe St., Joliet

The Virgin of Guadalupe made another less-than-glamorous appearance in the attic window of an abandoned house in Joliet. She was first noticed by eight-year-old Francisco Lopez in April 1999. Once word got around, police were needed to direct traffic.

Mary on a Tree Trunk

Rogers Ave. and Honore St., Chicago

In the summer of 2001 the Virgin of Guadalupe also appeared on the scar on a trimmed tree in Rogers Park. The robed image could be seen in the oozing sap where a branch had been cut off. The tree remains, but Mary has since left the burl.

The Archangel Michael and Opus Dei

So is the Devil alive and causing trouble in the Windy City? Not if you believe the statue in the entryway of St. Mary of the Angels Church. The sculpture depicts the Archangel Michael standing on the Devil with a spear jammed into the Dark One's throat. Just the thing you want to see on a Sunday morning, particularly if you belong to the pain-loving organization Opus Dei of *The Da Vinci Code* infamy.

St. Mary of the Angels is the only parish in the United States run by the mysterious Catholic group. Followers regularly beat themselves with a knotted whip, called a discipline, and wear a cilice, a band of spikes that digs into the thigh, for two hours a day. This "mortification of the flesh" is intended to remind them of Jesus's suffering. Visitors can find a shrine to St. Josemaría Escrivá de Balaguer, who founded Opus Dei in 1928, in the basement of the church. It is not guarded by an albino.

St. Mary of the Angels Church, 1850 N. Hermitage Ave., Chicago, IL 60622

Phone: (773) 278-2644

Hours: Daily 7 AM–7:15 PM

Cost: Free

Website: http://sma-church.org, www.opusdei.org

Directions: Two blocks south of Armitage Ave., five blocks west of Ashland Ave.

Devil in a Little Parish

It isn't just Mary and Jesus that come to visit Chicago's churches; the Devil has dropped by, too. In fact, he's come to St. Michael's on the North Side. Twice.

According to parishioners' stories, the first time Satan dropped by, he appeared in the form of an old woman. She reportedly followed a priest out of the church, but he figured out who she was when he noticed her cloven hooves. The padre then chased the Evil One off.

But so much for learning from experience. When the Devil returned in the 1980s in a hooded cloak and tried to take communion during mass, he again forgot to cover his goatlike tootsies and was refused the sacrament. No shoes. No toes. No service!

St. Michael's Church, 1633 N. Cleveland Ave., Chicago, IL 60614

Phone: (312) 642-2498

Hours: Services Saturday 6 PM, Sunday 8 AM, 9:15 AM, 11 AM, and 7 PM

Cost: Free

Website: www.st-mikes.org

Directions: One block north of North Ave., two blocks east of Larrabee St.

The Athenian Candle Company and Augustine's Spiritual Goods

So let's say you don't have time to get to church but still want a visitation from on high. Why not conjure up your own spirits? There are two shops on Halsted Street that can help you in your quest.

The Athenian Candle Company stocks not only votive candles and statues of the saints for Christians, but spiritual goods for a wide variety of religions. Buddha statues sit side by side with tarot cards and oversized glow-in-the-dark rosaries. Need a Pope hologram or gris-gris bag of spells? They've got that, too.

Athenian Candle Company, 300 S. Halsted St., Chicago, IL 60661

Phone: (312) 332-6988

Hours: Monday–Tuesday and Thursday–Friday 9:30 AM–6 PM, Saturday 9:30 AM–5 PM

Cost: Free

Website: www.atheniancandle.com

Directions: In Greektown at Jackson Blvd.

Be careful what you wish for.

If you're a novice at all this do-it-yourself conjuring, perhaps you should take a class. In addition to its well-stocked shelves of New Age potions, elixirs, and how-to books, Augustine's Spiritual Goods offers courses in candle magic, numerology, Kabbalah, tarot reading, and more.

Augustine's Spiritual Goods, 3327 S. Halsted St., Chicago, IL 60608
Phone: (773) 843-1933
Hours: Thursday 11 AM–7 PM, Friday–Saturday 11 AM–6 PM, Sunday noon–4 PM
Cost: Free
Website: www.authenticspiritualgoods.com
Directions: Between 33rd and 34th Sts.

God on the Radio

For the money, there is no better theatrical performance in Chicago than the radio drama "UNSHACKLED!" recorded at the Pacific Garden Mission each Saturday. They have been producing the show without interruption since 1950, so they know what they're doing.

"UNSHACKLED!" is a throwback to the early days of radio. Each episode is a new "true story" of a sinner or sufferer who finds redemption, and while that might not sound like a barrel of laughs, it's surprisingly entertaining. At least two-thirds of each play chronicles the downward spiral of random tragedy and/or sin of the main character, every event punctuated with the soap-opera burst of organ music. Just when you think the hero (or heroine) can't endure another hardship, he is stricken with a new disease, mugged on a street corner, or watches his home burn to the ground.

And then the main character finds God. This doesn't always free him from his troubles, but at least he feels better about his life-threatening disease or dire situation. And of course, he is unshackled from the sin that got him into the mess in the first place.

Visitors are allowed to sit in the studio audience during the taping. The Pacific Garden Mission staff point out that the actors in the plays are union professionals and not all of them are "saved." That's probably just as well; if everyone was "saved," there would be no material for next week's episode of . . . "UNSHACKLED!" (cue organist).

Pacific Garden Mission, 1458 S. Canal St., Chicago, IL 60607
Phone: (312) 492-9410
Hours: Saturdays at 4:30 PM; seating begins at 4:15 PM
Cost: Free
Website: www.pgm.org, www.unshackled.org
Directions: Three blocks east of I-94 at 14th Pl.

Pushin' Up the Wild Onions

Dead in Chicago

Being dead in Chicago isn't all bad. For one thing, you can still vote. For another, the worms that eat you may be the same worms that devoured some famous Americans, as long as you choose the right spot to be buried.

Chicago's most visible grave site isn't a grave site at all—it's home plate at Wrigley Field. Songwriter Steve "City of New Orleans" Goodman asked that his ashes be interred beneath home plate in a song titled "A Dying Cubs Fan's Last Request," and since he was the first and only celebrity who had asked for the privilege, the stadium allowed it. They won't do it again, so don't bother asking or writing your own song.

Chris Farley Death Site

When you die a premature, tragic death, folks come out of the woodwork to praise you and contemplate what might have been had you survived. After 33-year-old Chris Farley died on December 18, 1997, he was hailed as a comic genius. But what were the same folk saying about *Beverly Hills Ninja* when Farley was alive?

Most people, perhaps even Farley himself, anticipated his early death. Friends say he idolized John Belushi, even to the point of admiring Belushi's premature demise. That's taking hero worship a bit far.

One of Farley's most well-known *SNL* characters was the Chicago Superfan. During a Bears call-in show, his character inevitably had multiple heart attacks, but always revived himself through self-administered CPR. That's pretty much how the real Farley died, according to the coroner, with one main difference: he forgot to administer CPR. Farley's brother found the 300-pound actor in the front foyer of his condominium, right where a stripper admitted leaving him after a long night of partying.

John Hancock Center, 60th Floor, 875 N. Michigan Ave., Chicago, IL 60611

No phone

Hours: Private residence; view from outside

Cost: Free

Website: www.johnhancockcenterchicago.com

Directions: Just north of Water Tower Place.

Eugene Izzi Death Site

Eugene Izzi was a mystery writer whose death was as puzzling as his crime novels. Police found Izzi hanging from his 14th-floor office balcony on the morning of December 7, 1996. Izzi was being treated for depression and his office door was locked from the inside, so police ruled his death a suicide.

But was it? The author was found wearing a bulletproof vest and had three computer disks in his pocket. On the disks were 800 pages of a crime story that paralleled his own murder, suicide, or accidental death—whatever it was. In the outline, members of an Indiana militia try to kill an author by hanging him out the window of his 14th-floor office. Friends of Izzi's claim he was a stickler for details and might have been trying out one of his plot twists when the experiment went horribly wrong.

Or was it an Indiana militia? Izzi had been telling his friends that a white supremacist group was after him because of his research on the new novel. Or perhaps the guy wanted folks to talk about him after his death, which is just what people did. Dying young never hurt James Dean's image, just Dean himself. You be the judge.

6 N. Michigan Ave., Room 1418, Chicago, IL 60602

No phone

Hours: Always visible

Cost: Free

Directions: At Madison and Michigan Aves.

Clarence Darrow's Ashes

Before Clarence Darrow died on March 13, 1938, he made a promise to his friends: he claimed he would return to them on the anniversary of his death if there was an afterlife. If he didn't, they could safely assume they too would be food for worms.

Darrow's ashes were scattered over Wooded Island in the Jackson Park Lagoon, adjacent to a bridge that today bears his name. Each year on March 13 people gather there. Some people claim to have seen his ghost from the bridge at night, standing on the back steps of the museum. Witnesses admit the figure is nondescript and stays hundreds of feet away, so until the specter clears up, the agnostic lawyer has yet to speak from the great beyond.

Jackson Park, Clarence Darrow Memorial Bridge, 5900 S. Lake Shore Dr., Chicago, IL 60637

No phone

Hours: Always visible

Cost: Free

Directions: The bridge crosses the lagoon at about 59th St. east of Cornell Ave.

Camp Douglas and the Douglas Tomb

Abraham Lincoln's 1860 Democratic presidential opponent, Stephen A. Douglas, died on June 3, 1861, shortly after the Civil War began. His body was then interred on his Oakenwald estate south of downtown. But it's hard to imagine he rested in eternal slumber because the Union built a prison camp in Oakenwald's backyard, naming it in his honor: Camp Douglas. Conditions in the stockade bound by Cottage Grove Avenue, 31st Street, Giles Avenue, and 33rd Street were nothing short of deplorable. Of the 30,000 Confederate troops imprisoned here from 1862 to 1865, 6,129 died. Most were buried in Oak Woods Cemetery (see below).

After the war, a fitting monument to Douglas was planned. During its construction, for two years during the late 1860s, the public could view Douglas through the glass-topped lid of his sarcophagus. (He has since been shielded from the elements—too bad.) The statue atop the 96-foot tomb is 9 feet, 9 inches tall, almost twice the height of the man for whom it was fashioned.

Stephen A. Douglas Tomb, 636 E. 35th St., Chicago, IL 60616

Phone: (312) 225-2620

Hours: Wednesday–Sunday 9 AM–5 PM

Cost: Free

Website: www.state.il.us/hpa/hs/douglas_tomb.htm

Directions: At Cottage Grove Ave. at the end of 35th St., across from Ellis Park.

Oak Woods Cemetery

Oak Woods is the South Side's largest and most beautiful cemetery. It is the final resting place for Jesse Owens, Harold Washington, "Big Jim" Colosimo, Ida B. Wells, Enrico Fermi, and thousands of Confederate prisoners.

Jesse Owens won four gold medals and broke three world records at the 1936 Berlin Olympics, much to Adolf Hitler's dismay. You'd think a

star athlete would stay away from cigarettes. He didn't, and he died of lung cancer later in 1980. His grave site overlooks the small lake to the west of the main entrance.

Chicago mayor Harold Washington was buried in Oak Woods after his lifelong attachment to food got the better of him. Every week since his death, a red rose has appeared on his grave. Washington is buried in a gray granite mausoleum toward the southwest of the main gate. His epitaph reads, "Remember me as one who tried to be fair."

Behind Washington's tomb is a tall obelisk marking the grave of "Big Jim" Colosimo, Al Capone's Mob predecessor. He was gunned down on May 11, 1920, in a hit organized by "Little John" Torrio (see page 275).

Civil rights leader Ida B. Wells, the crusading journalist who documented lynchings of African Americans throughout the United States, is also buried in Oak Woods. She died in 1931.

Physicist Enrico Fermi is buried here not far from where he produced the world's first nuclear chain reaction at the University of Chicago (see page 95). He died of stomach cancer on November 28, 1954.

Finally, about 6,000 Confederate prisoners who died at Camp Douglas, only 4,200 of whom were "official," are buried in Oak Woods under the Confederate Monument in the southwest corner of the cemetery. When you stand on the mound, you are standing over thousands of Rebel bodies laid out in radiating concentric circles.

1035 E. 67th St., Chicago, IL 60637

Phone: (773) 288-3800

Hours: Daily 9 AM–5 PM

Cost: Free

Website: www.oakwoodscemetery.net

Directions: Bounded by 67th and 71st Sts., between Cottage Grove and the Illinois Central railroad tracks; enter from 67th St.

Graceland Cemetery

As cemeteries go, Graceland is drop-dead gorgeous. It's the perfect place for a picnic, though that's not exactly encouraged. Some of Chicago's best-known citizens are planted at this cemetery, but three lesser-known residents get most of the attention these days, at least from ghost lovers: Inez Clarke, Ludwig Wolff, and Dexter Graves.

Inez Clarke died in 1880 at a young age from tuberculosis. According to legend, her parents were so overcome with grief they marked her grave with a life-sized replica of the girl sitting on a bench so that they could then see her angelic face whenever they visited. To protect it from the pigeons, they encased the statue in glass. It may keep out the birds, but the case isn't strong enough to hold Inez's restless spirit. Her statue is said to cry real tears and run around the tombstones at night while the bench and box sit empty, filled only with a faint mist. This event usually takes place on August 1. If you live in the area, expect a heavy police presence around Graceland's perimeter to discourage devil worshippers as well as the merely curious.

Sit still, Inez.

Ludwig Wolff, unlike Inez, is entombed in an underground mausoleum and cannot escape. Apparently he's not too happy about it, because people have heard him howling from inside his granite tomb. Others claim it isn't Wolff but a green-eyed ghost dog that lives inside and protects his dead master. Either way, would you want to find out?

Graceland's scariest monument, however, is the hooded figure over Dexter Graves's plot dubbed *Eternal Silence*, carved by Lorado Taft in 1909. It has also been called the "Statue of Death." It is said to be impossible to photograph, but anyone with a camera knows that's not true.

4001 N. Clark St., Chicago, IL 60613

Phone: (773) 525-1105

Hours: Daily 8 AM–5 PM

Cost: Free

Website: www.gracelandcemetery.org

Directions: Enter from Irving Park Rd. and Clark St.; Inez Clarke is along the road to the left; Wolff is along the north wall; Graves is east of the crematorium.

ALSO PLANTED IN GRACELAND

John Peter Altgeld: Former Illinois governor who pardoned the three surviving Haymarket Eight.

Philip Armour: Made his fortune selling canned meat for Civil War troops; he later revolutionized the meatpacking industry by utilizing refrigerated railcars.

Daniel Burnham: Chicago's city planner had his ashes planted on an island on Lake Willomere in the northeast corner of the cemetery.

August Noel Dickens: Younger brother of Charles Dickens and general ne'er-do-well.

Marshall Field: The mercantile genius rests beneath a seated figure atop a platform called Memory. The statue was an early inspiration for the Lincoln Memorial in Washington, D.C. Both were done by Daniel Chester French and Henry Bacon. Field died January 1, 1906, of pneumonia contracted while playing golf in December.

William A. Hulbert: Baseball's first National League president is buried beneath a giant granite baseball with the league's first eight cities etched upon it.

Jack Johnson: America's first black heavyweight boxing champion (1908) is buried in an unmarked grave next to his wife, Etta.

John Kinzie: The first European settler to the area, he survived the Fort Dearborn Massacre of 1812 when 52 settlers were killed near 1600 S. Indiana Avenue. This is Kinzie's fourth resting place.

Cyrus McCormick: The inventor of the harvesting machine was planted here after he was harvested by the Grim Reaper.

Ludwig Mies van der Rohe: Architect of the glass box skyscraper who stated "Less is more."

Walter Newberry: Founder of the Newberry Library, he died overseas and was shipped back to Chicago in a barrel of rum. He was buried here in the same barrel.

Potter and Bertha Honoré Palmer: Developer of State Street and focal point of High Society, they've got the snazziest sarcophagi in the cemetery. Part of *Damien: Omen II* was filmed near the Palmers.

Allan Pinkerton: Founder of the Secret Service, Pinkerton became the nation's first private eye after botching the Lincoln job. Several of his faithful employees, one of whom was killed pursuing Jesse James, are buried by his side.

George Pullman: Sleeping car magnate and union buster, interred in a lead-lined casket in a cement vault beneath steel railroad tracks (and more cement). These precautions were to deter grave robbers and angry former employees. Rumors have long circulated that he was actually preserved in formaldehyde in the basement of his Pullman mansion, but odds are he's here, and nobody is getting him out.

Louis Sullivan: The influential architect died penniless. His gravestone was placed here years after his death by admirers and includes two half-profiles of skyscrapers on the sides. Sullivan designed the nearby Getty Tomb, called "a symphony in stone" by Frank Lloyd Wright.

Rosehill Cemetery

Rosehill is no Graceland in terms of beauty, celebrities, or spooks, but it runs a close second. And if acreage means anything, Rosehill is the city's biggest boneyard.

Filed away in Rosehill's large mausoleum, retailers Montgomery Ward and Richard Sears are locked together in eternal combat. They didn't get along in life any better than they seem to in death. Late-night visitors have spotted Sears's ghost stepping out of his tomb and moving toward Ward's crypt, and nobody believes he's bargain hunting.

The ghosts of Frances Pearce and her infant daughter are less famous than Sears but more disturbing. After they died during childbirth in 1864, Pearce's husband, Horatio Stone, commissioned a "sleeping" statue of the pair to be placed in a glass case over their graves. Each year in May, on the anniversary of their deaths, the box is said to fill with a white mist and the two statues sit up to say hello to visitors . . . who then run away screaming.

Rosehill also has many weird monuments. Life-sized renderings of Charles Hull (namesake of Hull House) and Leonard Volk (sculptor of both Lincoln and Douglas) sit comfortably in chairs on top of their respective graves. George Bangs has a three-foot-long railroad car entering a tunnel for his monument; Bangs perfected the mail car while head of the Railway Mail Service.

A couple of spurned lovers round out the odd monuments. A 16-foot phallus was erected over the grave of Lillian Jenkins by her ex-husband, S. A. Jennings. Jenkins divorced Jennings after finding him in an affair, and this is how he repaid her. Lifelong bachelor Charles DuPluesses's monument reads, "Now Ain't That Too Bad." He went to his grave believing women should have paid him more attention.

5800 N. Ravenswood Ave., Chicago, IL 60660

Phone: (773) 561-5940

Hours: Daily 9 AM–5 PM

Cost: Free

Website: www.rosehillcemetery.com

Directions: Just south of Peterson Ave. between Western and Ravenswood Aves.

ALSO PLANTED IN ROSEHILL

Jack Brickhouse: Baseball broadcaster and forerunner to Harry Caray.

Leo Burnett: Advertising mogul who loved apples.

Milton Florsheim: Chicago's shoe king.

Bobby Franks: Fourteen-year-old murder victim of Leopold and Loeb.

Otis Hinckley and George Schmitt: Founders of Chicago's Hinckley & Schmitt bottled water.

Oscar Mayer: Head hot-dog man and creator of the Wienermobile.

Reinhart Schwimmer: Gangster-loving optometrist caught in the crossfire during the St. Valentine's Day Massacre.

Ignaz Schwinn: Bicycle manufacturing pioneer.

Frances Willard: Leader of the Women's Christian Temperance Union. Her ashes were buried in the same casket as her mother, as per Willard's wishes. The elder Willard was exhumed and her daughter's urn was placed inside the casket.

Bohemian National Cemetery

Further down on the Chicago cemetery ladder is Bohemian National. You once had to be Czech to be planted here, but the ethnic restriction has been lifted. What it lacks in famous residents it makes up for in cool headstones and monuments. You won't find a larger collection of carved angels, cherubic babies, and soldiers anywhere in the Windy City.

Bohemian National contains perhaps the spookiest monument in all of Chicagoland. *Pilgrim Mother* was created by Albin Polasek for the Stejskal-Buchal crypt and depicts a hooded old hag coming to claim the souls of the people interred within. Rest in peace? Not likely! There's a long-repeated legend that if you look into the hag's face you'll see how you will die. So, just how curious are you?

This graveyard also contains the dead hopes and dreams of several Cubs fans—Beyond the Vines (http://beyondthevines.net/default.aspx), a special burial plot for fans of the North Side losers. They've got a short red brick wall with a stained glass insert of the scoreboard, a couple of uncomfortable dugout benches, and grass from the field. Living fans are welcome to pray here, but they might get more action if they head to the South Side. No, not the White Sox's US Cellular Field, but the National Shrine of St. Jude (3200 E. 91st St., (312) 544-8230, http://shrineofstjude.claretians.org), patron saint of lost causes.

It's not just their dreams of a pennant that are dead.

5255 N. Pulaski Rd., Chicago, IL 60630
Phone: (773) 539-8442
Hours: Daily 9 AM–5 PM
Cost: Free
Website: www.bohemiannationalcemeterychicago.org
Directions: At the corner of Pulaski Rd. and Foster Ave.

Day of the Dead

With all this talk of death, you might feel depressed. Here's the antidote: stop on by the National Museum of Mexican Art in October for its annual Day of the Dead show. That ought to cheer you up! Its popular exhibition is said to be the nation's largest of its kind and includes many elaborate memorial altars created by Chicago artists, decorated sugar skulls, tissue paper cutout demonstrations, and more.

National Museum of Mexican Art, 1852 W. 19th St., Chicago, IL 60608
Phone: (773) 738-1503
Hours: Tuesday–Sunday 10 AM–5 PM
Cost: Free
Website: www.nationalmuseumofmexicanart.org
Directions: Two blocks west of Ashland Ave., four blocks north of Cermak Rd.

Birthplace of the Bomb

And last, no tour of Chicago death sites would be complete without a visit to where what will likely be our ultimate end first began: the birthplace of the bomb. The first nuclear chain reaction took place on December 2, 1942, in Enrico Fermi's lab at the University of Chicago. The lab was located in a converted squash court under the west grandstands of Stagg Field. Thrilled as his team was at their accomplishment, it was revealed years later that the crew wasn't entirely sure that the chain reaction would stop once started. Perhaps that's why they were so happy.

Stagg Field was torn down years ago due to, among other problems, radiation contamination. (A new Stagg Field has been erected a few blocks away.) Much of the stadium rubble was trucked out to Palos Hills and buried in Red Gate Woods, along with other "hot" waste from the Manhattan Project. The worst of the contaminated material came from the "Site B" uranium production facility at 61th Street and University Avenue. Signs at Red Gate Woods today read: CAUTION, DO NOT DIG. BURIED IN THIS AREA IS RADIOACTIVE MATERIAL.

In 1967 a sculpture by Henry Moore titled *Nuclear Energy* was placed on the exact spot where that first chain reaction took place. Some say Moore's work looks like a human skull. Others say it resembles a modified mushroom cloud. But no matter which way you look at it, it's not encouraging.

5651 S. Ellis Ave., Chicago, IL 60637
No phone
Hours: Always visible
Cost: Free
Website: http://hep.uchicago.edu
Directions: On the east side of Ellis between 56th and 57th Sts.

Radioactive Waste Dump, Red Gate Woods, Lemont, IL 60465
No phone
Hours: Daily 7 AM–10 PM
Cost: Free
Website: www.lm.doe.gov/land/sites/il/sitea/sitea.htm
Directions: Near Archer Ave. and 107th St.

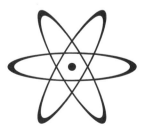

2

CHICAGO SUBURBS

Many people see the suburbs as dull, featureless nowhere-villes, hardly worth visiting on valuable vacation time, and for the most part, they're right. But there are a few spots in the Chicago suburbs where you can enjoy yourself and give people the idea you actually went someplace exotic. All you need is a camera and the ability to lie through your teeth.

Get a shot of you toasting with a tropical drink at the Hala Kahiki and tell everyone you went to Hawaii. Pose in front of the Leaning Tower of Niles—instant Italy! The Tropic World exhibit at the Brookfield Zoo can double as the Amazon rainforest or the jungles of Cameroon. And if you're extremely daring, bring a shot of you at Medieval Times and tell your friends you have a time machine. They'll either be impressed or think you're a freak. Or both.

Alsip
Rose Mary and Mayor Daley

Mary Alice Quinn was a pious 14-year-old who had dedicated herself to St. Therese of Lisieux (see page 100), "The Little Flower," but that didn't prevent the teenager's death in 1935. Some who knew her believed she had been given the gift of healing, and that it continued even after her untimely death. Visitors to her grave reported the smell of roses even in the dead of winter, then received miraculous cures. Mary Alice Quinn was nicknamed Rose Mary.

Word got around and soon hundreds went to pray at her grave. Reportedly, if Rose Mary answered your prayers, you would smell roses on the ninth day after your request. Anxious to connect with her, some pilgrims would take soil from her grave, and groundskeepers needed to keep replacing the soil lest she be slowly unearthed. Fewer people visit Rose Mary's grave today, but you're still likely to see somebody there if you visit.

If you go to Holy Sepulchre Cemetery (a former horserace track) on the morning of a Chicago election, you're likely to find somebody famous at a grave other than Rose Mary's: Richard J. Daley at the plot of his father, Richard M. Daley. The young Daley has made a tradition of visiting the man who defined machine politics on the most important day of the year, at least for deceased Cook County residents—this is the one day where their votes count!

Holy Sepulchre Cemetery, 6001 W. 111th St., Alsip, IL 60803

Phone: (708) 422-3020

Hours: September–April, daily 8:30 AM–5 PM; May–August, daily 8:30 AM–7 PM

Cost: Free

Website: www.catholiccemeterieschicago.org/locations.php?id=9

Directions: Enter from 111th St. at Austin Ave.; Daley is to the immediate left as you enter.

Quinn is buried in section 7, to the right, just behind the large red "Capone" monument.

Berwyn
Horrorbles

Calling all fans of zombies, spacemen, vampires, evil clowns, reanimated mummies, radioactive Japanese monsters, and masked serial killers: you'll feel right at home in Berwyn. No, this city of charming bungalows isn't populated with the walking undead, at least not entirely, but it's where you'll find Horrorbles, the official store of Fangoria Entertainment and your one-stop shop for all things ghoulish. The main floor is cram-packed with toys, action figures, magazines, models, DVDs, posters, books, and masks of every movie monster and space alien that ever crawled this doomed earth. All very terrifying, indeed, but wait until you see the basement. Deep in the bowels beneath Horrorbles is a gallery of gruesome art, cemetery dioramas, and a mini-theater that shows classic monster and horror flicks—descend those stairs only if you dare!!

So why Berwyn? Any fan of Chicago's Saturday night "creature feature" host Svengoolie (http://svengoolie.com) knows the answer. Horrorbles has embraced the city's biggest booster, offering rubber chickens and Svengoolie T-shirts to commemorate your spooky trip to Berrrrrwynnnn.

6729 W. Roosevelt Rd., Berwyn, IL 60402

Phone: (708) 484-7370

Hours: Tuesday–Saturday 11 AM–7 PM, Sunday 11 AM–5 PM
Cost: Free
Website: www.horrorbles.com
Directions: Just east of Oak Park Ave. on Roosevelt Rd. (12th St.).

World's Largest Laundromat

So you're on a coast-to-coast road trip, and though you've done your best to keep clean, things are getting a little gamey in the car. What to do?

Make Berwyn your next destination, home of the World's Largest Laundromat. This 13,500-square-foot operation has 153 washers and 148 dryers so you can wash every load simultaneously and get back on the road. That's assuming you'll be in a hurry to get out of this place, which you may not be—this washeteria has Wi-Fi, flat-screen televisions, microwaves, a playground for the kids, and even a small aviary. There's free coffee and doughnuts every morning and free pizza on Wednesday nights. And if all this seems rather decadent, it's probably more eco-friendly than anything you have at home; all of the WLL's hot water comes from 36 solar panels on the roof. It's like heaven with a spin cycle.

6246 Cermak Rd., Berwyn, IL 60402
Phone: (708) 749-1545
Hours: Always open
Cost: Wash, $2.75–$4.75 per load; dry, 25¢ for 10 minutes
Website: www.worldslargestlaundry.com
Directions: At Highland Ave.

Brookfield
Binti-Jua, Mother of the Year

On August 16, 1996, a three-year-old boy crawled over a guardrail and planter box to get a better look at the critters in Brookfield Zoo's Tropic World. He got it, falling 24 feet into a pit filled with gorillas. Luckily for him, one gorilla, Binti-Jua, was a recent mother who had been trained to be nurturing by her human jailers. She picked up the unconscious child and dragged him 40 feet to an outside gate. Meanwhile, zoo keepers hosed down the other gorillas to keep them away.

In Illinois, monkeys have done time for shoplifting, so it was encouraging to hear news that one of our primate relatives had done something positive. "Ideas Man" Newt Gingrich seized the opportunity to observe that Binti-Jua was more nurturing than some welfare mothers and was rightfully criticized. Still, Binti-Jua was proclaimed Mother of the Year and received worldwide attention. She even got a rhinestone pendant from the American Legion. Nobody seemed to entertain the notion that perhaps she dragged the child over to the door in exchange for a banana.

Brookfield Zoo, 3300 Golf Rd., Brookfield, IL 60513

Phone: (800) GO-TO-ZOO or (708) 688-8000

Hours: Monday–Friday 10 AM–5 PM; Saturday–Sunday 10 AM–6 PM

Cost: Adults $13.50, seniors (65+) $9.50, kids (3–11) $9.50

Website: www.czs.org

Directions: At First Ave. and 31st St.

Darien
National Shrine of St. Therese Museum and Gift Shop

Relic lovers know the problem: if you want to see the bone chip of a saint, you usually have to catch a church when it's open, and that means getting up early on a Sunday morning. But at the National Shrine of St. Therese, you can stop by whenever's convenient.

The relics on display here are only those of St. Therese of Lisieux, but they've got some good ones. The best? "A particle of St. Therese's uncorrupted flesh, discovered when her decomposed body was exhumed in the municipal cemetery of Lisieux, September 6, 1910." Was she uncorrupted, or decomposed? The placard seems to want it both ways.

But that flesh blob isn't all. They've got bone chips, locks of hair, her toy tambourine, prayer books, and a chair from her cell in a French convent. There are also plenty of spooky statues and the Largest Religious Wood Carving in the United States, a tableau of St. Therese's life.

Carmelite Visitors Center, 8501 Bailey Rd., Darien, IL 60561

Phone: (630) 969-3311

Hours: Daily 10 AM–4 PM

Cost: Free

Website: www.saint-therese.org

Directions: Take the Cass Ave. exit from I-55, north to Frontage Rd., then west to Bailey Rd.

IS THAT THE WHITE HOUSE?

Illinois congressman Martin Madden must have dreamed of bigger political things when he built a one-tenth-scale version of the White House in Darien in 1903. Madden was instrumental in the planning for the Panama Canal, so he didn't suffer a lack of ambition or ego. **Castle Eden,** as he dubbed it, was later converted to a restaurant, but today it is the Aylesford Retreat Center of the Carmelite Fathers. It can be seen on North Frontage Road at Bailey Road, adjacent to the National Shrine of St. Therese.

Des Plaines and Oak Brook
The First McDonald's

To call this fake restaurant-museum the "First McDonald's" is more than a little misleading. The first McDonald's Restaurant was located in San Bernardino, California, and was run by Maurice and Richard McDonald. The first McDonald's with a golden arch was built in Downey, California. It too was owned by the McDonalds. But the brothers' Multimixer salesman, Ray Kroc, bought the right to franchise their operation in 1954, and that is where the modern corporation's revisionist history begins. On April 15, 1955, Ray Kroc opened a McDonald's in Des Plaines, and it was a huge success. By 1960, Kroc had amassed enough wealth to buy the brothers' entire operation for $2.7 million, then proceeded to run them out of business. They weren't even allowed to continue using their own last name.

Today, only the sign in front of the Number One Store Museum is original. The restaurant was torn down in the name of progress in 1984, then rebuilt for burger-loving tourists. Look through its windows at wax dummies serving plastic food to nonexistent customers. Marvel at the 15-cent price of a hamburger. Visit the basement museum and audit Ray's accounting ledgers. Learn about McDonald's early sexist policy of refusing to hire women. (They relented in 1968, but the sixties were a crazy time!) And reflect on how much has changed from the company's early years; a manager's handbook once directed, "Personnel with bad teeth, severe skin

blemishes, or tattoos should not be stationed at service windows." How things have changed!

Number One Store Museum, 400 N. Lee St., Des Plaines, IL 60016

Phone: (847) 297-5022

Hours: June–August, Thursday–Saturday 10:30 AM–2:30 PM

Cost: Free

Website: www.aboutmcdonalds.com/mcd/our_company/museums/first_store_museum.html

Directions: Two blocks south of River Rd., just west of Des Plaines River Rd.

The Ray Kroc Museum

Judging from this museum's nonexistent advertising and its weekday-only hours, the Ray Kroc Museum seems intended more for prospective franchisees than the general public. But if you can find the time, you're welcome to visit. Located on the ground floor of the Corporate Headquarters, accessed through a McStore gift shop, the Ray Kroc Museum is a tribute to the tireless enterprise of one man, a man so driven he once said of his competitors, "If they were drowning to death, I'd put a hose in their mouths."

Yes, you'll follow Kroc's exploits when he first sold paper cups for Lily, how the flat-bottomed paper cup revolutionized the industry, and how the Multimixer years (1940–54) led him to the McDonald brothers and his eventual fortune. A multimedia presentation and mechanical diorama shows how the greasy, character-filled diners of yesteryear were transformed into the sanitized, bland food factories of today. Final thoughts are offered by the sanitized, bland blather factory George Will.

There are plenty of things to learn about Kroc and McDonald's that you might not have known, such as how Ray was in American Red Cross Company A during World War I, the same as Walt Disney, and that the first Ronald McDonald was Willard Scott. Did you know about Kroc's many failures, such as the Hula Burger (a Friday-only pineapple sandwich for Cincinnati Catholics), Jane Dobbins Pies, or the San Diego Padres in the years Ray was alive?

Got a question? You can still "Talk to Ray" in a phone-filled theater! Select McDonald's-related questions from a video menu and Ray will resurrect before your eyes and answer them. When Kroc stated, "McDonald's is not a restaurant. . . . It's a religion," he definitely cast himself as the Messiah.

McDonald's Corporation, 1 McDonald's Plaza, Oak Brook, IL 60521

Phone: (630) 623-3000

Hours: Monday–Friday 9 AM–5 PM

Cost: Free

Directions: Just east of Oak Brook Shopping Center, north of Cermak Rd.

FAST FOOD FUN

If you've seen *Supersize Me* and can't stomach the idea of visiting a McDonald's museum, there are a few other fast-food attractions in Chicagoland.

Birthplace of Dairy Queen

501 N. Chicago St., Joliet (closed)

In 1938 John McCullough and his son Alex developed a new type of soft-serve ice cream, and in 1940, along with Sherb Noble, opened the first Dairy Queen store in Joliet. The original building is now a storefront church. No museum, no plaque, no nothing. The first Dairy Queen franchise opened on the corner of Wall and Station Streets in Kankakee. Nothing there, either. What's the Dilly-o?

Burger King Time Machine

506 S. Washington St., Naperville, (630) 717-1261

The very first Burger King ever erected in Illinois looks pretty much as it did when it was built in 1965, which is quite different from what you're used to today. The Naperville building has two large red arch-like structures soaring over the roof that look suspiciously McDonald's-esque. Were they hoping to attract the illiterate color-blind?

Breakfast on a train.

The Choo-Choo

Just two blocks from McDonald's monument to restaurant homogeneity stands a burger joint with real character: the Choo-Choo. The restaurant opened in May 1951, the brainchild of Roy and James Barlowe. It draws its name from its method of presentation. Your order is taken by a waitress but delivered by a toy train! Plastic baskets straddle flatbed cars that ride on a track from the kitchen. However, only the stools and booths around the central island receive train service, so come during off-peak hours if you want your hamburger on rails.

Be sure to saddle up in the corner on a still-operating mechanical pony. For 10 cents you can pretend you're Roy Rogers or Dale Evans.

600 N. Lee St., Des Plaines, IL 60016

Phone: (847) 391-9815

Hours: Thursday–Friday 10:30 AM–8 PM, Saturday–Wednesday 10:30 AM–3 PM

Cost: Meals $5–$8

Website: www.thechoochoo.com

Directions: One block north of Miner St., two blocks west of Des Plaines River Rd.

Elmhurst
American Movie Palace Museum

The Theatre Historical Society of America is dedicated to cataloging and preserving theater buildings regardless of their primary usage, be they for movies, opera, dancing, theater, nickelodeons, or vaudeville. While the archives occupy more space than the exhibits, the museum does have an impressive collection of artifacts from many now-leveled movie palaces.

By far the most impressive display is a scale model of the interior of Chicago's 1927 Avalon Theatre (today known as the New Regal Theater, 1641 E. 79th St.). The Avalon Video Theatre was constructed over three

years by THSA member Frank Cronican. The former set builder paid close attention to detail, down to the exact paint shades from the original structure. Plaster lions on chains crouch on the balconies, fake trees pop up on the horizon, and a large video screen rests on the stage.

Also on display are architectural remnants of many famous theaters, such as an arch finial and a house phone from New York's demolished Roxy. You can see Radio City Music Hall's Wurlitzer Organ reproduced in miniature by Robert Longfield. They've also got EXIT signs, ushers' uniforms, velvet-covered seats, and lighting fixtures from across the nation.

Theatre Historical Society of America, 152 N. York St., Second Floor, Elmhurst, IL 60126

Phone: (630) 782-1800

Hours: Tuesday–Friday 9 AM–4 PM, third Saturday 9:30 AM–1:30 PM

Cost: Donations encouraged

Website: www2.hawaii.edu/~angell/thsa/welcome2.html

Directions: Two blocks south of North Ave.; enter just north of the York Theater entrance.

Lizzadro Museum of Lapidary Art

What is lapidary art? This museum's brochure defines it best: "Lapidary art combines the miracles of nature, the mysteries of science, and the creative genius of man in the medium of stone." Today, about the only places you still see lapidary art practiced in abundance are in onyx chess sets and jade figurines, both of which are decorating no-no's.

The museum began as the personal collection of master carver Joseph F. Lizzadro. Many the pieces were done by Lizzadro himself. Though the world's largest collection of carved Chinese jade is impressive, the best pieces are the small dioramas along the outer wall of the museum. Look closely for the animal figures made of semiprecious stones: a barnyard with glassy pink pigs, Iggy the Elephant out for a walk (carved partly with the real dead Iggy's tusks!), the "Age of Dinosaurs" with species from conflicting geologic eras, and a herd of buffalo on the Great Prairie.

220 Cottage Hill Ave., Elmhurst, IL 60126

Phone: (630) 833-1616

Hours: Tuesday–Saturday 10 AM–5 PM, Sunday 1–5 PM

Cost: Adults $4, seniors (60+) $3, teens $2, kids (7–12) $1

Website: www.lizzadromuseum.org

Directions: In Wilder Park, three blocks north of St. Charles Rd., two blocks west of York Rd.

Elmwood Park
World's Largest Wagon

Everyone knows that childhood obesity is epidemic, and while we hope it never happens, should it get waaaaaay out of hand the folks at Radio Flyer are ready—in 2003 they built the World's Largest Wagon. The shiny red bed is 27 feet long and 13 feet wide and can comfortably hold 75 of today's children. Tomorrow's, who knows?

The wagon was created to mark the 80th anniversary of the first Red Flyer, which was invented in Chicago during the 1920s by Antonio Pasin of the Liberty Coaster Company. It was parked at several locations around Chicagoland, but today it sits outside the factory where the regular-sized models are manufactured.

6515 W. Grand Ave., Elmwood Park, IL 60707

Phone: (800) 621-7613

Hours: Always visible

Cost: Free

Website: www.radioflyer.com/worlds-largest-wagon

Directions: At Fullerton Ave., two blocks west of Narragansett Ave.

Hop in, butterballs!

Evanston

Rest Cottage and the WCTU Headquarters

In the US Capitol's Statuary Hall, each state has selected one native son or daughter to represent it. Illinois chose Frances Willard, a woman barely known today to most in this state. But in her day, Willard was a monumental figure.

Frances Willard was the Women's Christian Temperance Union's second president, from 1879 to 1898, and its most influential. She wrote and promoted the Polyglot Petition in 1885, asking Congress to outlaw alcohol, opium, and tobacco. Though 7.5 million people signed it worldwide, the petition didn't have any immediate effect, except to demonstrate the political muscle of active women. Willard died in 1898, years before women's suffrage and Prohibition, but both constitutional amendments can be strongly attributed to her efforts and those of the WCTU.

Willard lived in an 1865 Victorian home built for her father near Northwestern University, which her mother dubbed "Rest Cottage." The home appears much as it did when Willard lived there, preserved by her companion and secretary, Anna Gordon. Family mementos and WCTU artifacts fill this large but comfortable home, including a begonia propagated from one first potted by Willard. You'll see rolls of the Polyglot Petition, the family Bible signed with each member's temperance pledge, dolls representing each Willard family member, and a huge bell cast from 1,000 confiscated opium and tobacco pipes.

Rest Cottage, 1730 Chicago Ave., Evanston, IL 60201

Phone: (847) 328-7500

Hours: First and third Sundays of every month, 1–4 PM, or by appointment

Cost: Adults $10, kids (12 and under) $5

Website: www.franceswillardhouse.org, www.wctu.org

Directions: At Elgin Rd./Clark St.

EVANSTON

➡ Unless there is a fire, it is illegal to change clothes in a car without drapes in Evanston.

➡ Actors William Christopher (10/20/32), Barbara Harris (7/25/35), Elizabeth McGovern (7/18/61), Joan Cusack (10/11/62), and John Cusack (6/28/66) were all born in Evanston.

A WOMAN AHEAD OF HER TIME

Worried about who you might run into at Rest Cottage? Do you have visions of tour guides badgering you to swear off Demon Rum, pointing bony, accusatory fingers in your face, demanding to know if you have ever smoked a cigarette or worse?

Fear not. The Rest Cottage volunteer docents give sermon-free tours punctuated with healthy laughs and fascinating information. Their task is formidable, trying to educate the public on one of the 19th century's most remarkable women, all this during only six hours a month.

It is hard not to be impressed by Willard's forward-thinking advocacy on many topics, including an eight-hour workday, suffrage for women, uniform laws regarding women and men, pure food and drug reform, and passive resistance as a method of bringing about social change. Her motto? "Do everything."

Also astounding is the way in which Willard conducted her personal life, even from childhood. When denied the right to ride a horse on her family's farm, young Frances—or Frank, as she liked to be called—taught a cow to take a bridle, then saddled it up. After the cow tossed her off, Willard's father relented. She refused to hold to the Victorian convention that a woman was obligated to marriage and motherhood. And at the age of 53, when presented with a bicycle by Lady Somerset, Willard taught herself to ride. The Rest Cottage docents proudly point to "Gladys," Willard's bike, in an upstairs room and revel at the image of Willard in corset and full-length dress, peddling this behemoth around Evanston to the shock of the bluebloods.

Prehistoric Life Museum

Tucked away in the basement of a quiet Evanston rock shop is a remarkable collection of prehistoric creatures. Arranged in order by geologic age, these 1,000-plus specimens are the collection of Dave and Sandra Douglass, along with a few pieces from their family and friends.

Dave started collecting fossils when he was in high school and has made some amazing discoveries over the years. One fossil, a giant scorpion, was named *Titanoscorpio douglassi* in his honor. His parents caught the rockhounding bug, and they too discovered new extinct species; his father found a dragonfly nymph (*Mischoptera douglassi*) that filled a gap in dragonfly evolution, and his mother unearthed the oldest known fossilized squid (*Jeletka douglassae*).

The Douglasses' specimens are attractively displayed, still embedded in rock but cleaned so as to be easily examined. Most of the critters are creepy and unfamiliar, like the Tully Monster, the Illinois state fossil. *Tullimonstrum gregarium* was a one-foot, tube-shaped invertebrate that lived from 280 to 340 million years ago in the Illinois Sea. The Tully Monster had two paddle eyes that scientists have not yet been able to explain.

They've also got a fair share of dinosaur samples, both footprints and bones, as well as a makeshift cave where they're displayed. For the money, this place beats the Field Museum, and might even if it wasn't free.

Dave's Down to Earth Rock Shop, 704 Main St., Evanston, IL 60202

Phone: (847) 866-7374

Hours: Monday–Tuesday and Thursday–Friday 10:30 AM–5:30 PM, Saturday 10 AM–5 PM

Cost: Free

Website: www.davesdowntoearthrockshop.com

Directions: One block west of Chicago Ave., on the other side of the railroad tracks.

Forest Park
Haymarket Martyrs Monument and Emma Goldman's Grave

The four men executed for the Haymarket Massacre (see pages 68–69), along with the one who committed suicide before his hanging, were not allowed to be buried in Chicago, so their bodies were laid to rest just outside the city's border in Forest Park. Two of their three pardoned comrades were also buried here after they died, as were anarchist Emma Goldman, labor activist Lucy Parsons, and part of Wobbly Joe Hill's ashes. This "Dissenter's Row" is sometimes called the "Communist Plot."

A monument to the Haymarket Martyrs was erected and dedicated in 1893 and has been the location of many labor rallies since. Every year on the Sunday closest to May 4, you can join the Black Sunday gathering for long speeches to small crowds.

Forest Home Cemetery was built on an old Indian burial ground, and bones have been unearthed when graves have been opened, so be wary of poltergeist activity. To spook yourself, check out the monument erected by the United Ancient Order of Druids. There are three concentric rings around a central monument topped by a guy looking like Willie Nelson. He carries a walking stick, the top of which is a carved child's head. You can also find monuments to the International Alliance of Bill Posters and Billers, the Cigar Makers International Union, and the Independent Order of Odd Fellows.

Forest Home/German Waldheim Cemetery, 863 S. Des Plaines Ave., Forest Park, IL 60130

Phone: (708) 366-1900

Hours: Daily 9 AM–5 PM

Cost: Free

Website: http://ucblibrary3.berkeley.edu/Goldman

Directions: Three blocks north of Roosevelt Rd., 11 blocks west of Harlem Ave.

ALSO PLANTED IN FOREST HOME

William C. Gunrow: Founder of the Majestic Radio Corporation; you can identify his mausoleum by the Greek goddess Athena wearing a radio headset.

Dr. Clarence and Grace Hall Hemingway: Ernest Hemingway's parents; Dr. Hemingway shot himself with a Civil War pistol.

Dr. Ben Reitman: The "King of the Hoboes" was Emma Goldman's lover.

William "Billy" Sunday: Preacher-baseballer Sunday bad-mouthed liberals and freethinkers, the very folks with whom he shares his final resting place. Sinclair Lewis's *Elmer Gantry* was based upon Sunday's life.

Mike Todd: Elizabeth Taylor's husband, who directed *Around the World in 80 Days* and perished in a plane crash, is buried here.

Glencoe
Frank Lloyd Wright's Only Bridge

To the best of anyone's knowledge, Frank Lloyd Wright designed only one bridge that was ever built. It spans the "ravine"—little more than a ditch—in what was the Ravine Bluffs Development in Glencoe. Six of the surrounding houses were also designed by Wright, and the bridge functioned as the north entrance to the miniature subdivision. The bridge has two distinct Prairie Style streetlights and a large square urn at one end. The bridge was erected in 1915, but fell into disrepair and was closed to traffic in 1977. It was rebuilt in 1985.

Sylvan Road, Glencoe, IL 60022

No phone

Hours: Always visible

Cost: Free

Directions: Turn east on Maple Hill Rd. from Green Bay Rd., then north on Franklin Dr. to
 Sylvan Rd.

Justice
Resurrection Mary

Ghost stories of phantom hitchhikers are not uncommon, but perhaps the best known is that of Resurrection Mary. Her tale goes something like this: a lonely guy driving along Archer Avenue at night comes across a beautiful, young, blond woman in a white dress. She asks for a ride home, sometimes after they go to a dance, then she leads him to the gates of Resurrection Cemetery. She hops out of the car, runs toward the gate, and vanishes. During the night the driver had learned Mary's mother's address and goes to visit her, only to discover that Mary was killed years ago while driving home from a dance at the Oh Henry (now Willowbrook) Ballroom (8900 S. Archer Ave., (708) 839-1000, www.willowbrookballroom.com).

Resurrection Mary was first spotted in 1939, and the stories of encounters remained fairly consistent. Then, during the 1960s and '70s, Mary took on a more political agenda. She not only wanted a ride back to her grave but also to warn the human population about the End of the World, including the Second Coming of Christ. In 1977, she vandalized the gates to the cemetery, this time trying to get out—a witness spotted her glowing fig-

Need a lift?

ure inside the gate, pulling on the bars. Some claimed you could see her handprints embedded into the metal, but the bars have since been removed, or bent back with a welding torch, depending on who you ask.

Many have speculated as to which Mary in the cemetery she is, but because there are so many young, dead Marys at Resurrection, there is disagreement. Top contenders are Mary Bregovy and Mary Duranski, both of whom died in 1934 in car crashes while coming home from dances. Or perhaps Anna "Marija" Norkus, who met a similar fate going to a 1927 soiree. If you happen to run into her, be sure to ask her full name so this can be cleared up.

Resurrection Cemetery, 7201 S. Archer Ave., Justice, IL 60458

Phone: (708) 458-4770

Hours: Daily 9 AM–5 PM

Cost: Free

Website: www.catholiccemeterieschicago.org/locations.php?id=15

Directions: Ask Mary; cemetery is bound by Archer Ave. (Rte. 171), 79th St., and Roberts Rd.

Lansing
First Lady Dolls

If you can't make it to the Smithsonian to see the real inaugural gowns of the First Ladies, perhaps this little museum will do. Each dress has been reproduced and placed on foot-tall dolls by Sophie Drolenga. Many have two-inch plastic husbands by their sides.

You'll notice that the First Ladies' faces are identical; only their hair color and clothing changes. The only exceptions are Barbara Bush and Hillary Clinton, both of whose faces are hideously bloated. It works for Barbara, not for Hillary. Michelle Obama should be added soon.

The rest of this museum is filled with the standard historical society fare: spinning wheels, quilts, old plates, mementos from the Columbian Exposition, and stuffed dead animals.

Lansing Historical Society and Museum, 2750 Indiana Ave., PO Box 1776, Lansing, IL 60438

Phone: (708) 474-6160

Hours: Monday 6–8 PM, Wednesday 3–5 PM, Saturday 10 AM–noon

Cost: Donations encouraged

Website: www.lansing.lib.il.us/historical.html

Directions: One block north of Ridge Rd., just west of School St., in the basement of the Lansing Public Library.

Lemont

Ghost Monks

St. James at Sag Bridge is Cook County's oldest church, and its most haunted. Parishioners should have expected as much when they built it on an old Indian burial ground! When the church foundation was excavated in the 1830s, workers uncovered Native American bones, but they continued building the church anyway. Originally the parish was made up of Irish immigrants, many of whom died early, ghastly deaths while working on the nearby Sanitary and Ship Canal.

But it isn't the canal workers who haunt the grounds, nor the defiled Indians, but instead a group of ghost monks. They were first sighted floating along the ridge near the church in 1847, and as the cemetery filled up around the chapel, more monks were reported. Witnesses often claimed to hear them chanting in Latin. The most recent sighting occurred in November 1977, when policemen chased seven monks up the hill after receiving a report of intruders in the graveyard after dark. When the monks reached the peak, they vanished.

A more ominous specter associated with St. James at Sag Bridge is a horse-drawn hearse spotted along Archer Avenue. The driverless carriage races through the night, horses frothing, with a baby's glowing casket seen through the viewing window.

St. James at Sag Bridge Church, 10600 S. Archer Ave., Lemont, IL 60439

Phone: (630) 257-7000

Hours: Daily 9 AM–5 PM

Cost: Free

Website: http://historicstjames.org

Directions: Northeast of town, just east of the Rte. 83/107th St./Rte. 171 intersection.

Bugs's bizarro brother.

Lincolnwood
Novelty Golf and the Bunny Hutch

This 60-year-old miniature golf course could never be accused of being the slickest course around, but it is perhaps the one with the most character. Suburban miniature golf courses tend to be polished, prefab enterprises, but Novelty Golf looks like it's been slapped together with leftover objects from everywhere. Mismatched statues appear to have had previous lives as business advertisements, the buildings look like they were built in a junior high shop class, and there is nothing that even remotely resembles a theme. Over the two 18-hole courses you'll see tiki heads, the Hancock Tower, an out-of-water mermaid, and the scariest-looking Humpty Dumpty on the planet.

The Bunny Hutch, a classic burger shack, sits adjacent to Novelty Golf. They don't serve bunny burgers, so tell the kids not to worry. Guarding the hutch is another fiberglass creature, but this one looking like Bugs Bunny on speed.

3650 W. Devon Ave., Lincolnwood, IL 60712

Phone: (847) 679-9434

Hours: April–October, daily 10 AM–midnight

Cost: $7–$9, depending on day of the week and tee time

Website: www.noveltygolf.com

Directions: At the corner of Devon and Lincoln Aves.

Midlothian

Bachelors Grove Cemetery

Most Chicago-area spook experts agree: Bachelors Grove Cemetery is the most haunted spot in the region. The cemetery was established during the Blackhawk Wars; few people have been buried there since the 1940s. It fell into disrepair and was vandalized by bored teenagers and beer-guzzling boneheads. Tombstones were kicked over and spray-painted. Caskets were pulled from the ground. House pets and chickens were sacrificed. Not good.

Bachelors Grove's "residents" reacted with an all-out effort to scare off the intruders. People began seeing floating blue lights, misty figures, faces on tombstones, and red streaks through the sky along the road. Others spotted the ghost of an unfortunate farmer whose jittery plow horse pulled them both into a nearby swamp to drown. A two-headed man was once seen rising from the same swamp, crawling toward the highway. Ghost sedans raced along the turnpike where gangsters once dumped bodies. A phantom farmhouse appeared along the dirt road, but faded into the distance whenever anyone approached it. And on full moons, the Madonna of Bachelors Grove (aka Mrs. Rogers, aka the White Lady) walked the haunted ground in a white gown with a dead baby ghost in her arms.

Sadly, there isn't much left to see these days, but you'll probably run into somebody looking for ghosts if not the ghosts themselves. Police guard the place on Halloween, though on most days it's easy to sneak onto

How not to fake a ghost photograph.

the property . . . not that you should . . . wink, wink. But bring a camera if you do, just in case.

Rubio Woods, 6000 W. Midlothian Turnpike (143rd St.), Midlothian, IL 60445

No phone

Hours: Daily 9 AM–5 PM

Cost: Free

Website: www.bachelorsgrove.com

Directions: On the south side of the road, across from the soccer fields east of Ridgeland Ave., then down the abandoned road.

Niles
The Bradford Exchange

The Bradford Exchange is the industry leader in collector's plates, the kind you hang on the wall, not the kind you use to serve dinner. They sell these plates at jacked-up prices by assuring you of two things: (1) they really are "collectible," and (2) you can sell them through brokers at any time. That reasoning may fly on QVC, but let's face it, during the recent global economic meltdown, how secure did that 1987 Precious Angels plate make you feel?

Still, the Bradford Exchange puts on a good show. Old plates fill the lobby museum. Two attention-getters are the "Remembering Elvis" plates, complete with rhinestones, and the "Visions of Our Blessed Virgin Mary" 3-D plates. In each, the Virgin miraculously arises from her porcelain bond.

9333 Milwaukee Ave., Niles, IL 60714

Phone: (866) 907-3607

Hours: Monday–Friday 8 AM–4 PM, Saturday–Sunday 10 AM–5 PM

Cost: Free

Website: www.bradfordexchange.com

Directions: East of the Golf Mills Shopping Center, four blocks south of Golf Rd.

Leaning Tower of Niles

Why go to Europe to see the Tower of Pisa when there's one right here? This half-scale replica of the Italian blunder is a cleverly disguised water tower and works just fine for photos. It was built in 1933–34 to supply water to three swimming pools. Industrialist-with-a-heart Robert Ilg wanted a park

This mistake was planned.

for his employees to enjoy, and it had to look classy. This was his solution. Architect Albert Farr was criticized for building a heavy, tilted structure—some dubbed it Farr's Folly—but it has withstood the test of time,

and could outlast its namesake. That might be due in part to the fact that it leans only half as steeply as the one in Pisa.

Today the 96-foot structure serves as an attention-getter for the Leaning Tower YMCA, but it is no longer filled with water. A new park was built around its base, complete with a Leaning Telefono Booth of Niles. Niles became a sister city to Pisa in 1991.

6300 W. Touhy Ave., Niles, IL 60714

Phone: (847) 410-5108

Hours: Always visible

Cost: Free

Website: www.ymcachicago.org/leaningtower

Directions: Two blocks east of Caldwell Ave. (Rte. 14).

Oak Lawn
World's Largest Cigar Store Indian

Cigar store Indians originated years ago in Europe when public illiteracy necessitated that shop owners advertise with visual images rather than words. Since Native Americans introduced the European invaders to tobacco, carved Indians became synonymous with smoke shops. The tradition made its way to the United States and can still be seen in a big way in Oak Lawn.

When the Cook County Tobacco Warehouse first opened, it commissioned an Indian that was proportional to its stature as the area's biggest cigarette outlet. What it got was a 40-foot chief in a headdress, cigars in hand, who gazes off to the southern horizon, looking for a light. Eventually the store went out of business, but it has since reopened as a liquor store. I'm not sure if that's an improvement.

Cardinal Liquor Barn, 9630 Southwest Hwy., Oak Lawn, IL 60453

Phone: (708) 499-0332

Hours: Always visible

Cost: Free

Directions: Two blocks south of 95th St.

OAK LAWN

➡ A tornado cut through Oak Lawn on April 21, 1967, killing 33, most around the intersection of 95th and Southwest Highway.

Smoking is bad for you. Try booze!

BIG INDIANS

The Oak Lawn statue isn't the only oversized Indian in northern Illinois. It isn't even the largest—that honor goes to the Lorado Taft sculpture in Oregon (see pages 168–69). And there are three others you can see, though they're a bit less artistic.

Eye Care Indian

Midwest Eye Clinic, 6254 S. Pulaski Rd., Chicago, (773) 581-1515

First erected in 1966, "Geronimo" was a rooftop advertisement for a tobacco shop, though the two-story Native American doesn't resemble a traditional cigar store Indian. Instead, his arm is upraised in a gesture of "Howdy!" or "Halt!" The storefront now houses an optician who has fitted him with black frame glasses and a sign around his neck that reads EYE CAN SEE NOW.

Greenhouse Indian

The Greenhouse of Crystal Lake, 4317 S. Highway 31, Crystal Lake, (815) 893-6313, www.thegreenhousecl.com

Though he is missing his feet, the Indian outside a Crystal Lake greenhouse offers roadside Americana buffs the opportunity to directly investigate this iconic statue's origins. At the same greenhouse is a Muffler Man statue (see pages 150–51); a simple inspection reveals that the Indian and the Muffler Man are identical from the waist down. The International Fiberglass Company manufactured its statues in four pieces—head, torso, arms, and lower body. Buyers could swap out pieces for a variety of models and poses, but their legs were always the same.

Orchard Indian

Curtis Apple Orchard, 3902 S. Duncan Rd., Champaign, (217) 359-5565, www.curtisorchard.com

The arrow-shooting Indian at an orchard on the southwest side of Champaign was originally located in Danville. It was created by Herb Drews in 1949, but it was moved here in 1994. Today he guards the trees from apple rustlers.

Oak Park
Frank Lloyd Wright Studio and Museum

Frank Lloyd Wright, no matter what you might think of him, is arguably one of America's most influential architects. His first home in Oak Park is situated in the neighborhood where many of his early designs came to fruition. Wright built the place in 1889 at the age of 22 with a $5,000 loan from his employer, architect Louis Sullivan. Wright was fired four years later after Sullivan learned Wright was designing "bootleg" houses behind Sullivan's back. (You'll see two of these homes on the walking tour.) Being out on his own apparently didn't hurt business—Wright added the large adjoining studio in 1898.

Seeing Wright's work from the outside is always impressive, but visiting the interior is better: take the Home and Studio Tour. The guides on the Home and Studio Tour are quick to point out Wright's forward-thinking vision. The house was wired before Oak Park even provided electricity, baseboards vents were installed long before central air, and don't even ask them about that as-yet-unused teleportation room off the library. Jokes in the shadow of a genius are not welcome!

951 Chicago Ave., Oak Park, IL 60302

Phone: (312) 994-4000

Hours: Daily 11 AM–4 PM

Cost: Adult $15, seniors (65+) $12, kids (4–17) $12

Website: www.gowright.org

Directions: At Forest St., three blocks east of Harlem Ave.

"Broad Lawns and Narrow Minds"

Oak Park's most famous native son, Ernest Hemingway, once described this Chicago suburb as a place with "broad lawns and narrow minds," though some dispute that he ever said it. Whatever the case, the folks here have since forgiven Ernie for the wisecrack . . . though you don't often hear them repeating it.

Ernest Hemingway was born in Oak Park on July 21, 1899. To announce the birth, his father, Clarence, stood on the front porch and blared his cornet. Ernest was also the apple of his mother's eye. She dressed Ernie and his big sister as twins until he turned two.

The family moved from Ernest's birthplace to a new home (161 N. Grove Ave.) when he was six years old, then soon to a third house (600 N. Kenilworth Ave.), where Ernest would live until he left Oak Park. Hemingway attended Holmes Elementary School (508 N. Kenilworth Ave.) and Oak Park High School (today the Hemingway Museum), where he wrote for the school paper, the *Trapeze*, played the cello, and managed the track team. There are many photos of Hemingway during this time, and in almost every one he looks pissed off.

The Hemingway Foundation has an excellent museum filled with Hemingway family artifacts, including Ernest's first book, written at age two, zebra skin rugs, the manuscript of *Across the River and into the Trees*, and the "Dear Ernest" letter he received from nurse Agnes von Kurowsky after returning to Oak Park to recuperate from war wounds.

Hemingway Birthplace, 339 N. Oak Park Ave. (formerly 439), Oak Park, IL 60302

Hemingway Museum, 200 N. Oak Park Ave., Oak Park, IL 60302

Phone: (708) 848-2222

Hours: Sunday–Friday, 1–5 PM, Saturday 10 AM–5 PM

Cost: Adults $8, seniors (65+) $6, kids (5–18) $6 (includes birthplace)

Website: www.ehfop.org

Directions: Museum, one block north of Lake St.; birthplace, two blocks north of Lake St.

Palatine
Ahlgrim Acres

If you're ever thinking of becoming a funeral director, be aware that the job can be somewhat sporadic—you'll need a hobby to keep you busy during the down time. Undertaker Roger Ahlgrim loved miniature golf, so in

1964, shortly after opening a new funeral parlor in Palatine, he set about converting the basement into a nine-hole course. But instead of windmills and castles he built death-themed hazards on each hole. Players would need to dodge headstones and guillotines or putt though a mummy's crypt . . . if they dared. Ahlgrim Acres was born.

For years the basement was just an awesome playroom for his kids; the family lived at the funeral home. As they grew older Ahlgrim added foosball and ping-pong tables, pinball machines, and a shuffleboard court. Word got around, and once the kids left home, Ahlgrim decided to open it up for community events such as Boy Scout meetings and local club functions. Today you can book the Community Room for gatherings or stop by for a visit and a round on the links, as long as no funeral is in progress.

Ahlgrim Funeral Home, 201 N. Northwest Hwy., Palatine, IL 60067

Phone: (847) 358-7411

Hours: By appointment

Cost: Free

Website: www.ahlgrimffs.com/golfcourse.htm

Directions: Two blocks north of Palatine Rd. on Rte. 14 (Northwest Hwy.).

Miss it and it'll cost you a stroke, or a heart attack.
Photo by author, courtesy
Ahlgrim Funeral Home

Park Ridge
Museum of Anesthesiology

This museum won't leave you numb . . . but it could! Using the private collection of Dr. Paul Wood to start, the American Society of Anesthesiologists has amassed an impressive collection of literature, instruments, and numbing agents related to the history of anesthesiology. Displays are arranged topically in somewhat chronological order.

The first anesthetics were administered as inhalants: ether, chloroform, and nitrous oxide. Though these gases' properties were known for years, it took some time before doctors suggested their use during surgery in the 1840s. There is debate as to who deserves the credit for the first use of ether, William Morton or Dr. Crawford Long, but whoever launched the idea, the practice caught on quickly.

Although patients could be knocked out by inhalants, it wasn't until Dr. Richard and Ruth Gill brought rain forest curare to the medical establishment's attention that anesthesiology began resembling its modern form. Curare temporarily paralyzes a patient who has been knocked out—important!—making it much easier for a surgeon to operate.

You'll learn about curare, laughing gas, and much more of the world of "doctors without patients" at the Wood Museum. Before you leave, you'll know the difference between an anesthetist and an anesthesiologist, how it was once common to administer ether rectally during childbirth, that opiates and cannabis were at one time tools of the trade, and why merger mania is changing the face of anesthesiologists' equipment. Gas tanks, masks, monitors, acupuncture needles, Ecuadorian blow darts—they're all here!

Wood Library–Museum of Anesthesiology, 520 N. Northwest Hwy., Park Ridge, IL 60068
Phone: (847) 825-5586
Hours: Monday–Friday 9 AM–4:45 PM; tours by appointment
Cost: Free
Website: www.woodlibrarymuseum.org
Directions: At the intersection of Northwest Hwy. and Greenwood Ave.

PARK RIDGE
➡ Harrison Ford attended Maine Township High School (1131 S. Dee Rd.) in Park Ridge, graduating in 1960. He was in the Model Railroad Club.

River Grove
Hala Kahiki

"No food. No beer. Just tropical drinks." That's the way it was described on the phone. Could any place be that wonderful?

Well, Hala Kahiki comes close. South Seas decor. Hawaiian-dressed waitresses. And a tropical drink menu the size of a small phone book. Missionary's Downfall, Dr. Funk of Tahiti, Pineapple Boomerang, Skip & Run Naked, Suffering Bastard, Preacher's Panic Punch—where to start? Try them all, as long as you have a designated driver. The waitress will take the menu away between drinks just in case you get a little sloppy . . . and you probably will. The drinks are cheap, and umbrellas are included.

The Hala Kahiki looks like it was built one room at a time. As you walk toward the rear, each turn through a doorway reveals another grouping of dimly lit tables. Finally you reach a gift shop bursting with carved coconut monkey heads, fake grass skirts, shell lamps, and racks of Hawaiian shirts and muumuus. If you're staggering, stay away from the tiki mugs on the shelves.

2834 River Rd., River Grove, IL 60171

Phone: (708) 456-3222

Hours: Monday–Tuesday 7 PM–2 AM, Wednesday–Thursday and Sunday 4 PM–2 AM,
   Friday–Saturday 4 PM–3 AM

Cost: Drinks $3 and up

Website: www.hala-kahiki.com

Directions: One block north of Grand Ave. on River Rd.

RIVER GROVE

➡ John Belushi's parents, Agnes and John, are buried in River Grove's Elmwood Cemetery (2905 Thatcher Ave., (773) 625-1700, www.elmwoodcemeteryandmausoleum.com). Their headstone implies that John might be laid to rest beside them, but he's actually planted on Martha's Vineyard.

ROCK ISLAND

➡ Eddie Albert was born Edward Albert Heimberger in Rock Island on April 22, 1908.

Rolling Meadows
1950s House

Ahhhh, the 1950s! Sock hops, Ike, McCarthyism, and the threat of nuclear annihilation. It was a great decade, as long as you weren't black, or gay, or an independent woman, or on a blacklist. Flush with babies and the pride of beating the Nazis, Americans rushed to the suburbs, some of which popped up from the cornfields just months before they arrived. Rolling Meadows was one of those suburbs, most of it built in 1953 by developer Kimball Hill.

The Rolling Meadows Historical Society has built a unique tribute to Hill and the town's earliest inhabitants: 1950s House. Walk through the door of this one-story ranch and you'll think you stepped onto the set of *Leave It to Beaver*, only the Cleavers don't live here. Instead, it's Fred and Mildred and their three youngsters, none of whom are around to greet you. Maybe they're down in a fallout shelter. No matter, you're free to look around. Mildred was cooking dinner when the air raid siren blew, so boxes of 1950s food clutter the counters. The kids were watching *I Love Lucy* in the once-again-stylish living room and have left the TV on. And Fred was apparently in the bedroom, where his underwear drawer is still open—no doubt he'll need an extra pair when the big ones start to drop.

Rolling Meadows Historical Museum/1950s House, 3100 Central Rd., River Grove, IL 60008
Phone: (847) 577-7086
Hours: Wednesday 10 AM–2 PM, Sunday 1–4 PM
Cost: Adults $3, kids $1
Website: www.ci.rolling-meadows.il.us/HTML/historical_museum.htm
Directions: One block west of Lathrop Ave.

Opera in Focus

Face it—attending an opera is expensive, not just for the tickets but having to dress up to impress, or at least not be mocked by, the social set. But there is an alternative that doesn't involve a PBS fund drive: Opera in Focus. It started in Chicago in 1958 under the vision of William B. Fosser, but this unique puppet theater has been based in Rolling Meadows since 1993.

Performances last about an hour and include a half-dozen scenes from famous operas or classic musicals, all acted out by intricately costumed

puppets controlled by rods from below the five-foot-wide stage. The theater has a large repertoire, so you can see as many as 10 different shows in a single season. And when compared with a ticket to a typical opera, 10 performances at Opera in Focus just might be cheaper.

3000 Central Ave., Rolling Meadows, IL 60008

Phone: (847) 818-3220

Hours: Wednesday 4 PM, Saturday 1:30 PM

Cost: Adults $12, seniors (60+) $11, kids (under 12) $7

Website: www.operainfocus.com

Directions: Four blocks west of New Wilke Rd.

PUPPETS ON PARADE

So maybe opera isn't your thing, but you really, really like puppets—perhaps you're a fan of *The Sound of Music*, have a Muppet fetish, or find something compelling about pulling another's strings. That's your business. In addition to Opera in Focus, there are several other puppet-based attractions in Chicagoland for you to enjoy.

PuppetBike

All Over Town, Chicago, www.puppetbike.com

There's no telling where you might run into the PuppetBike, but it's a safe bet you can find the three-wheeled theater wherever tourists with spare change congregate—Navy Pier, Millennium Park, or Michigan Avenue. This converted pedicab transports a pop-up stage and an eight-puppet ensemble directly to the eager public. The cast includes Clover, an aspiring starlet bunny; Amtrak, a cowboy-philosopher dog; and Namy, a one-eyed kitten who once hijacked the PuppetBike and pedaled it to the lake. Bad Namy! Bad!

Von Orthol Puppets

4541 N. Ravenswood Ave., Chicago, (773) 878-8337,
www.vonorthalpuppets.com

Von Orthol Puppets is dedicated to the idea that both kids and adults can enjoy the same richly cultural puppet experience. Their shows range from fables to jazz showcases to meditations on the origins of the universe; check the website for what's new on their schedule and you're bound to find something of interest. They also offer classes in puppet building and performance if you want to start your own troupe.

Kukla and Ollie, but Not Fran

Chicago History Museum, 1601 N. Clark St., Chicago, (312) 642-4600,
www.chicagohs.org

Adults of a certain age remember *Kukla, Fran and Ollie*. It ran from 1947 to 1957, and though it originally aired in Chicago, it became the first coast-to-coast TV puppet show with rabidly devoted fans including John Steinbeck and Tallulah Bankhead. Kukla and Ollie can be found today on display at the Chicago History Museum, but not Fran—she wasn't a puppet, and she's buried in California.

Garfield Goose

Museum of Broadcast Communications, 676 N. LaSalle St., Suite 424, Chicago, (312) 245-8200, www.museum.tv

At the present time, the Museum of Broadcast Communications' new multimillion-dollar facility is "in development," but when it reopens in River North, curators will certainly pull WGN's old Garfield Goose puppet out of mothballs. The MBC also has Macintosh Mouse, Beauregard Burnside III, and Romberg Rabbit in its collection.

Schaumburg
Medieval Times Dinner & Tournament

If eating dinner with your bare hands, wearing a paper crown for an entire evening, or cheering on Fabio lookalikes as they battle on horseback doesn't sound appealing, then you should pass up Medieval Times. Then again, maybe you should lighten up. This 11th-century dinner theater is surprisingly entertaining, if you let it be.

Your banquet is served by teenage serfs and wenches in an arena divided into six colored sections. Each section cheers for its designated knight. The show begins with a display of the horses used in the tournament and a visit from the Royal Falconer. They're followed by a parade of the night's knights. At the behest of the king, the men spear rings with their lances at a full gallop and heave javelins at a target. But soon they are locked in hand-to-hand battle, striking each other with swords, maces, and battle-axes, yet you do not receive so much as a fork for your meal! The victorious knight is allowed to choose the Queen of Love and Beauty from the audience, usually a girl about five years old. This child is brought to the throne where she must watch her Prince Charming battle with the Black Knight and eventually threaten to chop off his head. Talk about entertainment!

When the show is over, you can visit the Torture Chamber for $2 and dance the night away at the disco. If Medieval Times has a fault, it is the constant pestering you receive at the hands of strolling merchants. Over the course of the evening, you're given the opportunity to purchase a photo of yourself with the king and queen (nobody gets through the front gate without them snapping it), a photo of yourself with the members of your party, flags for your knight, glowing necklaces, swords and shields, and illuminated plastic roses, not to mention all the junk in the gift shop. Just tell them you're a lowly peasant.

2001 N. Roselle Rd., Schaumburg, IL 60195

Phone: (866) 543-9637

Hours: Check website for show times

Cost: Adults $59.95, kids (12 and under) $35.95; group rates available

Website: www.medievaltimes.com/chicago.aspx

Directions: North of I-90 at Roselle Rd. exit.

HORSING AROUND CHICAGOLAND

If you like both horses and theater but aren't crazy about eating with your hands or wearing a paper crown, you do have options.

Noble Horse Theatre

1410 N. Orleans St., Chicago, (312) 266-7878, www.noblehorsechicago.com

Housed in an 1872 riding hall on the edge of Chicago's Old Town neighborhood, the Noble Horse Theatre specializes in live horse productions of *The Nutcracker* (mice in saddles!), *The Legend of Sleepy Hollow*, and *Quadrille*, a European adventure of "the romantic bond between horse and man." Hmmmm . . . isn't that *Equus*?

Leapin' Lipizzans!

Tempel Farms, 17000 W. Wadsworth Rd., Wadsworth, (847) 623-7272, www.tempelfarms.com

There's only one place in the United States that regularly puts on performances by the famous leaping Lipizzan stallions: Tempel Farms, a horse-breeding operation near Gurnee. Check its website for show times.

Alcala Horses

Alcala's Western Wear, 1733 W. Chicago Ave., Chicago, (312) 226-0152, www.alcalas.com

It's hard to miss the two fiberglass horses that frame the 1700 block of Chicago Avenue—both are reared up on their hind legs, and one has a rider outlined in neon. No, Alcala's isn't a theater; it's a giant Western wear store where you'll find all you need to dress up as a cowboy or cowgirl. Giddyup!

South Holland
Midwest Carver's Museum

The Midwest Carver's Museum is much more than a static display of regional artists; it's an active club of local carvers and whittlers (the South Suburban Chiselers), a gift shop, and a library covering all aspects of the pastime. It was founded in 1988, and it shows no sign of slowing.

The museum is the first building you enter. It is guarded by two carved "busy beavers." On display are 1,000-plus pieces from Midwestern woodworkers and a few samples from farther away. Many reflect common themes—cowboys, ducks, and more cowboys—but there is the

Ed Stockey points out some mighty fine whittlin'.

occasional odd duck, like the Odd Duck statue of a man's head on a mallard's body, or a whittling of Richard Nixon holding a bowling ball.

Adjoining the museum is a gift shop where you can buy knives, wood, and books. In back, small replicas of a saloon, a blacksmith shop, and homes are filled with small pieces from club members, none of which are for sale. A woodworking shop filled with jigsaws and hundred of templates made by cofounder Ed Stockey stands to the south, and a converted home acts as a meeting place for people to try their hands at carving. Amateurs and pros gather around tables to swap advice and stories and pass along their craft.

16236 Vincennes Ave., South Holland, IL 60473

Phone: (708) 331-6011

Hours: Monday–Saturday 10 AM–4 PM

Cost: Donations encouraged

Website: www.southholland.org/index.php?page=Community/Org/carvers

Directions: Five blocks east of Halsted St. and one block south of 162nd St. (Rte. 6).

Wheaton

Billy Graham Center Museum

Long called the "Button of the Bible Belt," Wheaton is home to 24 different religious organizations, the most prominent being Wheaton College, alma mater of Billy Graham. The evangelist graduated with a degree in anthropology in 1943. It is here that he met his wife, Ruth Bell, and where they set up their first and only pastorate: a Baptist church in Western Springs (4475 Wolf Rd., (708) 246-1530, www.westernspringsbaptistchurch.org).

Though it is called the Billy Graham Center Museum, it actually traces the history of evangelism. The exhibits tend to skip over much of the burn-in-Hell stuff and spend more time talking about the Underground Railroad and their wonderful work with the underprivileged through the Salvation Army and the YMCA. In other words, this is a one-sided presentation.

One uncensored part of the museum, however, is its collection of Billy-abelia. They've got his traveling pulpit, a B+ paper he once wrote about Christopher Columbus, a plaque commemorating his star's placement on the Hollywood Walk of Fame, and photos of him with all the US presidents since Truman, as well as Johnny Cash, Sammy Davis Jr., and Muhammad Ali.

Wheaton College, 500 E. College Ave., Wheaton, IL 60187

Phone: (630) 752-5909

Hours: Monday–Saturday 9:30 AM–5:30 PM, Sunday 1–5 PM

Cost: Suggested donations—adults $4, seniors $3, teens $3, children (12 and under) $1

Website: www.wheaton.edu/bgcmuseum

Directions: On campus off Main St., three blocks west of President St.

WHEATON

➡ John Belushi attended Wheaton Central High School (now called Wheaton Warrenville South), graduating in 1967. He was the Homecoming King. Reporter Bob Woodward, author of *Wired*, also attended this school.

Willowbrook

Flower Pot and Arap

Flower Pot was a skunk. A very special skunk. So special, in fact, that when he died his owner buried him in a formal cemetery and topped the grave with a life-sized sculpture of the stinker.

There have been plenty of deceased pets lovingly laid to rest like Flower Pot in Hinsdale Animal Cemetery since it opened in 1926. While most are dogs and cats, there are the occasional birds, turtles, horses, and a deer named Bambi. The most impressive monument is for a dog named Arap whose headstone reads, "He Gave Up His Life That a Human Might Live. Greater Love Hath No Man." Walking through the well-kept cemetery, it is hard not to be touched by the sentiments of these animals' owners, especially as you see tombstones etched with photos of beagles in Santa hats and Persian cats on big, fluffy pillows.

Hinsdale Animal Cemetery, 6400 S. Bentley Ave., Willowbrook, IL 60527

Phone: (630) 323-5120

Hours: Monday–Friday 9 AM–5 PM, Saturday–Sunday 8 AM–3 PM

Cost: Free

Website: www.petcemetery.org

Directions: One block south of 63rd St., two blocks west of Clarendon Hills Rd.

Wilmette
Bahá'í House of Worship

Looking like a gigantic, nine-sided orange juice squeezer on the shores of Lake Michigan, the Bahá'í House of Worship is the only such structure in North America. It was designed by Louis Bourgeois and is constructed of cement panels made with a concrete/quartz mixture that turns into a sparkling beacon at night. The white panels were cast in Washington, D.C., and shipped by rail to Wilmette, where they took more than 40 years to assemble. Chicagoland's largest jigsaw puzzle was dedicated on May 2, 1953, and is open to the general public.

100 Linden Ave., Wilmette, IL 60091

Phone: (847) 853-2300

Hours: Temple, daily 6 AM–10 PM; visitors' center, daily 10 AM–5 PM

Cost: Free

Website: www.bahai.us/bahai-temple

Directions: Along the lake, off Sheridan Rd. north of Central St.

WILMETTE

➡ Bill Murray was born in Wilmette on September 21, 1950. He graduated from Loyola Academy (1100 Laramee Ave.) in 1968.

MORE FUNKY HOUSES OF WORSHIP

To you-know-where with storefront churches—if you want to get right with God (or gods), you need to worship someplace splashy. Here are a few options:

BAPS Shri Swaminarayan Mandir

4N739 IL Route 59, Bartlett, (630) 213-2277, www.chicago.baps.org

This $30 million Hindu temple was manufactured in India and shipped to Illinois in 40,000 pieces, the last of which was put in place in 2004. The ornate structure, a large central dome surrounded by five pinnacles and sixteen smaller domes, does not contain a single piece of steel or iron.

Unity Temple

875 Lake St., Oak Park, (708) 848-6225, www.unitytemple.org

Designed by Frank Lloyd Wright and built between 1906 and 1908, Unity Temple was one of the first concrete structures built in the United States. Because of Wright's signature flat/leaky roof, this breathtaking building has been undergoing restoration since 1987, though it is still open for services and events.

Sri Venkateswara Swami Temple

1145 W. Sullivan Rd., Aurora, (630) 844-2252, www.balaji.org

Better known as the Balaji Temple, this structure is one of the largest Hindu temples in the country. It was modeled after a shrine in Tirupati, India, honoring Balaji (modern-day Vishnu), though there are eight other smaller shrines around the interior—take your pick.

Annunciation of the Mother of God Byzantine Catholic Parish

14610 Will Cook Rd., Homer Glen, (708) 645-0241, www.byzantinecatholic.com

The golden domes of this suburban church rise like the Emerald City above a reclaimed prairie. Built in 1998–99 using environmentally conscious construction methods, they still found room for hundreds of gilded icons and murals inside.

St. Joseph's Ukrainian Catholic Church

5000 N. Cumberland Ave., Chicago, (773) 625-4805, www.stjosephukr.com

This unique structure near O'Hare Airport, built from 1975 to 1977, looks like a bundle of bright blue, gold-topped missiles. If your mind wanders to something more perverse, get it out of the gutter—this is a church!

Winnetka
Birthplace of the Jungle Gym

Kids have been climbing through trees like monkeys since they were monkeys, but it took Chicago lawyer Sebastian Hinton to come up with the idea of making a compact fake jungle for children to play on, a jungle that could be erected anywhere. When Hinton was a child he enjoyed climbing around on a structure his mathematician father made from bamboo to teach his son Cartesian coordinates. As an adult he translated it into a boxy tower of pipes that he patented in 1920 under the name "Jungle Gym."

The first Jungle Gym was erected on the playground of Winnetka's progressive Crow Island School that same year. You can still see the structure today in all its unpadded, tooth-chipping glory, though you should come in the evening or on a weekend when school isn't in session or you'll freak out the teachers.

Crow Island School, 1112 Willow Rd., Winnetka, IL 60093
Phone: (847) 446-0353
Hours: Always visible
Cost: Free
Website: www.winnetka36.org/CrowIsland
Directions: At the south end of Glendale Ave., south of Willow Rd.

Burglars beware.

Home Alone Home

The 1990 John Hughes movie that launched Macauley Culkin's short-lived career was filmed in this posh northern suburb. And in a small, creepy coincidence, this movie about thieves battling with a young child was filmed in a town best known as the site of the attack against Hubbard Woods Elementary by the psychotic Laurie Dann only two years earlier.

When you drive down the street, the home is immediately recognizable by the many NO STOPPING OR STANDING signs along the curb. But this is private property—you could be hit in the face with a paint can or burned with a blowtorch if you try to approach. The home was put up for sale in 2011 for $2.4 million.

671 Lincoln Ave., Winnetka, IL 60093

Private phone

Hours: Private residence; view from street (while moving)

Cost: Free

Directions: Two blocks east of Green Bay Rd., one block north of Pine St.

OTHER JOHN HUGHES FILMING LOCATIONS

John Hughes used Chicago's north and northwest suburbs as his personal backlot, and though he made a lot of regrettable and forgettable flicks (*Beethoven's 5th*, really?), there are a few worth mentioning.

Sixteen Candles (1984)

High School: Oakton Community College, 7701 Lincoln Ave., Skokie

➡ This building was Niles East High School when the movie was filmed. The now-hard-to-recognize exterior was also used for the high school in *Risky Business*.

Baker Home: 3022 Payne St., Evanston

➡ Molly Ringwald's family lived in this Evanston home.

Church: Glencoe Union Church, 263 Park Ave., Glencoe

➡ Ringwald's sister gets married here at the end of the film.

The Breakfast Club (1985)

"Shermer" High School: Illinois State Police Station, 9511 Harrison St., Des Plaines

➡ Maine North High School had been vacant for about two years before the movie was filmed there in 1984. Anyone who attended Maine North wouldn't recognize the library seen in the film—it was a set built in the school's old gymnasium. Today the building is used by the Illinois state police, and though the interior is very different, the exterior looks much like it did in the movie.

Ferris Bueller's Day Off (1986)

"Shermer" High School (exterior): Glenbrook North High School, 2300 Shermer Rd., Northbrook

"Shermer" High School (interior): Illinois State Police Station, 9511 Harrison St., Des Plaines

➡ Though Bueller attended the same named high school as in *The Breakfast Club*, the outside looked entirely different . . . because it was. Bueller's "Shermer" was a real high school on Shermer Road. The interior, however, might have looked familiar because Hughes used old Maine North for the hallway shots. Confused?

Ferrari House: 370 Beech Street, Highland Park

➡ Bueller convinces his friend Cameron to take a spin in his father's Ferrari, but when Cameron learns his dad recorded the mileage before leaving town, they put the car up on blocks inside this modern house, its wheels spinning in reverse, with mixed results.

Planes, Trains, and Automobiles (1987)

"Those Aren't Pillows" Motel: Sun Motel, 140 S. Hickory St., Braidwood

➡ Forced by circumstances to bunk together in a hotel room in Wichita, Steve Martin and John Candy are robbed while they sleep and share an intimate encounter that didn't involve pillows.

El Rancho Motel: River Trails Gardens and Inn, 36355 Route 41, Gurnee

➡ After nearly being incinerated on the highway, Martin can't pay for his room at the El Rancho with his melted

credit cards and is forced to hock his watch; in the morning, while trying to get their car unstuck from a snowbank, Candy backs it into the room.

Home Sweet Home: 230 Oxford Rd., Kenilworth

➡ After parting ways on the Chicago El platform at LaSalle/ Van Buren, and then returning, Martin invites Candy home for Thanksgiving at this typical North Shore house.

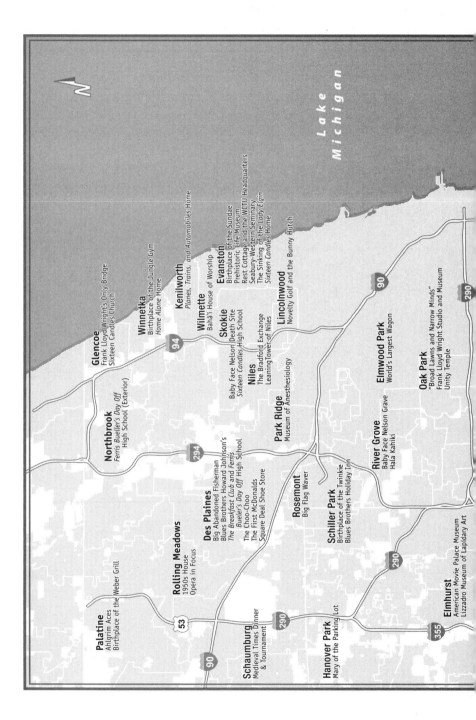

Lake Michigan

Glencoe
Frank Lloyd Wright's Only Bridge
Sixteen Candles Church

Winnetka
Birthplace of the Jungle Gym
Home Alone Home

Kenilworth
Planes, Trains, and Automobiles Home

Wilmette
Bahá'í House of Worship

Evanston
Birthplace of the Sundae
Prehistoric Life Museum
Rest Cottage and the WCTU Headquarters
Seabury-Western Seminary
The Sinking of the Lady Elgin
Sixteen Candles Home

Skokie
Baby Face Nelson Death Site
Sixteen Candles High School

Niles
The Bradford Exchange
Leaning Tower of Niles

Lincolnwood
Novelty Golf and the Bunny Hutch

Northbrook
Ferris Bueller's Day Off
High School (Exterior)

Park Ridge
Museum of Anesthesiology

Elmwood Park
World's Largest Wagon

Oak Park
"Broad Lawns and Narrow Minds"
Frank Lloyd Wright Studio and Museum
Unity Temple

Des Plaines
Big Abandoned Fisherman
Blues Brothers Howard Johnson's
The Breakfast Club and Ferris
Bueller's Day Off High School
The Choo-Choo
The First McDonalds
Square Deal Shoe Store

Rosemont
Big Flag Waver

River Grove
Baby Face Nelson Grave
Hala Kahiki

Schiller Park
Birthplace of the Twinkie
Blues Brothers Holiday Inn

Rolling Meadows
1950s House
Opera in Focus

Palatine
Ahlgrim Aces
Birthplace of the Weber Grill

Schaumburg
Medieval Times Dinner
& Tournament

Hanover Park
Mary of the Parking Lot

Elmhurst
American Movie Palace Museum
Lizzadro Museum of Lapidary Art

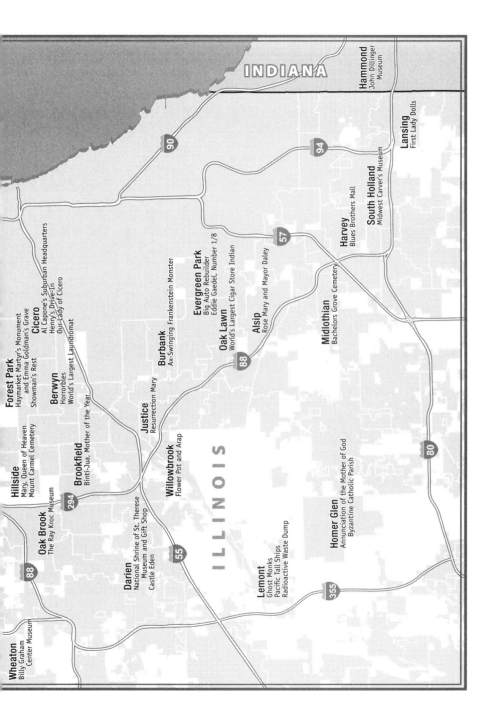

INDIANA

Hammond
John Dillinger Museum

Lansing
First Lady Dolls

South Holland
Midwest Carver's Museum

Harvey
Blues Brothers Mall

Midlothian
Bachelors Grove Cemetery

Alsip
Rose Mary and Mayor Daley

Oak Lawn
World's Largest Cigar Store Indian

Evergreen Park
Big Auto Rebuilder
Eddie Gaedel, Number 1/8

Burbank
Ax-Swinging Frankenstein Monster

Forest Park
Haymarket Martyr's Monument
and Emma Goldman's Grave
Showman's Rest

Cicero
Al Capone's Suburban Headquarters
Henry's Drive-In
Our Lady of Cicero

Berwyn
Horrorbles
World's Largest Laundromat

Justice
Resurrection Mary

Hillside
Mary, Queen of Heaven
Mount Carmel Cemetery

Brookfield
Binti-Jua, Mother of the Year

Willowbrook
Flower Pot and Arap

Homer Glen
Annunciation of the Mother of God
Byzantine Catholic Parish

Oak Brook
The Ray Kroc Museum

Darien
National Shrine of St. Therese
Museum and Gift Shop
Castle Eden

Lemont
Ghost Monks
Pacific Tall Ships
Radioactive Waste Dump

Wheaton
Billy Graham
Center Museum

ILLINOIS

3

NORTHERN ILLINOIS

Were it not for the vision of Nathaniel Pope, this might have been a very short book. When drafting the original borders for Illinois, Congress marked its northern boundary at the southern tip of Lake Michigan, 61 miles south of where it is today. But Pope, a territorial senator from the region, offered a proposal to move the boundary farther north, from 42°30" to 41°37", in order to give the future state a port on the lake. The proposal passed, and when Illinois became a state in 1818, Fort Dearborn, the future Chicago, was on the Illinois side.

Think about it. If Congress had kept its original boundaries, folks in northern Illinois might be wearing cheese-head hats! And would the Badger State have spawned such wonder-filled regional attractions as Donley's Wild West Town, the Feet First museum, or the Volo Auto Museum, at least outside the Dells tourist vortex? Maybe. Maybe not. But this I know for sure: because these places are in Illinois, their gift shops aren't crammed with black-and-white cow-abilia and coolers full of cheese and summer sausage. That's something.

Aledo
A Night Spent in Jail

If you're ever ordered to spend the weekend in jail as part of some plea bargain, do it in Aledo. The food's fantastic, they've got a sauna and a Jacuzzi, and they hand you the keys to come and go as you please. Sound like they're coddling criminals? Did I mention that this is a bed-and-breakfast?

Housed in the former Mercer County Jail, the Great Escape lacks the rifle-toting guards and shower fights of most correctional facilities. Instead, they've got comfy rooms, free popcorn and soda, and friendly "jailers." If all prisons were this nice, people would be killing one another to get in.

Downstairs is the Slammer Restaurant, offering entrees like a Fishy Story, an Executioner's Order, or a Final Request. Each booth is its own

cell, circa 1909, and the waiters and waitresses wear striped uniforms. If you're rowdy, there's a padded cell, and if the kids act up, you can always threaten them with the electric chair. It's on the second floor.

The Great Escape B&B/Slammer Restaurant, 309 S. College Ave., Aledo, IL 61231
Phone: (309) 582-5359
Hours: Year-round
Cost: Rooms $65–$85
Website: http://theslammer.net
Directions: One block southwest of the town square.

Amboy
Amboy Sculpture Park

Dennis Hastert's head is solid wood.

If life gives you tornadoes, make tornado-ade . . . or something like that. Back in 1999 a violent storm blew through Amboy's Green River City Park, toppling more than 50 old oak trees. So, with the blessing of city leaders, Bob and Marie Boyer pulled out their chainsaws and got to work transforming every salvageable stump into a work of art.

Their subject matter transcends the traditional bear-with-fish or Indian-with-cigars genre, with most of their creations celebrating small town life, community heroes, wild critters, and the Republican Party. Among the more than two dozen pieces are soldiers from World Wars I and II, a jumbo ear of corn, a fireman, a mom with a loaf of bread, a Little League baseball player, Ulysses S. Grant, Abraham Lincoln, Ronald Reagan, Dennis Hastert, Willie Morrisey (an area farmer), and Louie Scott, a local railroad worker who lived to be 105.

Amboy Green River City Park, 800 E. Main St., Amboy, IL 61310
Phone: (815) 857-3814
Hours: Daylight
Cost: Free
Website: www.cityofamboy.org/citypark.htm
Directions: Six blocks east of downtown on Main St.

Batavia
Mary Todd Lincoln in the Cuckoo's Nest

After her husband's assassination, Mary Todd Lincoln went off the deep end. She told people that gas lamps were sent from the Devil, that unknown persons were pulling wires from her eyes and bones from her left cheek, and that an Indian spirit lived in her head, causing her constant headaches. He even, on one occasion, removed and replaced her scalp, according to Mary.

In 1875 her son Robert had her committed to a sanitarium after an embarrassing public trial pitting son against mother. Mary ended up in the Bellevue Place Rest Home on May 20, an unconventional "rest home" by any standards. According to *The Insanity Files* (Neely and McMurtry, 1986), "patients received quinine, morphia, marijuana, cod-liver oil, beer or ale. . . . The staff seems only to have kept order while allowing the patients to play croquet, go for walks around the grounds, take carriage rides, or play the piano." Well if that's institutionalization, sign me up!

Mary didn't stay long; she was soon released on an "experiment." During that time, those around her learned that she was planning to kill her son Robert, even carrying a pistol in her pocket. It never happened, but she did send him a long series of letters demanding gifts back that she had previously lavished on Robert, "the monster of mankind," and his wife. Mary went to live with her sister in Springfield and almost drove her nuts, living in the dark until her death on July 16, 1882.

The building where Lincoln was held, stoned and playing croquet, is now a private condominium complex. She did not stay in the main "Ell" of the building but in the residence adjacent to the main structure. Though you can't enter the building, you can see a replica of her room at the nearby Batavia Depot Museum, which has the bed and dresser she used during her stay.

Bellevue Place Building (private), 333 S. Jefferson St., Batavia, IL 60510

Mary Todd Lincoln Display, Batavia Depot Museum, 155 Houston St., Batavia, IL 60510

Phone: (630) 406-5274

Hours: March–November, Wednesday, Friday–Monday 2–4 PM

Cost: Free

Website: www.bataviahistoricalsociety.org/mtodd.htm

Directions: Bellevue Place, two blocks south of Main St., one block west of Batavia Ave.
(Rte. 31); museum, one block north of Wilson St., one block east of Batavia Ave.

WAS HONEST ABE RESPONSIBLE?

Various explanations have been offered as to why Mary went cuckoo. It could have been an 1863 carriage accident in Washington in which she bashed her head on a rock, or it could have been that three of her four children died before reaching adulthood. Also, having your husband shot in the head while sitting beside you has to make you a little loopy. But could it have been syphilis?

Some historians believe that Abraham Lincoln might have contracted syphilis from a Beardstown whore, then passed it on to his wife. This theory is based upon recollections of Lincoln's Springfield law partner, William Herndon, a man of sometimes questionable motives and no friend of Mary's.

Because Abe died relatively young, he didn't suffer from the advanced stages of the disease, but Mary was another story. Her mental state could very well have been a result of rampant syphilis. Her autopsy revealed physiological deterioration of her brain, which bolsters the theory.

Belvidere
Big Thunder Park

Chief Big Thunder of the Potawatomi tribe wanted to be buried so that he would be able to command future generations in battle, which is to say, he did not want to be buried at all. After dying in the 1830s he was wrapped in a blanket and placed in a chair on the tallest hill in the area. A stash of earthly belongings and tobacco were laid out around him. Big Thunder's body was guarded only by a six-foot-tall stockade fence through which a hole had been cut for him to peer out at the Squaw Prairie. This land was where he predicted the future battle would take place.

The elements and vultures had their way, but it was the tourists who did him in. Stagecoach passengers who stopped at Doty's Tavern in Belvidere were encouraged to stretch their legs by walking up the hill to view

Big Thunder's body and leave a tobacco offering. After the chief's skull disappeared—some think it ended up in the hands of an East Coast phrenologist—the rest of the bones were up for grabs.

Local residents then faced a dilemma: see their tourist trap disappear or come up with a plan. Kids began tossing animal bones into the stockade so visitors never went away empty-handed. Many travelers went home with a soup bone from a local slaughterhouse, and many local kids collected free tobacco from the city suckers.

The scheme didn't work forever. The first Boone County Courthouse was built on the same hill, and a flagpole was erected on the spot where Big Thunder's chair had sat. The DAR attached a plaque to a boulder by the flagpole, and that's all you'll see today.

Big Thunder Park, 601 N. Main St., Belvidere, IL 61008

No phone

Hours: Always visible

Cost: Free

Directions: At the Boone County Sheriff's Department, two blocks east of State St. at Menomonie St.

BELVIDERE

➡ On April 21, 1967, a tornado struck Belvidere High School (1500 East Ave.) just as students were being released from class. The twister overturned 12 of the school's 16 buses and killed 24 people. An aluminum tornado sculpture marks the spot today.

Big Rock
Mount Barry

Jutting up from the banks of Welch Creek is a teetering tower of red rock. A natural formation? Hardly. It looks more like a movie set from a Road Runner cartoon. Saguaro cacti made of rebar cling to the mountain, as do several plastic barrel cacti and a small concrete deer.

Welcome to Mount Barry, aka Arizona Mountain, the creation of John Van Barriger. This Big Rock resident has always had an affection for the Southwest, and he decided to make his own Monument Valley in the heart

Wile E. Coyote would feel right at home.

of corn country. Building permits be damned, Mount Barry went up, made mostly of concrete slabs and other salvaged construction material.

Kane County officials were not happy about the new big rock in Big Rock. They've tried to fine Van Barriger for toxins supposedly leaching into the creek, but they were hard-pressed to prove concrete is poisonous. For the time being, Mount Barry stands tall, but you'd better get a look before the county killjoys fire up a bulldozer.

Route 30, Big Rock, IL 60511

Private phone

Hours: Always visible

Cost: Free

Directions: South of Rte. 30 where it intersects with Dauberman Rd., across the railroad tracks.

Bourbonnais
Big Lincoln Lift

In Illinois you get fairly accustomed to seeing Abraham Lincoln's image being used to hawk everything from mattresses to auto insurance. But the 28-foot-tall statue of our 16th president at a heavy equipment rental company in Bourbonnais—what's that all about? Is it that Abe was our tallest president at six feet, four inches, the 19th-century version of a cherry picker?

Nope. Turns out the statue is just owner Jerry Alexander's way of communicating with the thousands of drivers who pass his business every day along I-57. Lincoln holds up a sign facing the highway that has read, in the past, LINCOLN WAS A REPUBLICAN and WANT $7.00 GAS? VOTE DEMOCRAT. Not quite as elegant as the Gettysburg Address, nor as profound, but then Lincoln was a better writer.

Alexander Construction, 1511 Commerce Dr., Bourbonnais, IL 60914

Phone: (815) 933-1121

Hours: Always visible

Cost: Free

Website: www.aeriallifetequipment.com

Directions: North on Rte. 50 from I-57, left on Larry Power Rd., then left on Commerce Dr.

President, emancipator, cherry picker.

Bull Valley
Stickney Mansion

What darkness is to Dracula, square corners are to the Devil. Satan loves to hide in square corners . . . or at least that's what George and Sylvia Stickney believed. When their Bull Valley mansion was constructed in 1849, masons were under strict orders not to build it with any 90-degree corners. From the outside, it appears that they did a good job rounding off the points, but apparently they overlooked the meeting of two interior walls.

Sylvia and George were Spiritualists, and through séances they confirmed their worst fear: the Devil was going to pay them a visit. One day, George was found huddled in the only square corner of the house, dead from no apparent cause. Sylvia packed up and never returned.

Subsequent owners reported hearing George's ghost, including a band of "devil worshippers" in the 1960s. Well, the locals thought they were devil worshippers, but they were actually a hippie commune. The building fell into disrepair in the '70s until it was put into service as the Bull Valley Village Hall. You're welcome to stop by during business hours, but the upper floor is off-limits. Could it be the Village knows something you don't?

1904 Cherry Valley Rd., Bull Valley, IL 60098

Phone: (815) 459-4833

Hours: Always visible on outside; inside Monday–Friday 10 AM–5 PM

Cost: Free

Directions: Just north of Crystal Springs Rd., southeast of Mason Hill Rd.

Crystal Lake
The Giants of Crystal Lake

There must be something in the water—growth crystals, perhaps—in Crystal Lake. What else would explain the oversized Amish gardener in the neon green shirt, and the huge Indian wearing no shirt at all, outside a

greenhouse north of town? And just a few miles away as the big bird flies, there's another gargantuan guy—this one a lumberjack outside a firewood and mulch emporium. What's going on here?

Turns out that two of these fiberglass monsters were, until recently, part of the Ozzi Waterpark and Go Cart Park in Palatine. To prevent their kidnapping by high school pranksters, their feet were once set in cement. But when Ozzi went out of business, the Indian and the Amish guy were pried off their bases, repainted, and given cinder block feet outside their new greenhouse home. The nearby lumberjack still has his shoes.

The Greenhouse of Crystal Lake, 4317 S. Highway 31, Crystal Lake, IL 60012

Phone: (815) 893-6313

Hours: Always visible

Cost: Free

Website: www.thegreenhousecl.com

Directions: One mile north of Rte. 176 on Rte. 31.

Lumberjacks Firewood, 2316 Highway 176, Crystal Lake, IL 60012

Phone: (815) 337-1451

Hours: Always visible

Cost: Free

Website: www.lumberjax.com

Directions: Two miles east of Rte. 31 on Rte. 176.

Something in the water.

BIG MEN OF NORTHERN ILLINOIS

The giants of Crystal Lake represent a species of roadside attraction commonly known as Muffler Men. The first such giant was manufactured in 1962 for the PB Cafe in Flagstaff, Arizona. He looked like Paul Bunyan—PB—and he drew in a ton of customers. Soon the International Fiberglass Company of Venice, California, was cranking out these statues for other eateries as well as filling stations, repair shops, amusement parks, and more. Built in four pieces that could be interchanged depending on the buyer, the most common configuration was to have its forearms outstretched with its right hand palm up and the left hand palm down. Muffler shops in particular liked to install a complete exhaust system in its hands (hence the nickname), but they've been know to hold axes, rockets, hot dogs, flags, golf clubs, miniature cars, you name it.

International Fiberglass later branched out to create other colossal characters, including the "Noble Savage" Indian (see page 120), the Uniroyal Gal (page 209), and the A&W Root Beer Family.

In addition to those listed below, there are other Muffler Men scattered around the state: the Gemini Giant in Wilmington (pages 177–78), the Paul Bunyan in Atlanta (page 190), the Lauderbach Giant in Springfield (page 223), and the biker guy outside the Pink Elephant Antique Mall in Livingston (page 246).

Lambs Farm Giant

Lambs Farm, 14245 W. Rockland Rd., Libertyville, (847) 362-4636, www. lambsfarm.org

This bucolic petting zoo, bakery, and miniature golf course has a rather unsettling Muffler Man on its grounds: a bearded logger holding an ax over the head of an innocent milk cow. He has obviously scared the milk out of her, as there is a 20-foot-tall bottle of the stuff nearby.

Ax-Swinging Frankenstein Monster

Haunted Trails Amusement Park, 7759 S. Harlem Ave., Burbank, (708) 598-8580, www.enchanted.com/indexBurbank.html

Another ax-swinging monstrosity can be found in the southwest suburb of Burbank, and he's even scarier. Decked out in a purple suit and yellow tie (the horror!), this two-story Frankenstein's monster guards a miniature golf course, batting cages, and go-kart track.

Big Auto Rebuilder

Guardian Auto Rebuilders, 8939 S. Kedzie Ave., Evergreen Park, (708) 422-5600

The Muffler Man atop this body shop was blown off its perch in 1998. His owners used the opportunity to give him a spiffy new paint job—a sparkly red shirt and a pair of neon blue disco slacks.

Mr. Bendo

Ced's Muffler & Brakes, 3940 W. Grand Ave., Chicago, (773) 384-3646

A similar fate struck Mr. Bendo on Chicago's West Side in 2010, but rather than being knocked over entirely, just his upper body was blown off. Today all you'll see is an empty pair of white pants on top of the building. Hopefully the garage will replace his torso, head, and upraised arms that once held a long, bent tailpipe.

Big Flag Waver

Wolff's Flea Market, 6920 N. Mannheim Rd., Rosemont, (847) 524-9590, www.wolffs.com

The lumberjack inside this mega-market stood outside a lumber warehouse in Melrose Park until a few years ago, but he is now protected from the elements in the loading dock of a flea market. Just to make sure nobody confuses him with a Canadian, he waves an American flag in his outstretched hands.

Big Onan Man

Onan Garage, 3500 Sunset Ave., Waukegan, (847) 336-7777,
www.onangarage.com

Though he's not a Muffler Man, the guy on top of the Onan Garage warehouse in northwest Waukegan is just as big. He holds a hammer in one hand and one of the company's prefab structures under his other arm, which tells you how they save overhead on a forklift.

Big Abandoned Fisherman

9665 Golf Rd., Des Plaines

Also not a Muffler Man, and not long for this world, is the huge fisherman of Des Plaines. He's landing a 10-foot trout that he caught in the defunct (and funky smelling) Fisherman's Dude Ranch, long since closed to make room for more condos. The abandoned fisherman is best seen in the winter, as the statue/sign is obscured by vines and trees in the summer.

Big Vegas Elvis

Rides Unlimited, 908 E. Rte. 71, Newark, (815) 695-5029,
www.ridesunlimitedchicago.com

Elvis Presley never sold mufflers, but he did once drive a delivery truck. Still, that was years before he squeezed into a white jumpsuit to play the Vegas strip, which is what he's wearing outside this used car lot east of Newark. The nine-foot crooner takes care of business with a large black guitar on the front patio.

DeKalb
The Egyptian Theatre

Built in 1928 and opened in 1929, the Egyptian Theatre puts the modern moviegoing experience to shame. Architect Elmer Behrns used features from the tomb of Ramses II to make the Egyptian a special place, including a scarab skylight, linen curtains, and two seated Ramses II statues flanking the stage. A ceiling peppered with twinkling stars and a cloud generator gave visitors the illusion they were seated in a desert oasis, as did the murals depicting the Pyramids of Giza, the Great Sphinx, and the tableaus of Abu Simbel.

But the Egyptian fell on hard times. It was to be torn down in 1976, but it was purchased by a group of volunteers calling themselves P.E.T.: Preserve the Egyptian Theatre. It was not until 1983 that the building was renovated. P.E.T. managed to keep 80 percent of the original structure intact, including the antique carbon-arc projector. The murals were restored with a few minor revisions; look for the tablets showing the restorers' names at the front left, or the cat on the rock at the front right. A stray cat became the constant companion of restoration crews, so it was immortalized.

The 1,475-seat Egyptian does not just show movies on weekends. It also has 40 to 50 live performances a year. Call ahead for a schedule.

135 N. Second St., DeKalb, IL 60115

Phone: (815) 758-1215

Hours: Check website for schedule; closed January, July, and August

Cost: Movies, adults $4.50, kids $3; events, check website; tours, free

Website: www.egyptiantheatre.org

Directions: One block north of Lincoln Highway (Rte. 38), two blocks west of Fourth St. (Rte. 23).

DEKALB

➡ Supermodel Cindy Crawford was born in DeKalb on February 20, 1966.

➡ Actress Barbara Hale was born in DeKalb on April 18, 1922.

Corn? Corn? What's corn?

Dixon
Ronald Reagan's Boyhood Home

Ronald Reagan's family moved to Dixon in 1920 when "Dutch" was just nine years old. It was here, in the "Petunia Capital of the World," that Ronnie learned to swim at the YMCA, where he ran around with his brother, Neil, or "Moon" as the other kids knew him, and where he was art director for the 1928 school yearbook.

The Reagan family lived in this home from 1920 to 1923. None of the furnishings here are original; they were chosen by the president from a pre-1920 Sears catalog according to what he remembered, which wasn't much. (Actually, his brother Moon later admitted that neither he nor Ron remembered too much about this place, moving around as much as their family did.) In front of the home stands a statue of Reagan as president, staring into his upturned palm. A plaque reads ILLINOIS IS FAMOUS FOR ITS PRODUCTION OF AGRICULTURAL PRODUCTS, SO IT SEEMS APPROPRIATE FOR HIM TO BE ADMIRING THE KERNELS OF CORN IN HIS HAND.

Three other Dixon homes in which his family lived—338 W. Everett Avenue, 226 Lincoln Way, and 107–108 Monroe Avenue—are not open to the public. You can, however, step inside the old South Central School where he attended classes, today the Dixon Historic Center (205 W. Fifth St., (815) 288-5508, www.dixonhistoriccenter.org), as well as the First Christian Church (123 S. Hennepin Ave., (815) 288-1222) where the Reagans worshipped. And finally, there are two other Reaganesque photo ops in town. A statue of Ronnie riding a horse can be found along the riverfront at the Dixon Welcome Center (106 W. River St., (815) 284-3496); the sculpture is based on a 1950 photo of Reagan riding in Dixon's Injun Summer Days Parade. There's also a fake chunk of the Berlin Wall at the nearby Wings of Peace and Freedom Park (Galena Ave. and Second St.); it's a reproduction of the wall Reagan didn't really tear down, but it was made by a Bulgarian.

816 S. Hennepin Ave., Dixon, IL 61021
Phone: (815) 288-5176
Hours: April–October, Monday–Saturday 10 AM–4 PM, Sunday 1–4 PM
Cost: Adults $5, kids (12 and under) free
Website: http://reaganhome.org
Directions: One block west of Galena Ave. (Rte. 26), between Eighth and Ninth Sts.

WHY THE FOLKS OF DIXON NEED LIFEGUARDS

During his high school years, from 1926 to 1933, Ronald Reagan was a lifeguard at Lowell Park (2114 Lowell Park Rd., (815) 288-5209), three miles north of town on the Rock River. He was credited with saving 77 people, though rumors are that some young women, and perhaps a few men, faked distress in order to have young, strapping Dutch pull them to safety. Reagan notched a log every time he "saved a life."

But for the folks of Dixon, Dutch might have been born too late. Forty-two people died and 100 were injured when a footbridge over the Rock River near Dixon collapsed on May 4, 1873. The crowd had gathered to watch a submersion baptism.

Essex
Jack Barker's Sculpture Park

If you fly by too fast, you might mistake this roadside wonder for a scrap metal yard. In a sense it is, but on closer inspection you'll notice the haphazard piles of rusted machinery and car parts have been welded together to make hundreds of interesting sculptures. They're all the creations of Jack Barker, who's been at it for five decades and shows no sign of slowing. Many are fantastical creatures of his imagination, while others are more identifiable: Donald Duck, clowns, Jesus on the cross, a pink elephant, and a horse raised on its hind legs, ready to gallop. They crowd the front entryway to his garage/studio and wrap around to the back, and if Barker's around when you visit he'll show you what he's got inside.

Take your time, and make sure you've had your tetanus shot.

Most of Barker's works are located at this workshop on East Street, though there are a few others just down the block at 333 North Merchant Street, where he lives. He's carefully mounted those works on pivots so that they turn in the wind.

600 N. East St., PO Box 155, Essex, IL 60935

Phone: (815) 365-4045

Hours: Always visible

Cost: Free

Directions: Just North of Merchant St. on Rte. 41 (East St.).

Freeport
Little Cubs Field

Though it is a regulation ballpark, Chicago's Wrigley Field seems more intimate than most ballparks. Little Cubs Field in Freeport is a replica of Wrigley but measures 100 feet down the lines rather than 355 feet. *That's* intimate. It was built by volunteers and opened in 2008, and it has all the

features of the original, including the red brick outfield wall and scoreboard but minus the grandstands, skyboxes, and overpriced beer.

Any team is welcome to rent out the field, though it's mostly booked for T-ball, ages 6–8 Little League, kickball, and whiffle-ball games . . . more along the skill level of the real Cubs.

1160 W. Empire St., Freeport, IL 61032

Phone: (800) 369-2955

Hours: Always visible

Cost: Free; $45 per hour to rent

Website: www.littlecubsfield.com

Directions: In Read Park at S. McKinley Ave.

Galena
Tara's Green Drapes

Contrary to what was depicted in *Gone with the Wind*, Miss Scarlett did not make Tara's drapes into a dress. Need proof? They're hanging right here in Galena's Belvedere Mansion! And that's not all. This place has also got oil paintings from Tara and Victorian trinkets picked up at Liberace's estate sale. This Galena abode is the restored Italianate mansion of a former ambassador to Belgium, J. Russell Jones, and it's one of the fanciest homes in "The Town That Time Forgot."

Belvedere Mansion, 1008 Park Ave., Galena, IL 61036

Phone: (815) 777-0747

Hours: Tours, May–November, Sunday–Friday 11 AM–4 PM, Saturday 11 AM–5 PM

Cost: Adults $12, kids $6

Website: www.galenabelvederemansion.com

Directions: One block south of Rte. 20 (Spring/Decatur St.), just east of the Galena River.

Harvard
Harmilda the Cow

As big roadside cows go, Harmilda is kind of puny, but don't equate size with power. While other tacky statues are routinely shuffled around or dragged off by teenage pranksters, Harmilda is afforded a lot of respect by the Harvard locals. She's been around since 1966, unveiled at Harvard Milk

Nobody messes with Harmilda.

Day (from which she draws her name), still held each June in the "Milk Center of the World."

Harmilda stood for years on a pedestal in the middle of the intersection of Routes 14 and 173, but in 1991 the Illinois Department of Transportation determined she was a traffic hazard and demanded that she be removed from her perch. She was so beloved by this point, however, that the Chamber of Commerce sacrificed its offices for the cow's new home; the COC took a wrecking ball to its own building for a minipark at the same intersection, and Harmilda was mounted in front of a new bovine mural. A few years later some "tourism consultant" jackanapes suggested that Harvard replace its favorite fiberglass monument with a classy bronze version and was all but run out of town.

Ayer and Division Sts., Harvard, IL 60033

Phone: (815) 943-4614

Hours: Always visible

Cost: Free

Website: www.milkdays.com

Directions: At the intersection of Rte. 14 and Rte. 173.

HAVE A BIG COW

You don't have to go to Harvard, or Wisconsin for that matter, to find a big roadside cow. There are plenty of larger, and in some cases meaner, cows to be found in northern Illinois.

Gas City Cow

Sager and S. Manheim Rds., Frankfort

Once located at 55th Street and Pulaski Road, this black and white Holstein can now be found guarding the corporate offices of Gas City. What does a big cow have to do with gas production? Do you have to ask?

Gertrude, the Giant Guernsey

Lockwood Park Trailside Equestrian Centre and Children's Farm, 5201 Safford Rd., Rockford, (815) 987-8809, www.rockfordparkdistrict.org

Though horses are the focus of this Rockford park, it's hard to ignore the giant Guernsey on the hill overlooking it all. Gertrude stands 19 feet tall and is 21 feet long and can be found across the bridge, above and behind the playground.

Bessie

Lambs Farm, 14245 W. Rockland Rd., Libertyville, (847) 362-4636, www.lambsfarm.org

Big Bessie stands watch over the miniature golf course at this petting zoo, farm, bakery, and home for persons with developmental disabilities. Why, might you ask, would Bessie need to stand sentry in such a peaceful, happy place? Perhaps to protect the young 'uns from the ax-wielding giant standing beside her (see page 152). Now kids, relax and focus on your stroke . . .

Cow Cannibal

Country Cottage Café, 101 E. South St., Durand, (815) 248-4159

If you thought Bessie was frightening, wait until you see the Cow Cannibal of Durand. Not content to chew her cud, this murderous mooer has developed a taste for flesh—cow flesh! The goofy chef's cap doesn't hide the fact that this steak griller is eating one of her relatives.

Baby Bull

Baby Bull's Restaurant, 1025 W. Reynolds St., Pontiac, (815) 844-5757

The namesake of this Pontiac restaurant stands at the far end of the parking lot where it attracts customers on busy Route 116. Though just a baby, it looks pretty much like an adult steer, only smaller. . . . OK, who are we kidding? The restaurant obviously bought the economy model.

Moomaw's Big Bull

Lowell Moomaw Elevator, 2800E and 300N, Stewardson, (217) 682-5741

A large, bug-eyed black bull balances atop four posts adjoining this rural business. For some reason, small statues of a pig, a lamb, and a goat stand nearby.

Lincolnshire
Par-King

When you tee up at the Par-King miniature golf course, you'll think you stepped through a time warp. And you have. This attraction started in the 1950s as George's Gorgeous Golfing Gardens, then in 1964 moved to a new location with a new name: Par-King in Morton Grove. It later expanded to a second site in Lincolnshire, which is the only course still open today.

Each hole on "America's Most Unusual Golf Course" is unique, including a Mount Rushmore hole, a Roulette hole, a Sears Tower hole, and plenty of clowns, toy soldiers, and tiki totems everywhere you look. The

most elaborate is the Roller Coaster hole; if you can putt into the coaster's "loading area," your ball goes on a journey around an old-fashioned wooden coaster before being dumped near the final green. Unlike many miniature golf attractions, everything's freshly painted and the hedges are cleanly trimmed.

21711 Milwaukee Ave., Lincolnshire, IL 60069

Phone: (847) 634-0333

Hours: June–August, Monday–Saturday 10:30 AM–11 PM, Sunday 11:30 AM–10 PM; mid-April–
May and September, Saturday 10:30 AM–11 PM, Sunday 11:30 AM–10 PM

Cost: Days, Monday–Friday $7, Saturday–Sunday $8; evenings (after 6 PM), Monday–Friday
$7.50, Saturday–Sunday $8.50

Website: www.par-king.com

Directions: One mile south of Half Day Rd. (Rte. 22).

Dance, puppets, dance!

Morris
Truck Stop Marionettes

Quick—what's the last thing you'd expect to find at an interstate truck stop? A mechanical marionette show, you say? Welcome to Morris! For just a

quarter, the R Place Band will strike up a German polka while 18 hand-carved puppets jump to life. There's a drunken old man and his broom-swinging wife, a clown on the piano with a spotted dog, two clogging couples, and three shimmying sailors, all dancing on strings.

Is it worth getting off I-80 to take in a performance? What's your rush? Afraid of a little culture? The show only lasts a minute; then you can grab a Slim Jim and a Slushy and get right back on the road.

R Place Eatery, 21 Romines Dr., Morris, IL 60450

Phone: (815) 942-5690

Hours: Always open

Cost: Performances, 25¢; meals, $6–$12

Website: www.rplaceeatery.com

Directions: One block north of I-80 on Rte. 47, then right on Romines Dr.

Mt. Carroll
Raven's Grin Inn

To call Raven's Grin Inn a haunted house is to call Disneyland a kiddie park. It's so much more! Raven's Grin Inn is a childhood clubhouse gone haywire, an indoor junkyard fun house, a performance art piece that could have been built by the Marx Brothers but is actually the fevered brainchild of Jim Warfield.

Warfield promises "No chainsaws, no Jason, no Freddy!" but that doesn't mean you won't be frightened or entertained. Without revealing too much, it's safe to say you'll spend a full hour and a half crawling through passageways, bumping down slides, jumping at sight gags, meeting Mr. Tuxedo (Warfield's cat), and listening to creepy monologues worthy of a dead Henny Youngman.

The visit will take you at least an hour, more if you get lost, and you probably will, no thanks to your tour guide. When offered the "optional ride" midway through your visit, take it . . . and hold on. There are multiple paths through the 1870s structure, so no two visits will be the same.

Warfield hopes one day to make part of the Raven's Grin into a bed-and-breakfast where guests play a role in taunting the visitors. He already offers the Raven's Grin to hide-and-seek parties, so if you have a large group, call ahead.

411 N. Carroll St., Mt. Carroll, IL 61053

Phone: (815) 244-GRIN

Hours: Monday–Friday 7 PM–midnight, Saturday–Sunday 2–5 PM and 7 PM–midnight; call ahead for reservations, particularly during winter

Cost: Adults $13

Website: www.hauntedravensgrin.com

Directions: Two blocks west of Clay St. (Rte. 78) behind the True Value, just north of the business district.

Head ornament.

North Chicago
Feet First: The Scholl Story

Who would have thought the human foot was so interesting? Dr. Scholl, for one! William Scholl began his career as a shoemaker, but in 1904 he branched out into products for shoe injuries: bunion pads, callus protectors, corn pads, and sole inserts. They were a welcome offering to the foot-weary public, and they made Dr. Scholl a household name.

You'll learn all about the history of footwear and footcare—chiropody—at Feet First, a museum at the Rosalind Franklin University of Medicine and Science. You'll see historical footwear from an era before left and right shoes were common. Even after formfitting, arch-supporting shoes became the norm, modern shoes created problems. Read the warnings: "In the 1970s, these platform shoes were stylish, but the wearer risked falling because of their height and inflexibility." Damn you, gravity!

Feet First has many feets-on exhibits. Step on the Meet Your Feet pressure pads and learn why your dogs get so tired. Rest your tootsies in the EZ Your Feet Theater as you watch Scholl's life story. His credo? "Early to bed, early to rise, work like hell, and advertise." And check out foot-related oddities like the fluoroscope, an x-ray device for measuring feet in the 1950s, and the oversized shoes worn by professional basketball players and Alton's Gentle Giant, Robert Wadlow (see pages 262–64).

3333 Green Bay Rd., North Chicago, IL 60064

Phone: (847) 578-3200

Hours: Monday–Friday 9 AM–5 PM

Cost: Free

Website: www.rosalindfranklin.edu/dnn/scholl/home/schollcollegeofpodiatricmedicine/feetfirst.aspx

Directions: College on the south side of North Chicago; ask for directions to the museum at the front desk.

Norway
A Crashed Plane

You might be tempted to call 911 when you spot a plane crashed nose down on a country road near Norway, but you'd be reporting a tragedy that happened three decades ago, and it had nothing to do with airplanes. A sign in front of the wreck reads DEDICATED TO FARMERS AND ALL AG-RELATED BUSINESS FOLKS THAT HAVE LIVED THRU THE AGRICULTURAL CRASH OF THE 1980S. It was erected by Melvin and Phyllis Eastwold of the Norwegian Implement Company.

While you could stare at the empty shell and contemplate the farm crisis, it would be a shame to pass up a great photo opportunity. Lie on the ground as if thrown from the fuselage on impact, and you'll always be able to trump your friends' vacation horror stories.

Route 71 and 25th Rd., Norway, IL 60551
No phone
Hours: Always visible
Cost: Free
Directions: South of town on Rte. 71.

A double disaster.

Oregon
Big Chief Black Hawk

Overlooking the Rock River Valley is a stoic Native American figure, 48 feet from head to toe. The *Eternal Indian* is the world's largest reinforced-concrete statue, a massive monument weighing 268 tons and sitting on a foundation that goes 30 feet into the ground. It is commonly referred to as Big Chief Black Hawk, but the name is incorrect. While it could be many Native Americans, it looks nothing like Chief Black Hawk, who had a mohawk. In actuality, it was modeled after sculptor Lorado Taft's brother-in-law, dressed up in a robe.

The 1911 statue is the work of Lorado Taft, later the leader of the Eagle's Nest Artist Colony during the 1920s. This group of Chicago bohemians set up shop near Oregon each summer to escape the heat and frighten the locals. Taft's previous artist colony had been run out of Indiana, and the folks of Oregon were only slightly more receptive. Their suspicion could have been the constant fun everyone seemed to be having or the plaster sculptures the artist made one day and smashed the next, but most likely it was the themed evenings. One night the entire colony dressed in Egyptian garb, paraded around the bluffs, and presented two "slaves" to a visiting Egyptologist.

Lowden State Park, PO Box 403, 1411 N. River Rd., Oregon, IL 61061

Phone: (815) 732-6828

Hours: Daily, sunrise to sunset

Cost: Free

Website: http://dnr.state.il.us/lands/landmgt/parks/r1/lowdensp.htm

Directions: Rte. 64 east from Oregon, turn north on River Rd., and follow the signs in the park.

Ottawa
Effigy Tumuli

Many early American cultures built effigy mounds, earthen sculptures formed in the shapes of animals to honor great spirits (or to signal UFOs if you believe *Chariots of the Gods*). But there is another possibility for why some mounds exist: to cover up a big mess.

That was the plan behind *Effigy Tumuli*, designed by Michael Heizer. As part of a land reclamation project on the Illinois River, these five

modern earthen mounds were piled in the shape of a snake, a catfish, a water strider, a frog, and a turtle. Because they're a mile and a half long and mostly flat, they can only be truly appreciated from above via Google Earth, though you're welcome to hike all over them.

Buffalo Rock State Park, 1300 N. 27th Rd., PO Box 2034, Ottawa, IL 61350
Phone: (815) 433-2224
Hours: Daily, sunrise to sunset
Cost: Free
Website: www.dnr.state.il.us/lands/landmgt/PARKS/i&m/east/buffalo/home.htm,
   http://doublenegative.tarasen.net/effigy_tumuli.html
Directions: Three miles west of town on Dee Bennett Rd., along the Illinois River.

Ottawa Scouting Museum

W. D. Boyce was a world traveler, yet somehow he got lost on a foggy London evening in July 1909. A young boy emerged from the mist and helped him find where he was going. When Boyce offered the lad a tip, the boy refused, saying it was his duty as a Boy Scout to "Do a good turn every day." Boyce knew he wouldn't be the only guy who would ever get lost in the fog, so he met with British Scout founder Colonel Robert Baden-Powell. In 1910, Boyce established an American chapter to assist others with a poor sense of direction.

Boyce was able to fund the early Scouts using money he made through the unscoutsmanlike enterprise of publishing tabloid newspapers in Chicago. He had enough left over to purchase an estate near Ottawa. When he died in 1929, Boyce was buried in the Ottawa Avenue Cemetery (1601 Ottawa Ave., http://ottawaavenuecemetery.com), and a scouting monument was placed over his grave in 1941.

Because of Ottawa's Boyce connection, it is the natural place for a Scouting Museum. The newly opened collection has an impressive array of memorabilia associated with the Boy Scouts of America, the Lone Scouts, the Girl Scouts, the Brownies, the Camp Fire Girls, and others. Its most recent exhibit is a room re-created from Boyce's Ottawa home.

1100 Canal St., PO Box 2241, Ottawa, IL 61350
Phone: (815) 431-9353
Hours: Thursday–Monday 10 AM–4 PM
Cost: Adults $3, kids (17 and under) $2
Website: www.ottawascoutingmuseum.org
Directions: Four blocks west of Columbus St. (Rte. 23), four blocks south of Norris Dr. (Rte. 6).

That's-a spicy statue!

Rochelle
Vince, the Pizza Guy

It's been a downhill slide for Italian stereotypes since Alka-Seltzer's "Mamma mia—that's-a spicy meatball!" campaign of the 1970s. Where have all the Guidos gone . . . besides MTV? Thankfully, you can still find a mustachioed pizza flipper today in Rochelle: Vince, the Pizza Guy. This gargantuan goombah stands 10 feet tall and guards the parking lot of this puny pizzeria. Personally, I think it's a good thing that somebody's keeping the pepperoni-slinging image alive, otherwise people will fugetaboutit.

Vince's Pizza and Family Restaurant, 1701 N. Seventh St., Rochelle, IL 61068
Phone: (815) 562-7300
Hours: Always visible; restaurant, daily 4–9 PM
Cost: Free
Directions: One block south of Rte. 38 (May Mart Dr.) on Rte. 251 (Seventh St.).

Rockford
Baby Jane

Forget Sue and avoid the Chicago crowds—if you want to see a *Tyrannosaurus rex* up close, come to Rockford where you'll find Jane, the most complete juvenile *T. rex* skeleton ever unearthed. Jane was born about 66,000,011 years ago, and though she wasn't even a teenager when she died, she did stand seven and a half feet tall at the hip and measured 21 feet end to end. (And you thought you had an awkward adolescence.) Her fossilized bones were discovered in the Montana Badlands in 2001, but it took four years to prepare them for display. She was named in honor of one of the Burpee Museum's benefactors, Jane Solem, and no, there is no resemblance between the two.

Jane has recently been joined by Homer, a juvenile Triceratops, who also was found in the same Montana beds. Burpee dig volunteer Helmuth Redschlag came across the skeleton in 2005 and named it for his favorite character on *The Simpsons*, also a lumbering, boneheaded oaf.

Burpee Museum of Natural History, 737 N. Main St., Rockford, IL 61103

Phone: (815) 965-3433

Hours: Daily 10 AM–5 PM

Cost: Adults $8, kids (3–17) $7

Website: www.burpee.org

Directions: Just southwest of the Whitman St. bridge.

World's Largest Sock Monkey

Any home crafting enthusiast will tell you that 1932 marked a quantum leap forward in sock monkey technology. That was the year the Nelson Knitting Company of Rockford introduced the Red Heel sock; the location of the colored heel was perfect to form the monkey's gaping mouth. Of course it didn't hurt that the country was in the midst of the Great Depression, when a stuffed old sock was just the type of toy a family could afford.

Was it made from Paul Bunyan's socks?

Though the Red Heel is no longer manufactured in Rockford, the city has embraced its place in folk art history. You can see the original patents for both the signature sock and the first sock monkey design at Midway Village, as well as a seven-foot stuffed simian named Nelson, the world's largest. Each March the museum hosts the Sock Monkey Madness Festival, where a Miss Sockford is crowned. (The pageant is for dolls, not children.)

Midway Village and Museum Center, 6799 Guilford Rd., Rockford, IL 61107

Phone: (815) 397-9112

Hours: May–August, Tuesday–Friday 10 AM–4 PM, Saturday–Sunday 10:30 AM–4 PM; September–
   April, Tuesday–Friday 10 AM–4 PM, Saturday 10:30 AM–4 PM

Cost: Adults $6, kids (3–17) $4

Website: www.midwayvillage.com

Directions: Two blocks west of Perryville Rd., north of Rte. 20.

Roscoe
Historic Auto Attractions

Don't be bored off by this museum's name, nor worry that it's just for gear-heads. Quite simply, Historic Auto Attractions is one of the greatest private museums in the state. It seems that there's nothing owner Wayne Lensing won't buy and put on display, as long as it's cool.

Yes, there are the cars. See a twisted chunk of metal from James Dean's death Porsche, as well as vehicles owned by Conway Twitty, Evita Peron, Howard Hughes, Elvis Presley, Andy Griffith, and Colonel Sanders. Check out the *Back to the Future* DeLorean, the *Batman Returns* Batmobile and Batrocket, the *Ghostbusters* "Ecto-1" Cadillac ambulance, and the *National Lampoon's Vacation* station wagon. See the *Sanford & Son* pickup truck and the set from the TV show! The museum has even got Johnny Cash's "Psy-chobilly Cadillac," built one piece at a time (according to the Cash song) by Bill Patch with parts scavenged from 1949 to 1968 models—it has three headlights, one tail fin, and three doors.

And if you're not particularly interested in automobiles, there's still plenty here to keep you interested. Lensing's Abraham Lincoln collection includes locks of hair from the President and First Lady, Abe's straight razor, several White House chairs, handles from the slain leader's coffin, and manacles from Booth conspirator Lewis Payne. Are you a space nut? How about a tire from the Space Shuttle, a space glove from Apollo 17, or a one-quarter-scale model of the lunar lander?

But that's not all! You'll see leftover wax dummies of the *Happy Days*, *All in the Family*, and *Star Trek* casts, Lee Harvey Oswald's getaway taxi, Christopher Reeve's Superman cape (and tights), Bonnie and Clyde's death hats, a working guillotine, tons of White House bric-a-brac, Jackie Kennedy's mourning veil, JFK's golf balls, and on and on and on.

What more do you need to know? Don't wait—go visit now!

13825 Metric Dr., Roscoe, IL 61073

Phone: (815) 389-7917

Hours: June–August, Tuesday–Saturday 10 AM–5 PM, Sunday 11 AM–4 PM; September–October,
    Saturday 10 AM–5 PM, Sunday 11 AM–4 PM

Cost: Adults $12, seniors (65+) $10, kids (6–15) $7

Website: www.historicautoattractions.com

Directions: One block east of Second St. (Rte. 251), north of Rockton Rd. (Rte. 9).

St. Charles
Bicentennial Man

You have to hand it to Andrew Pakan—when he decided to erect a giant soldier to mark this nation's Bicentennial, he didn't order up a floor model from Big Fiberglass Statues 'R' Us. Instead, he built it himself. And since he was a furniture builder by trade, he made the whole thing out of wood. Huge hunks of wood.

The *Unknown Revolutionary Soldier* took more than a year to carve using trunks Pakan salvaged from trees on his property. The arms, legs, and head are held together using two-inch steel pipes. If he were standing he'd be 18 feet tall, but instead he reclines in a bright red rocking chair with a 14-foot musket draped across his lap. The sculpture sits in front of Pakan's former furniture store, today run by his children, and was recently given a fresh coat of paint.

Custom Furniture, 6N518 IL Route 25, St. Charles, IL 60174
Phone: (847) 695-7040
Hours: Always visible
Cost: Free
Website: www.customfurn.com
Directions: North of Army Trail Rd. on Rte. 25.

He's unknown, but not invisible.

Union
Wild Wild Midwest

If you want to see a shoot-out but can't make it to Chicago, you can always visit Donley's Wild West Town. The killings look realistic and you don't run the risk of getting caught in the crossfire—it's just acting! And that's not all, partner. You can pan for gold, knock back a few tall ones at the saloon, ride a pony, or get tossed in jail for a minor infraction. They've got roping demonstrations, a prairie dog town, a blacksmith shop, and a museum filled with guns, old phonographs, Beanie Babies, and other Old West artifacts.

Wild West Town used to have a wider and weirder collection of memorabilia on display, but more sensitive concerns have taken over. No longer will you see the Cook County gallows, bought from the city after it gave up hope of finding escaped murderer "Terrible" Tommy O'Connor. (Because he was explicitly sentenced to be hanged, they kept it until 1977, just in case.) The museum also had Hitler's 1908 red leather photo album from World War I, and a few of Adolf's *Mein Kampf*s, but they've been mothballed. However, you can still see six criminals' death masks from Pop Palmer's Freak Circus, including Bob Dalton and Cherokee Bill, as well as an autographed Tiny Tim album.

Donley's Wild West Town, 8512 S. Union Rd., Union, IL 60180

Phone: (815) 923-9000

Hours: May and September–October, Saturday–Sunday 10 AM–6 PM; June–August, daily 10 AM–
6 PM; shoot-outs at noon, 2 PM, and 4:30 PM

Cost: $15 per person, kids (2 and under) free

Website: www.wildwesttown.com

Directions: Four miles north of I-90 on Rte. 20.

Volo
Volo Auto Museum

If you like classic cars, go to Volo. This rambling attraction is part museum, part auto repair shop, and part picnic ground, but it's all about the internal combustion engine. Building after building is filled with immaculately preserved automobiles—some restored on site—parked bumper to bumper, five or six cars deep. Leave a trail of lug bolts or you'll never find your way back out.

If you're a film buff, the museum also has dozens of cars from TV shows and movies. It owns the Duke brothers' General Lee, the Love Bug from *Herbie Fully Loaded*, Kit from *Knight Rider*, the Batmobile, the Bluesmobile, the Mystery Machine, and the dried-out Porsche from *Risky Business*. They've also got strange concept cars, including SpongeBob SquarePants's Viking ship hot rod, a guitar-shaped dragster, Bugs Bunny's carrot-hooded touring car, and more.

And if the hundreds of cars in its collection aren't enough, plan your visit for one of Volo's Sunday Cruise-Ins, when collectors from around the upper Midwest pull their beauties into the picnic areas for an all-day gearhead get-together.

27582 Volo Village Rd., Volo, IL 60073

Phone: (815) 385-3644

Hours: Daily 10 AM–5 PM

Cost: Adults $9.95, seniors (65+) $7.95, kids (5–12) $5.95

Website: www.volocars.com

Directions: East on Belvidere Rd. (Rte. 20) from Rte. 12, then north on Volo Village Rd.

Wadsworth
Gold Pyramid House

When James Onan broke ground for his ultimate Dream House, a ¹⁄₁₀₀ replica of the Great Pyramid of Giza, the bulldozer struck a huge rock. Water spewed forth from the crack, flooding the site. Onan brought a chunk of the stone to a mineral assayist and learned that it contained gold, an element not found naturally in Illinois. Onan saw this as an omen to continue building.

The new natural spring feeds a moat around his six-story home, guarded by a large metal gate and a 40-foot, 200-ton Ramses II statue made by Walt Disney Studios. The pyramid is the world's largest 24-karat gold-plated structure and is surrounded by a moat filled with, at times, jellyfish and live sharks. If you didn't know better, you'd think Onan was a James Bond villain. He's actually quite friendly.

Inside the structure is a re-creation of King Tut's tomb along with a gold-plated chariot and anything else a mummy could need. You can take a tour, but you have to arrange it well in advance. Views from the road are free.

Pharaoh's phortress.

37921 Dilley's Rd., Wadsworth, IL 60083
Phone: (847) 244-7777
Hours: Tours by appointment only, five-person minimum
Cost: $20 per person
Website: www.goldpyramid.com
Directions: North of Great America, 2.5 miles on Rte. 132, just east of I-94.

Wauconda
Curt Teich Postcard Archives

The Lake County Museum is a better-than-average local historical museum, but the Curt Teich Postcard Archives make it exceptional. The archives house a collection of 1.5 million postcards, which includes every card produced by the Curt Teich Company between 1898 and 1975. Throughout its history, Teich's postcard salesmen were outfitted with cameras to take photos across the nation to make into cards. The company would later return to sell these cards to the communities in which the shots were taken, and as a result, they catalog a broad snapshot of America during the last century.

Though you can't actually dig through the physical archives unless you're a researcher or have a definable purpose, most of their collection is online for you to peruse, and there's always a rotating exhibit on display in the museum.

Lake County Museum, 27277 N. Forest Preserve Rd., Wauconda, IL 60084

Phone: (847) 968-3381

Hours: Monday–Friday 11 AM–4:30 PM

Cost: Adults $6, kids (4–17) $2.50

Website: www.lcfpd.org/teich_archives

Directions: On Rte. 176, west of Fairfield Rd. (Rte. 49).

Wilmington
The Gemini Giant

Never let it be said that the folks of Wilmington are behind the times. After a local business purchased a 28-foot, 500-pound lumberman at auction in 1965, they retrofitted the guy for a trip to the moon . . . and beyond! (Its helmet was an original accessory ordered up from the California manufacturer.) The newly crowned Gemini Giant— the Gemini space flights were taking place in the mid-1960s—has stood guard over this local burger joint ever since.

Contemplating the rocket.

Today the Gemini Giant sports a glimmering green jumpsuit straight out of *Lost in Space*, and he stares out through his faceplate at a small rocket he holds in his hands. This is the third rocket the Giant has owned; two rockets have been stolen over the years, and the one he grips today was

ripped off in 1992. It was later found in a cornfield and returned, much to NASA's relief.

Sadly, this roadside icon's days may be numbered. The Launching Pad Café was sold to a new owner, Mory Szczecin, in 2007, who is now looking for a buyer. If you're looking to save a classic bit of Americana, do you dare go where a few people have gone before?

Launching Pad Café, 810 E. Baltimore St. (Route 53), Wilmington, IL 60481

Phone: (815) 476-6535

Hours: Always visible; café, Monday–Saturday 11 AM–8 PM

Cost: Free

Website: www.wilmington-il.com/rt66

Directions: On old Rte. 66 (current Rte. 53) at the east end of town.

Woodstock
Elvira in Seat DD 113

If you ever attend a performance at the Woodstock Opera House, don't sit in seat DD 113. That's Elvira's seat.

Who's Elvira? The legend goes that she was a young woman who hung herself in the bell tower, or tossed herself from the roof, after being jilted by an actor in 1903. (Another story says she was a bitter actress passed over for a choice role.) Ever since her untimely death, Elvira has acted as the theater's resident critic, letting her sentiments be known on the quality of the Opera House's productions. She usually shows up during rehearsals, getting up and sitting down many times in seat DD 113, causing the springs to squeak uncontrollably. The more the seat squeaks, the worse the show is. Both Orson Welles and Paul Newman claimed to have felt her presence at the theater.

Woodstock Opera House, 121 Van Buren St., Woodstock, IL 60098

Phone: (815) 338-5300

Hours: Box office, daily 9 AM–5 PM; they will let you go inside if the lights are on

Cost: Depends on the show; free without show

Website: www.woodstockoperahouse.com

Directions: On the south side of the square.

Groundhog Day

Do you remember that 1993 movie with Bill Murray where every morning he wakes up it's Groundhog Day? He plays a cynical reporter staying at the Cherry Street Inn (which is actually the Royal Victorian Manor) in Punxsutawney, Pennsylvania, there to cover the town's annual festival, and no matter what he does he can't escape. Well, it wasn't filmed in Punxsutawney but in Woodstock, Illinois. Today you can stay at the same B&B, or pick up a free map at the Chamber of Commerce to retrace Murray's steps.

Do you remember that 1993 movie with Bill Murray where every morning he wakes up it's Groundhog Day? He plays a cynical reporter staying at the Cherry Street Inn (which is actually the Royal Victorian Manor) in Punxsutawney, Pennsylvania, there to cover the town's annual festival, and no matter what he does he can't escape. Well, it wasn't filmed in Punxsutawney but in Woodstock, Illinois. Today you can stay at the same B&B, or pick up a free map at the Chamber of Commerce to retrace Murray's steps.

Do you remember that 1993 movie with Bill Murray . . .

Royal Victorian Manor, 344 Fremont St., Woodstock, IL 60098
Phone: (815) 308-5432
Hours: Always visible
Cost: Free; rooms $125–$175
Website: www.royalvictorianmanor.com
Directions: At the south end of Madison St.

Zion
Flat Earth Town

Zion was founded in 1901 by John Alexander Dowie, head of a movement he called the Christian Catholic Church. At its peak the church had 6,000 followers in the so-called City of God: Zion City. The town was essentially a theocracy with laws based upon the Old Testament and its streets given prophetic names like Gabriel, Ezekiel, and Jethro. And although Dowie was a stern patriarch, he was nothing compared to his deputy, Wilbur Glenn Voliva.

Tan shoes? Shorts?
A globe? A movie?
Four-time Zion felon!

Voliva took control in 1906. He ruled the town with an iron fist, outlawing alcohol, tobacco, circuses, opium, humming, movies, oysters, opera, pork, short pants, doctors, silk stockings, cosmetics, whistling on Sundays, tan-colored or high-heeled shoes, and most especially globes. Why globes? Voliva was sure of one thing: the Earth was flat. He scorned the "so-called fundamentalists [who] strain out the gnat of evolution and swallow the camel of modern astronomy."

According to Voliva, we live on a pancake with the North Pole at the center and the South Pole wrapping the edges. A wall of ice keeps the water from running off. The moon is lit from within, and stars are nothing more than small, bright disks. He offered $5,000 to anyone who could con-

vince him otherwise. Voliva never paid out, and he explained why: "I have whipped to smithereens any man in the world in a mental battle."

Voliva started the nation's first Christian radio station in 1922, WCBD. It transmitted an endless stream of snake oil and brimstone that is seldom matched today. On it he predicted he would live to be 120 years old, but he died in 1942 at the age of 72, just 48 years short of his forecast. That was the final straw for most of his followers. They'd put up with too much for too long. Anxious to purchase tan shoes, oysters, and pork, the sect dispersed into obscurity.

Zion Historical Society, Shiloh House, 1300 Shiloh Blvd., Zion, IL 60099

Phone: (847) 746-2427

Hours: June–August, Sunday 2–5 PM or by appointment

Cost: Adults $5, kids (6–12) $2

Website: www.zionhs.com

Directions: One block west of Sheridan Rd. (Rte. 137).

Roscoe
Historic Auto
Attractions

Rockford
Baby Jane
Gertrude, the Giant Guernsey
World's Largest Sock Monkey
Belvidere
Big Thunder Park

Harvard
Harmilda the Cow

Woodstock
Elvira in Seat DD 113
Groundhog Day

Bull Valley
Stickney Mansion

Crystal Lake
The Giants of
Crystal Lake

Union
Wild Wild Midwest

Barrington
Baby Face Nelson
Shootout

Libertyville
Lambs Farm Giant
and Bessie

Volo
Volo Auto Museum

Wauconda
Curt Teich Postcard
Archives

Lincolnshire
Par-King

Zion
Flat Earth Town

Wadsworth
Gold Pyramid House
Leapin' Lipizzans!

Gurnee
Plans, Trains, and Automobiles Motel

Waukegan
Big Onan Man

North Chicago
Birthplace of the Screw-Cap Bottle
Feet First: The Scholl Story

Highland Park
Ferris Bueller's Day Off
Ferrari House

Wheeling
Superdawg Drive-In #2

St. Charles
Al Capone's Hideaway
Bicentennial Man
Bowing Plastic Marys

Bartlett
BAPS Shri Swaminarayan
Mandir

DeKalb
The Egyptian Theatre

chelle
ce, the Pizza Guy

Batavia
Mary Todd Lincoln in the
Cuckoo's Nest

Big Rock
Mount Barry

Aurora
Sri Venkateswara
Swami Temple

Naperville
Burger King Time Machine
High School Mummy

Newark
Big Vegas Elvis

Norway
A Crashed Plane

Morris
Truck Stop Marionettes

Ottawa
Effigy Tumuli
Ottawa Scouting Museum

Frankfort
Gas City Cow

Joliet
Birthplace of Dairy Queen
Blues Brothers Prison
Mary of Joliet
Rich and Creamy Ice Cream Shop

Wilmington
The Gemini Giant

Braidwood
"Those Aren't Pillows" Motel

Burbonnais
Big Lincoln Lift

Essex
Jack Barker's Sculpture Park

Lake
Michigan

INDIANA

CENTRAL ILLINOIS

*C*entral Illinois is Lincoln Country. Lincoln statues. Lincoln hotels. Lincoln outhouses. That's right, when Abe's Springfield privy was excavated several years ago, its contents were big news: a broken chamber pot, two doll's heads, buttons, glass marbles, toothless combs, and other assorted other junk. That's news around here.

But the region is weirder than that. Much weirder. The agrarian society that formed the character of the Great Emancipator now generates folks who bury accordions in elaborate vaults, erect monuments to hippies, serve ice cream with eyeballs, and transform Cadillacs into Chickenmobiles. And you thought there was nothing between Chicago and St. Louis!

Abingdon
The Midwest's Tallest Totem Pole

When you think of totem poles you probably think of Alaska or the Pacific Northwest. But Abingdon, Illinois? True, none of the indigenous tribes of the Midwest ever carved these sacred objects . . . but Steve Greenquist did, and boy, is it huge!

The 83-foot-tall totem on an Abingdon parkway depicts popular state icons—Abraham Lincoln, Stephen Douglas, corn—and has two wings shaped like Illinois. It was erected in 1969 and is referred to as "Big Daddy" by locals. Others call it the Tallest Totem Pole East of the Rockies, which, considering the lack of competition, isn't that remarkable. (Want to see the Biggest Daddy? That 160-foot totem can be found in a shopping center in McKinleyville, California.)

400 N. Main St., Abingdon, IL 61410

No phone

Hours: Always visible

Cost: Free

Directions: Two blocks east of Monroe St. (Rte. 41), between Monmouth and Latimer Sts.

Arcola
America's One and Only Hippie Memorial

There are few places in America where you might *least* expect a memorial to the American hippie, but here it is. Based loosely on the Vietnam War Memorial, this monument attempts to show the quantum step upward, and back downward, that marked the beginning and end of the hippie movement. The piece is the work of the late Bob Moomaw, a man who split his time between Arcola and Michigan. Moomaw was not a hippie, just the town's eccentric artist-in-residence.

The 62-foot-long wall (one foot for each year in Moomaw's life) was originally planned for Arcola but was constructed in Michigan. After Moomaw's death the memorial fell into disrepair, so friends and family members brought it to Illinois. Folks here seem generally tolerant of this odd attraction, though on Memorial Day 2002 a World War II and September 11 memorial was erected just across the tracks, a bit of a counterprotest to the counterculture creation. The new monument has a large granite globe with quotes from the Bible, George Bush, General Patton, and Walt Whitman . . . a hippie in his own right. Oops!

175 N. Oak St., Arcola, IL 61910

No phone

Hours: Always visible

Cost: Free

Directions: Just north of the Train Depot Visitor's Center at Main St.

Far out, man!

Louis Klein Broom and Brush Museum and the Coffee Cup Collection

Arcola calls itself the "Broom Town," so it's little surprise that here you'll find the nation's only museum dedicated to the broom. Louis Klein collected more than a thousand different items used to sweep and brush, though not all of them are made from broom corn. Look over the shoe scrapers and feather dusters, "naughty" toothbrushes in the shape of a woman's body, makeup brushes with doll handles, bunny-shaped boot cleaners, toilet scrubbers, and other cleaning devices that you'd never expect to see in a display case. To fully celebrate the usefulness of the brush, come during the Broom Corn Festival (http://arcolatourism.com/festivals.html) in September, an annual event to mark the harvest of more sweeping material, and to face off in the National Broom Sweeping Contest.

The Welcome Center is also the repository of Arcola's famous coffee cup collection. For many years, the owner of Arrol's Drug Store served residents in the same coffee cup each morning. Each person's name was on his or her own mug, so they never had to share. To join the Coffee Club, you had to be an Arcola resident who'd drunk more than 100 cups already, and there had to be an opening on the rack. The only way that occurred was if somebody died or moved away. When Arrol retired, the cups were sent here.

Arcola Depot Welcome Center, 135 N. Oak St., PO Box 274, Arcola, IL 61910

Phone: (217) 268-4530

Hours: Sunday–Friday 9 AM–5 PM, Saturday 9 AM–3 PM

Cost: Free

Website: http://arcolatourism.com/visitors.html

Directions: West from I-57, turn right just before the railroad tracks.

Rockome Gardens

Rockome Gardens is America's only Amish amusement park. Sound like a contradiction in terms? Perhaps you should pay a visit; it's not all fudge making and buggy rides.

Strolling around the grounds, you might think somebody has been spiking the apple butter. Six-foot concrete toadstools grow between the pools of lily pads in the Water Garden. For a quarter, in the barn, a trained chicken will challenge you to a game of tic-tac-toe . . . and prob-

Do you dare?
Photo by author, courtesy Rockome Gardens

ably win! A piano-playing skeleton pounds the ivories in the Haunted Cave while a stuffed, one-eyed calf gazes on. And everywhere you look are fences, planters, birdhouses, and monuments built of broken glass, pottery, old Fresca bottles, and lots and lots of cement. The stunning gardens are filled with small placards with quaint Amish observations like IT TAKES TWO TO MAKE A MARRIAGE—THE ELIGIBLE GIRL AND HER ANXIOUS MOTHER and THE BEST GARDEN CLUB IS A HOE HANDLE.

If you only want to step back in time, Rockome Gardens has plenty of quilting demonstrations, candle dippers, and goats at the petting zoo. You can cut a log at the horse-powered buzz saw and have it branded at the blacksmith shop, all for one dollar. Or just snap photos of the stern-faced bearded and bonneted employees—it's all part of the fun!

Rockome is a one-of-a-kind place, at least for now. It was sold to a new owner a few years back and hasn't been drawing the crowds it once did. That means you, dear traveler, need to put this on your itinerary, or this old-world attraction will go the way of the buggy . . . even though it already has.

125 N. County Rd. 425 East, Arcola, IL 61910

Phone: (217) 268-4106

Hours: May–August, daily 9 AM–5 PM

Cost: Adults $10, seniors (60+) $8, kids (5–12) $6

Website: www.rockome.com

Directions: Five miles west of town off Rte. 133, then south on County Rd. 425 E.

Ashmore
World's Largest Abe Lincoln Statue

It's the World's Largest Abe Lincoln Statue, and it's cursed! Don't believe me?

It all started in 1968 when Charleston wanted to mark the 110th anniversary of the Lincoln-Douglas debate held in town. The city ordered up a 62-foot-tall fiberglass behemoth of the Great Emancipator, but by the time the statue arrived the funding for the park on East Harrison Avenue had fallen through. Regardless, up Abe went in an empty field, one hand clutching the Emancipation Proclamation, the other raising a finger to make some sort of point. And that was it—the project was abandoned.

Maybe it was their guilty consciences, but the more folks looked at Abe the more he appeared not to be pointing, but to be giving them the finger. What would you expect, given how he was treated? So, after a decade of this vulgarity he was sold to the Spring Haven Campground being built east of town near Ashmore. They stuck him in a hollow down by the Embarras River, though he was still tall enough to glare at drivers along Route 16. Somehow his index finger broke off, leaving Abe shaking an angry fist over his head. The campground later went belly up and the statue was left to deteriorate for another decade or so.

Then, in 2004, he was restored as part of the grand plan for the Lincoln Springs Resort, a restaurant–retreat center with big ideas and bigger dreams. Chain-

Damn you! Damn you all to hell!

saw artist Bill Monken was hired to create Abe's Garden around the statue's feet, and he populated it with a dozen odd-looking Lincoln statuettes depicting key moments in his life. But unlike the Field of Dreams, when the resort was finished the tourists did not come, and in the spring of 2011 it shuttered its doors.

You can still see Abe from a distance, but the closest you can get is the reviewing stands of the adjoining stock car track. And he looks maaaaaad.

9699 County Road 2000, Ashmore, IL 61912

No phone

Hours: Dawn to dusk

Cost: Free

Directions: Just east of Charleston on Rte. 16, behind the raceway to the north, along the Embarras River.

Atlanta
Tall Paul's Hot Dog

When H. A. Stephens opened a restaurant in Cicero in 1965, he was a little concerned that the PB (Paul Bunyan) Cafe in Flagstaff, Arizona (see page 152), might come after him for copyright infringement. After all, he'd purchased a 19-foot-tall fiberglass giant to put in front of his Route 66 establishment, a statue that was made from the exact same mold as the one standing out west. Crafty fellow that he was, Stephens purposely misspelled the name of his restaurant to be Bunyon's, took the axe out of the ogre's hands, and replaced it with an enormous hotdog. Lawsuit averted!

"Tall Paul" and his big wiener took a lot of abuse over the years—he was shot with arrows and at least one bullet, and was even rammed by a car. When Bunyon's closed in 2003, the statue was restored by the Illinois Route 66 Association (see pages 210–11). Though the Stephens family still owns him, Tall Paul is on permanent loan to the town of Atlanta, which has spruced up its two-block downtown for road-tripping tourists.

Race St. and Arch St./Old Route 66, Atlanta, IL 61723

No phone

Hours: Always visible

Cost: Free

Website: www.atlantaillinois.org/rt66/tourist_bunyon.html

Directions: One block north of South St., between Race and Vine Sts.

That's a mighty big hot dog . . .

Bloomington
Dead Dorothy

Literary historians believe Dorothy Gale, heroine of L. Frank Baum's *Wizard of Oz* series, was named after Dorothy Gage, Baum's late niece. Gage was born on June 11, 1898, and died on November 11 of the same year, and not from injuries sustained in a tornado. Dorothy's mother was the sister of Baum's wife, Maud, and the Baums were living in Chicago when Dorothy passed away in Bloomington.

Dorothy's original tombstone was recently discovered by a Baum biographer, just before the inscription became obscured by weathering. Former Munchkin actor Mickey Carroll heard about the discovery of Gage's grave and decided to donate a new marker. Because Carroll was a stonemason, he engraved it himself. Now her resting place is easy to find.

Also buried in Evergreen Memorial Cemetery are Adlai Stevenson I and Adlai Stevenson II. Presumably, Adlai Stevenson III will also be planted here, along with all future Adlais.

Evergreen Memorial Cemetery, 302 E. Miller St., Bloomington, IL 61701
Phone: (309) 827-6950
Hours: Daily 8 AM–4:30 PM
Cost: Free
Website: www.evergreen-cemetery.com
Directions: Two blocks east of 1100 S. Main St.; Dorothy is in Section 7.

Brimfield
Jubilee Rock Garden

The Jubilee Rock Garden is a prime example of what one person can do with a pile of rocks, a few bags of cement, and plenty of time on his or her hands. Built over many years by Bill Notzke on his dairy farm, the Jubilee Rock Garden is named after a local college. The terraced garden contains simple mosaic images—clubs, diamonds, hearts, and spades—fashioned from different colored quartzes, mica, geodes, and other colorful rocks.

When Bill's wife, Ethel, died in 1963, he built a Memorial Arch over his driveway entrance. He would light the arch from the inside, but only on Memorial Day and May 14, Ethel's birthday. Bill continued this tradition until his death. The home has since been sold, and the current owners request that you view the arch and garden from the road.

Rte. 150, Brimfield, IL 61517
Private phone
Hours: Private property; always visible from the road
Cost: Free
Directions: On Rte. 150 east of town.

Something for Ethel.

Carlock

The Partisan Dead

If you think politics is bad today, wait until you hear about Carlock. A long tradition of partisanship once separated this community, especially in death. It all started when Abraham Carlock, the town founder, was buried in the White Oak Cemetery under a monument that read, "Here Sleeps the Old Democrat." Carlock was a contemporary of Abraham Lincoln and was not at all impressed by the upstart GOP.

Local Republicans saw it as a slap in the face, particularly in the Land of Lincoln. So from that point on, Republicans were planted in the new Oak Grove Cemetery just across the road (and county line). Democrats continued to be buried with Carlock. No third graveyard was ever established for Bull Moosers, Libertarians, Communists, or Independents, so Ross Perot's puny body won't be welcome.

White Oak Cemetery (Woodford County/Democrats), N. Church St., Carlock, IL 61725

Oak Grove Cemetery (McLean County/Republicans), N. Church St., Carlock, IL 61725

No phone

Hours: Daily 9 AM–5 PM

Cost: Free

Directions: Three miles north on Church St. on the left.

Champaign
Sousa Archives and Center for American Music

Packed away on the second floor of the U of I's Band Building is a fascinating collection of artifacts related to America's favorite march composer: John Philip Sousa. The majority of this collection was a gift of Albert Austin Harding, a friend of Sousa's. It is roughly divided into three parts: Sousa's sheet music, his band's instruments and artifacts, and the personal collection of Herbert Clarke, a cornet soloist and assistant director for Sousa.

The archive's sheet music is of interest mostly to researchers. It contains 71 percent of Sousa's band performance collection, complete with annotations and notes from the band's travels. The library also has the original band parts for "The Stars and Stripes Forever."

The instrument collection will be of more interest to the casual visitor. If you didn't know better, you might think there had been a mix-up or accident when this 240-piece display was assembled. Many of the instruments look slapped together in mismatched combinations. A wrong mouthpiece here. A horn bell bent at a weird angle there. And who ever heard of an octavin, a rothophone, or a sarrusophone? For many reasons, most of these instruments never made it into popular use.

Many of Sousa's personal effects are also on display, including his traveling podium, Cuban cigars emblazoned with his image, band uniforms, a musical typewriter, a set of backfire brass used at the Battle of Bull Run, and a pewter ship that doubled as a decanter. Finally, you'll see the personal collection of Herbert Clarke. He was a soloist with Sousa for many years and willed his musical attic to the university on his death, expanding the scope of the Sousa collection from a band member's point of view.

236 Harding Band Building, 1103 S. Sixth St., Champaign, IL 61820

Phone: (217) 244-9309

Hours: Monday–Tuesday and Thursday–Friday 8:30 AM–noon, 1–4 PM; Wednesday 10 AM–noon, 1–4 PM

Cost: Free

Website: www.library.illinois.edu/sousa

Directions: Between Armory Ave. and Gregory Dr.

CHAMPAIGN

➡ Bow-tied columnist George Will was born in Champaign on May 4, 1941.

Imelda Marcos, eat your heart out.

Cornell
Friendship Shoe Fence

We've all been there—you're out on the road and look down at your feet and think, "You know, these shoes just don't go with my floor mats." But with today's economy, who can afford a new pair?

No problem—come to Cornell, friend! Here local humanitarian Gail Donze has established the Friendship Shoe Fence, basically a regular fence with hundreds of pairs of shoes tied to it. She got the idea while on a trip to New Zealand to visit a longtime pen pal; the Kiwis had one, and if they could pull it off, why couldn't she? So, with the help of her church, some neighbors, and a few thrift shops, Donze hung out 300 or so pairs in 2009. Leave a pair and take a pair, or if you have no shoes, just take a pair. It's all part of the Friendship Shoe Fence's creed.

County Rd. 28 (Sixth St.), Cornell, IL 61319

Private phone

Hours: Daylight

Cost: Free, or a pair of shoes

Directions: Head south out of town on Sixth St.

Dahinda
Sleep in a Barn

Barns have long been "hobo hotels," but you don't have to be a bum to stay here—it's a bed-and-breakfast! And as barns go, this is one of the nicest around, complete with pool table, claw-foot tub, outdoor shower, kitchen (in the horse stall), and no TV. What could be more relaxing? The Barn sits on a 150-acre working farm along the Spoon River and is a perfect getaway for hiking, fishing, or doing absolutely nothing. The hayloft sleeps up to nine and is only rented to one group a night, so you won't be bunking with strangers.

And don't worry that this place might smell like a sty; it has never been used to house animals. It was built in 1993 as a guesthouse for the owners' children and grandchildren, but at their friends' suggestions the couple started renting it as a B&B. It was constructed using traditional methods, from timbers cut on the farm and 700 hand-carved wooden pegs. Only the floorboards are held down with antique square nails. The space is homey and comfortable, air-conditioned or heated depending on the season. And if you'd like to build a bonfire, there's a place for that, too.

The Barn B&B, PO Box 92, 1690 Kenny St., Dahinda, IL 61428
Phone: (309) 639-4408
Hours: January–November; call ahead for reservations
Cost: $60 single, $80 double, $40 for each additional up to seven
Website: www.bbonline.com/il/thebarn
Directions: One-half mile west of the Dahinda post office, at the end of the road.

Decatur
Haunted Greenwood Cemetery

Ever since the Sangamon River overflowed through this cemetery in the late 1800s, things haven't been the same. The flood caused a mudslide that unearthed, washed away, and scattered caskets and skeletons of Civil War soldiers. Confederate prisoners, some of whom might have been buried alive during a yellow fever outbreak, were mixed together with Union soldiers, or worse yet, reburied beneath Yankee tombstones. Since then, strange ghost lights have been seen on the hill in the southwest corner of the cemetery.

People have also spotted the spirits of eight Native Americans murdered here in the 1820s. Moonshiners killed them in the Hell Hollow corner of the graveyard. Other people have reported seeing a spook with holes instead of eyes. And still others have bumped into the Greenwood Bride, a ghostly woman who committed suicide after the murder of her fiancé.

Greenwood Cemetery is a beautiful Victorian cemetery, but be careful if you visit, even during the daytime. Rumors have long circulated that crumbling tunnels lie just beneath the surface. They have been known to swallow up caskets . . . and perhaps snoopy tourists.

606 S. Church St., Decatur, IL 62522

Phone: (217) 422-6563

Hours: Daily 9 AM–5 PM

Cost: Free

Website: www.haunteddecatur.com/greenwood.html

Directions: Nine blocks south of Eldorado St. (Rte. 36), two blocks west of Main St. (Business 51).

East Peoria
Big Rooster

Talk about a cock-a-doodle-doozie! A 15-foot-tall rooster guards the entrance to an East Peoria bakery. For some unknown reason it wears a black top hat. Maybe it's to add a little class to the joint, like a jacket policy, or to honor our 14th president, though it looks more Amish than Abe-ish. The rooster has been out front for more than 40 years.

Carl's Bakery and Cafe, 819 E. Camp St., East Peoria, IL 61611

Phone: (309) 699-7275

Hours: Always visible; bakery, Tuesday–Saturday 5:30 AM–2 PM

Cost: Free

Directions: Just west of Washington St.

East Peoria and Mattoon
Twistee Treat's Giant Cones

These prefab fiberglass ice cream stands used to be a common sight on American highways. Today only a handful remain, with only two in Illinois. In East Peoria the two-story structure is a vanilla soft-serve atop a flat-bottomed sugar cone. The grills and the ice cream machines are located

But what if it melts?

inside the cone, but the seating area is in a small building attached in the rear. Twistee Treat serves a standard fast-food fare, but dipped cones are its specialty.

While enjoying your cone, be sure to step over to the Last Harvest Ministries church just behind the building—the strange-looking chapel is a modified Quonset hut.

1207 E. Washington St., East Peoria, IL 61611

Phone: (309) 699-2604

Hours: Always visible; store, daily 11 AM–10 PM

Cost: Free; baby cone 93¢, small $1.45, medium $1.65, large $1.95

Directions: On Washington St. (Rte. 8) and Leadley Ave., north of I-74.

Another giant cone can be found in Mattoon. Though the original Twistee Treat name is clearly visible on the rim of the cone, this stand has been named Rhoadside Custard.

Rhoadside Custard, 404 S. 32nd St., Mattoon, IL 61938

Phone: (217) 234-7449

Hours: Always visible

Cost: Free

Directions: On the east side of Lytle Park, one block north of Marshall Ave. (Rte. 16).

Findlay
Tower of Baaaabel

It should probably come as no surprise if you think about it: goats like to climb. Humans domesticated the modern species roughly 10,000 years ago in the mountainous regions of Asia Minor, and though we've long since taken the goats out of the mountains, we haven't quite taken the mountains out of the goats. If you don't believe it, check out the goat tower northeast of Findlay.

The owners of a private farm have constructed a four-story cylindrical goat hotel

A condo for Capricorns.

with 276 steps spiraling up its outer wall, and no railing. It looks like a giant wood screw, and the goats love to climb up and down the stairs. Though the farm is not open to the public, the Tower of Baaaabel is clearly visible from the road.

Wolf Creek Rd. (CR 2500E), Findlay, IL 82534

Private phone

Hours: Daylight

Cost: Free

Directions: South off County Hwy. 3, east of Wolf Creek Park.

A better idea than it appears.

Gays
Two-Story Outhouse

A two-decker outhouse sounds like a bad idea, but it works. When this crapper was built by Samuel Gammill in 1869, this structure backed up to a general store with an apartment above it. Residents on the second floor could unload their burdens without coming downstairs, and store customers used their own facility below. Each level had a two-seater, so the facility could accommodate four at a time.

How did it work? Waste from above dropped to the pit behind a false wall; the bottom poopers didn't need to dodge any gifts from above. Still, imagine their nervousness at hearing footsteps above their heads.

The apartment and general store were torn down in 1984, and only the outhouse remains. This makes for a fantastic photo opportunity: "Here we are at an Illinois rest area." Gays residents have built a nice park around the structure where you can sit on a bench and write postcards to your friends, and there's even a mailbox where you can drop them.

1022 Front St., Gays, IL 61928

No phone

Hours: Always visible

Cost: Free

Directions: Just north of the grain elevator off Rte. 16.

Kewanee
Woodland Palace

Fred Francis was a lot of things—an engineer, a vegetarian, a believer in reincarnation, an agnostic, a nudist—but most locals just thought he was a nut. They weren't entirely wrong, but Francis was also a brilliant nut.

A mechanical genius, Francis patented a watchmaking tool for the Elgin Watch Company during the 1880s and was able to retire in his early

30s, living only on his royalties. But his retirement was far from restful. Francis set out in 1890 to build Woodland Palace for himself and his new bride, Jeanette "Jeanie" Crowfoot.

Though small and not wired for electricity, Woodland Palace was air-conditioned in the summer, was warmed through radiant heat in the winter, and had hundreds of modern mechanical conveniences. Storm windows and screens rolled in and out of use depending on the season, and a windmill pumped running water from a filtered cistern. It also powered a workshop in his basement.

His land was surrounded by a large hedge because Francis was a Physical Culturalist and practicing nudist. He seldom wore shoes, wanting to keep his feet in contact with the soil, and when he was at home, he was usually naked. Jeanie did not participate in her husband's activities, but if she objected, she did not show it.

Francis was left heartbroken after Jeanie died of tuberculosis. He continued to live in the home they shared, but when a hernia became too painful to bear, he killed himself on December 22, 1926. His will asked that he be cremated in a coffinlike cage on the property, but Illinois killjoys prevented this final wish.

Francis Park, 29862 N. 900 Ave., Kewanee, IL 61443

Phone: (309) 852-0511

Hours: May–September, daily 1–5 PM

Cost: Adults $2, kids (5–12) $1

Website: www.cityofkewanee.com/francis.php

Directions: Rte. 34 northeast to 2800E, north to 900N, then east to Woodland Park.

Lincoln
Lincoln-Mania

Lincoln, Illinois, is the only town in the nation named for Abraham Lincoln while he was still alive. In fact, it was named Lincoln before Abe was elected to national office. Lincoln was an up-and-coming lawyer who was called upon in 1853 to draft the town's incorporation papers. He responded to the founders' suggested name with unlawyerly humility: "I think you are making a mistake. I never knew anything named Lincoln that ever amounted to much."

Don't read and drive.

Lincoln presided over the town's dedication on August 27, 1853. The official story says he poured out the juice from a watermelon to christen the ground, but another story claims he spit out a mouthful of watermelon seeds to make it official. A statue was erected in 1964 near the train station where it all took place. The statue isn't of Lincoln. It's of the watermelon.

But that's not all! If you're looking for Abe in a black suit and stovepipe hat, they've got one on the east side of town. A large Lincoln is sitting in an even larger covered wagon outside a Best Western motel, and for some reason he's reading a law book rather than watching the road. Kids those days!

If you think that two Lincoln monuments in this Lincoln-crazy town is enough, think again, because there's been a proposal circulating since 2001 to build a 300-foot-tall president in a new local park—the World's Largest Emancipator. The $40 million price tag raised a few eyebrows, but not enough contributors; it's still in the planning stages.

Watermelon Statue, 101 N. Chicago St., Lincoln, IL 62656

Abe in a Wagon, Best Western, 1750 Fifth St., Lincoln, IL 62656

Phone: (217) 732-8687

Hours: Always visible

Cost: Free

Website: www.abe66.com

Directions: Watermelon, at Broadway St. near the railroad depot; Wagon, at I-55 Business Loop.

Mattoon
The Mad Gasser of Mattoon

On the evening of September 1, 1944, a Mattoon couple on Grant Avenue was overcome by a sweet odor that made their lips swell, their vision blur, and their bodies go numb. Odd, certainly, but then a local snoop reported seeing a man in a tight-fitting black suit, skullcap, and gas mask hanging around the couple's home. Before long, rumors of a mysterious attacker—a Mad Gasser!—swept the city, fanned in part by the *Mattoon Daily Journal-Gazette*. Each night more people were overcome by whiffs of gas that sent "electric shocks" through their bodies. The resulting paralysis prevented the victims from running for help. Investigators found mysterious damp rags and empty lipstick tubes and sent them to chemists for analysis, yet nothing out of the ordinary was ever confirmed. Doctors attributed the illnesses to "war nerves" and lack of sleep.

But Mattoon residents weren't buying their explanations. They formed shotgun-wielding posses to patrol the streets, but the "escaped lunatic" was never caught. Paranormal experts claimed it was Spring Heel Jack, a phantom gasser who had terrorized London a century earlier. How he had lived so long and why he resurfaced in Mattoon wasn't exactly known.

Two weeks later, when local attention returned to World War II, the gassings ceased. The final "victim" was the town's only fortune-teller. She cornered the Mad Gasser in her house and claimed he looked like an ape man.

Psychologists later dismissed the Mad Gasser of Mattoon as a classic case of American mass hysteria, on par with the Salem witch trials and the *War of the Worlds* radio broadcast. No evidence was ever produced that anyone attacked the people of Mattoon. They did it to themselves.

Or did they? A 2003 book by Scott Maruna posits that the attacks were real and perpetrated by Farley Llewellyn, the kooky son of a powerful local businessman. Young Farley liked to dabble in chemistry, perhaps a little too much. The Llewellyns had him committed to an institution just before the attacks stopped. Coincidence?

First Attack Site, 1817 Grant Ave., Mattoon, IL 61938
Private phone
Hours: Always visible
Cost: Free
Website: www.freewebs.com/swampgasbooks/index.htm
Directions: Two blocks north of Dewitt Ave. (Rte. 121), between 18th and 19th Sts.

Monmouth
Wyatt Earp's Birthplace

Wyatt Berry Stapp Earp's family lived in so many places in Monmouth it was difficult to determine where he was actually born. But the owners of this small home are confident that it was here, in the home of his aunt, that the gunslinging baby drew his first breath on March 19, 1848. They've got several notarized affidavits from descendants posted on the walls of this museum, each saying something like, "I am the third cousin twice removed from Wyatt Earp's uncle, and he told me that 406 S. Third Street was where Wyatt was born." Though Wyatt might have been born here, it was not where his family lived. Their addresses included 125 North First Street and 409–411 South B Street, among other locations. None is open to the public.

Being just a child, Earp didn't earn much of a shoot-'em-up reputation until after he left Illinois. In fact, when he lived in Monmouth he once hid from a group of Indians at the corner of Third Street and Archer Avenue. Yellow-bellied coward! Still, the city of Monmouth has erected a monument to Earp in Monmouth City Park.

Wyatt Earp Birthplace, 406 S. Third St., Monmouth, IL 61462

Phone: (309) 734-6771

Hours: By appointment

Cost: Donations accepted

Website: http://earpmorgan.com/wyattearpbirthplacewebsite.html

Directions: Three blocks east and four blocks south of the town square.

Monmouth City Park, Monmouth, IL 61462

No phone

Hours: Sunrise to sunset

Cost: Free

Directions: Off Rte. 164 at 11th St., near the airport at the northeast end of town.

Monticello
The Sun Singer

Ah, to run through a meadow, naked as the day you were born! You may have never done this yourself, but don't act like it never crossed your mind. It certainly was a dream of Robert Allerton, who commissioned a bronze statue of Apollo, wearing nothing more than a helmet, to erect at his coun-

try estate. Allerton was the son of one of the founders of the Union Stock Yards (see pages 42–43), but he didn't much like the city life. With his partner, John Gregg Allerton, he built a mansion he dubbed "The Farms" in the middle of a 12,000-acre spread near Monticello. Both men loved art, and they built an elaborate sculpture garden with works from around the world. After they died, the whole spread was turned over to the University of Illinois.

Today *The Sun Singer* anchors the west end of the property. Allerton had requested a life-sized figure, but when the statue arrived it was 15 feet tall. Its arms are upraised to greet the dawn, and the statue appears to have been sculpted on a very cold day. It was restored in 2007.

Allerton Park and Retreat Center, 515 Old Timber Rd., Monticello, IL 61856

Phone: (217) 333-3287

Hours: Daily 8 AM–sunset; visitors' center, daily 9 AM–5 PM

Cost: Free

Website: http://allerton.illinois.edu

Directions: South of County Farm Rd. on Old Timber Rd., west of Monticello.

Mt. Zion, Springfield, Pawnee, and Decatur
Krekel's Kustard and the Chicken Cadillac

If you're hungry and passing through Mt. Zion, Pawnee, Springfield, or Decatur, you might want to call ahead to the nearest Krekel's Kustard to see if the Chicken Cadillac is around. This 1970s Caddy has a flaring, feathered tail and a six-foot, red-eyed head on the roof. Most days it's parked outside the Mt. Zion store, but it does make an occasional appearance at the chain's other locations. (To be honest, even if you miss out on seeing the Chicken Cadillac, the food alone is worth a stop.)

Mt. Zion Store, 1340 N. State Hwy. 121, Mt. Zion, IL 62549

Phone: (217) 864-5725

Pawnee Store, 310 Carroll St., Pawnee, IL 62558

Phone: (217) 625-4952

Springfield Store, 2121 N. Grand Ave. East, Springfield, IL 62702

Phone: (217) 525-4952

Decatur Store 1, 801 E. Wood St., Decatur, IL 62521

Phone: (217) 429-1122

Decatur Store 2, 2320 E. Main (Rte. 36), Decatur, IL 62521
Phone: (217) 423-1719

Decatur Store 3, 1355 N. Illinois Rte. 48, Decatur, IL 62526
Phone: (217) 362-0121

Decatur Store 4, 3727 N. Woodford St., Decatur, IL 62526
Phone: (217) 875-4044
Hours: Monday–Saturday 10:30 AM–8:30 PM
Cost: Meals $4–$6
Website: http://krekels.weebly.com
Directions: Five blocks north of Main St. (Rte. 30) on Rte. 121.

Part chicken, part Caddy.

Pekin
Eyes Cream

Who in the world would ever look at an ice cream cone and think, "You know what's missing? Eyeballs!" Well, give a hand to Double D's Ice Cream Factory, which answered the question nobody thought to pose. As the giant statue in front of the stand shows, Double D's cones come with two black sugar eyes.

Understanding that not everyone wants their food to stare back at them, to get eyes you have to request them. When I first called the store, I asked, "Is this the place where you put eyeballs on the ice cream?" and

the employee replied, "We'll put eyeballs on anything you order." That, my friends, is customer service!

Double D's Ice Cream Factory, 1434 N. Eighth St., Pekin, IL 61554

Phone: (309) 353-3322

Hours: Monday–Saturday 11 AM–10 PM, Sunday 1–10 PM

Cost: Free; small cone $1.55, medium $1.75, large $1.95

Website: www.facebook.com/group
.php?gid=103413683032184

Directions: One block south of Sheridan Rd.

Here's looking at you!

Peoria
Mini Solar System/Maxi Model

If you've ever looked at a model of the solar system or a diagram of the relative orbits of the planets, you probably understand the problem. If the planets' relative sizes are correct (as in a model), their orbits are too small in comparison, but if their orbits are drawn to scale (as in some diagrams), the planets are far too large. What's a scale-model-loving astronomer to do?

Come to Peoria, that's what! Starting with a "sun" drawn on the outside wall of the Lakeview Museum of Arts and Sciences, you'll venture farther and farther out to the eight planets and Pluto, each one properly scaled and adopted by a business, college, or community organization. By the time you reach Pluto, some 47 miles away in Kewanee, a puny ball about the size of a large marble in a furniture store, you'll no doubt wonder, How in the hell did anyone ever find this with a telescope? And as you contemplate the vastness of outer space, you might cross off one thing from your lifetime dreams: to be on the first manned trip to Mars.

This model was the brainchild of Bradley University professor Sheldon Schafer, director of Lakeview's planetarium, and was the nation's largest such model until 2003 when an even bigger one was built in Maine.

Pluto, Good's Furniture, 200–202 N. Main St., Kewanee, IL 61443

Neptune, Roanoke Motor Company, 1313 W. Front St., Roanoke, IL 61561

Uranus, Sundance Sundial Park, Park Ave. and Court St., Pekin, IL 61554

Saturn, Kroger, 201 S. Main St., East Peoria, IL 61611

Jupiter, Olin Hall, Bradley University, 1501 W. Bradley Ave., Peoria, IL 61625

Mars, The School House, 2301 W. Glen Ave., Peoria, IL 61614

Earth, Beachler's BP Gas Station, 2623 N. University St., Peoria, IL 61604

Venus, Brown Printing, 609 W. Glen Ave., Peoria, IL 61614

Mercury, Peoria Camera Shop, Metro Centre Merchants, 4700 N. University St., Peoria, IL 61614

Sun, Lakeview Museum of Arts and Sciences, 1125 W. Lake Ave., Peoria, IL 61614

Phone: (309) 686-7000

Hours: Monday–Friday 9 AM–5 PM

Cost: Free; museum, adults $6, seniors (60+) $5, kids (3–17) $4

Website: www.lakeview-museum.org

Directions: Just east of University St.

Where national monument meets the free enterprise system.

Peoria and Vandalia
Mini Gateway Arches

Oh sure, the Gateway Arch in St. Louis is big, but there's only one of them in Missouri. Illinois has two. Better still, this state's arches have been modified to promote the businesses that erected them. Tacky? Maybe, but let's hear it for free enterprise!

The better of the arches is in Peoria outside a used-auto-parts dealership—basically an organized, indoor junkyard. The market must not be strong for used Buicks, because they've taken a white two-door model and mounted it on a beam halfway up the arch. Something tells me, though, that if Neal's can't find a part in its inventory, a part that's up on that arch, they'd go up and get it for you.

Neal Auto Parts, 3407 W. Farmingham Rd., Peoria, IL 61604

Phone: (309) 677-JUNK

Hours: Always visible; store, Monday–Friday 8 AM–5 PM

Cost: Free

Website: www.nealautoparts.com

Directions: West of the intersection of Farmingham Rd. and Southport Rd. (Rte. 8)

The second Illinois arch is also retrofitted to attract customers, this time to a motel along I-70 in Vandalia. A large Travelodge sign hangs where the Buick does in Peoria. The owners also have added to Eero Saarinen's space-age design by erecting an adjacent jungle gym that looks like a rocket ship.

Travelodge, 1500 N. Sixth St., Vandalia, IL 62471

Phone: (618) 283-2363

Hours: Always visible

Cost: Free

Directions: Rte. 51 exit south from I-70, then west on the frontage road (Veterans Ave.).

Peoria and Mt. Vernon
The Uniroyal Gals

Back in the late 1960s, after it had introduced the Muffler Man (see pages 152–54) to American consumers, the International Fiberglass Company of Venice, California, came up with a female counterpart. So many of these curvaceous colossi were sold to tire stores, they were dubbed Uniroyal Gals. They stood 17.5 feet tall and their measurements were identical: 108-72-108. Va-va-varoom!

There are two Uniroyal Gals in Illinois, though the statue in Peoria has been renamed Vanna Whitewall.

Vanna Whitewall with her skirt still on.

Depending on the time of year you visit, Ms. Whitewall will be wearing a short skirt and blouse (fall to spring) or a shiny red bikini (summer). Look closely at the left hem of the skirt and top—though they're made of fiberglass, they unbuckle to reveal the painted bikini below.

Peoria Plaza Tire, 1800 SW Washington St., Peoria, IL 61602

Phone: (309) 673-8261

Hours: Always visible; store, Monday–Friday 8 AM–5 PM, Saturday 8 AM–12:30 PM

Cost: Free

Website: www.plazatire.com

Directions: Northwest of the river, two blocks southwest of the Cedar St. (Rte. 29) bridge.

The Uniroyal Gal outside Stan the Tire Man's shop in Mt. Vernon is a bit more modest, for her clothing is permanently attached to her frame. With a red top and a powder blue skirt, she still draws in business . . . just not that kind of business.

1213 Broadway St., Mt. Vernon, IL 62864

Phone: (618) 242-6400

Hours: Always visible

Cost: Free

Directions: Along Rte. 15 (Broadway St.) between 12th and 13th Sts.

Peoria Heights
Observation Watertower with Woodpecker

Believe me, you haven't seen Peoria until you've seen it from 200 feet above the ground! OK, technically the homes just below this watertower are in the village of Peoria Heights, but honestly, it's rather difficult to tell where Peoria Heights ends and Peoria begins. Let's just call it greater Peoria.

There are actually three observation decks on top of this structure, all accessed via the world's slowest elevator. There are three telescopes mounted around the decks should you want to see beyond the city limits. The tower was built in 1968, but it was renovated in 2003, at which time a 10-foot-tall woodpecker was installed on the side. If it ever succeeds in punching through a hole, the town will lose 500,000 gallons of drinking water, and then won't they feel silly for installing it?

Tower Park, 1222 E. Kingman Ave., Peoria Heights, IL 61616

Phone: (309) 682-8732

Hours: June–August, daily 11 AM–9 PM; April–May and September, daily 11 AM–7 PM

Cost: Adults $2, seniors (65+) $1.75, kids (5–12) $1.25

Website: http://villageofpeoriaheights.org/new/about-us/current/93-tower-park

Directions: North of Glen Ave. at Prospect Rd.

Pontiac
Bob Waldmire's Traveling Art Studio

Nobody catalogued Route 66 as fastidiously or completely as pen-and-ink artist Bob Waldmire, son of the founder of the Cozy Dog Inn (see pages 221–23). For more than 30 years he produced hundreds of detailed draw-

ings depicting every stop and attraction of note from Chicago to Pasadena, California. For months each year, Waldmire would travel the Mother Road in an orange VW microbus, making sketches of all he saw and compiling historical research that would accompany every drawing. He would then return to his converted school bus–studio in Springfield to complete the final renderings.

After Waldmire died in December 2009, his van was donated to the Illinois Route 66 Association. Today it is on display at its museum in Pontiac. The association also has a booth from the original Steak 'n Shake, a solar car that traveled from California to Chicago, and hundreds of historic photos and newspaper clippings. Come and get your kicks.

Route 66 Hall of Fame and Museum, 110 W. Howard St., Pontiac, IL 61764

Phone: (815) 844-6692

Hours: June–August, Monday–Friday 9 AM–5 PM, Saturday–Sunday 10 AM–4 PM; September–May, Monday–Friday 11 AM–3 PM, Saturday–Sunday 10 AM–4 PM

Cost: Free

Website: www.il66assoc.org, http://www.bobwaldmire.com

Directions: Six blocks east of Ladd St. (Rte. 23) on Rte. 116 (Howard St.).

Quincy
Hee Haw Pickup Truck

The *Hee Haw* pickup truck is not as famous as the *Beverly Hillbillies'* jalopy, but it runs a close second. It's the crown jewel of this 35-car museum run by the Mississippi Valley Historic Automobile Club, and they don't take it out for just any occasion. You can see it at the car club's annual Father's Day show and during the few hours the museum is open each summer. If you're a true fan, pull that Trans Am off the cinder blocks and come on over.

Given the number of cornball jokes uttered in the front seat of this bumpkin-mobile, you might think this thing runs on ethanol. Not true, unleaded gas works fine.

Antique Car Museum, All American Park, Quinsippi Island Rd., Quincy, IL 62301

Phone: (217) 223-1238

Hours: June–August, Sunday noon–4 PM

Cost: Adults $2, kids free (with adult)

Directions: On Quinsippi Island, down by the river.

Do you see it?

Jesus in a Tree

Seeing isn't necessarily believing, but seeing can still be creepy, even if you don't believe. Near the center of this otherwise humdrum cemetery is a

large birch tree with a seven-foot burl on its trunk. If you look at it just right, from a distance, you can make out the figure of Jesus carrying a lamb in his folded arms. Reading bark is about as precise as reading tea leaves, so for all anyone knows, it could be a dead band member from Lynyrd Skynyrd.

The Apparition Tree was first noticed in July 1998 and was visited by thousands of curious folk each day. Today, ropes mark paths to keep visitors from treading on the dead. The best view is from a distance, but unblocked sightlines are often difficult through the throngs of the faithful.

Calvary Cemetery, 1730 N. 18th St., Quincy, IL 62301

Phone: (217) 223-3390

Hours: Daily 9 AM–5 PM

Cost: Free

Directions: North of Rte. 104, west of Rte. 96.

Lincoln-Douglas Valentine Museum

No, Abraham Lincoln and Stephen Douglas did not send each other valentines. There's no indication that they even liked one another. The name of this tiny museum dedicated to decorated candy boxes is drawn instead from the building that houses the collection: the Lincoln-Douglas Apartments.

Covering the walls of the communal library in this senior high-rise is an interesting assortment of red, heart-shaped containers. The Quincy Paper Box Company manufactured valentine candy boxes for years, and they donated their production samples to create the museum when the plant closed. Residents have expanded the collection by adding other items related to the holiday. Though the museum takes only a few short minutes to see, it's worth a visit if you're in town.

Lincoln-Douglas Apartments, 101 N. Fourth St., Quincy, IL 62301

Phone: (217) 224-3355

Hours: Monday–Friday 9 AM–9 PM by appointment

Cost: Free

Directions: At the corner of Maine and Fourth Sts.

QUINCY
➡ Actress Mary Astor was born in Quincy on May 3, 1906.

Marrakesh on the Mississippi.

Villa Katherine

Villa Katherine looks like it would be more at home in Tunisia than it does in the Corn Belt, yet here it is. The castle was commissioned in 1900 by trust-funder George Metz, and it was constructed and furnished with scraps of Moorish architecture scavenged during Metz's two-year trek through North Africa, including lamps, tiles, keyhole windows, crescent ornaments, and more. Metz named the building after his mother, then went to Europe in search of a bride.

Turns out, having the grooviest pad in Quincy didn't impress Metz's German girlfriend; she refused to leave her homeland, no matter how fabulous his place was. Metz returned to Villa Katherine to live as a recluse with his dog, Bingo.

Disheartened, Metz eventually sold the place to a railroad agent in 1912. The buyer had misrepresented his motives, and rather than keep the place pristine, he sold its furnishings and slated the building for demolition. Metz visited Villa Katherine in 1913 to find it vacant and vandalized. He turned away and never came back. Metz spent the remainder of his life feeding the squirrels and birds in Quincy parks. He died in 1937. (Bingo

had died years earlier, in 1906, and was buried in Villa Katherine's rose garden.)

Luckily, the railroad agent never razed the structure. Villa Katherine sat empty until the 1980s, when funds were collected to restore it. Today it houses the local visitors bureau and is listed on the National Register of Historic Places.

532 Gardner Expressway, Quincy, IL 62301

Phone: (800) 978-4748 or (217) 214-3700

Hours: Monday–Friday 8:30 AM–4:30 PM

Cost: Adults $3

Website: www.seequincy.com

Directions: Overlooking the Mississippi River off Rte. 57 south of the bridge.

Rantoul
Octave Chanute Aerospace Museum

When you first enter the Chanute Aerospace Museum, you'll swear you've just walked into a boy's bedroom. Plastic model airplanes battle each other in crude dioramas. The walls are covered in roughly painted renderings of cartoon characters dropping bombs and tossing thunderbolts. But this isn't some preteen hell—it's an old air force base! When the federal government handed the folks in Rantoul a decommissioned facility, they turned it into a tourist destination.

Check out the commander's office with its original desk and carpeting. Visit the hangers filled with rusting jets and missiles. Hop in the cockpit of a B-52 or a C-133 transport and, as a promotional flyer says, "Remember living on the brink of destruction as huge C-133 Douglas Cargomasters transported ICBMs and their nuclear payloads to launching sites around the midwest." Awesome!

During the Cold War, Chanute Air Force Base was a primary training ground for Minuteman missile repair teams. The three trainers are now open for you to visit and inspect, whether you be a red-blooded American or a cold-blooded Red. Imagine launching ICBMs at all those who ever wronged you.

The irony of an aerospace museum at Chanute is lost on most, but not those who served in World War II. At the time, Chanute was akin to Siberia for washed-out or washed-up pilots. Among servicemen, the common phrase was "Don't shoot 'em—Chanute 'em!"

Chanute Air Base, 1011 Pacesetter Dr., Rantoul, IL 61866

Phone: (217) 893-1613

Hours: December–March, Monday-Friday 10 AM–5 PM, Saturday 10 AM–4 PM; April–November, Monday–Saturday 10 AM–5 PM, Sunday noon–5 PM

Cost: Adults $10, seniors (62+) $8, military $8, kids (4–18) $5

Website: www.aeromuseum.org

Directions: East from I-57 to Rte. 45, turn south and follow signs to museum.

Sadorus
National Museum of Ship Models and Sea History

Yes, it's hundreds of miles from any ocean and a long way from the Great Lakes, but if you're interested in nautical history, this landlocked museum is worth the trip. Charles Lozar opened his 250-ship museum in 2001. The collection spans centuries, from early Greek and Egyptian boats to Mississippi paddle-wheelers to today's nuclear submarines, including a model used in *The Hunt for Red October*. Because Lozar started his collection in California, he ended up with several other film models, including miniatures used in *Ben Hur*, *Cleopatra*, and *Tugboat Annie*. The most amazing model, however, is a 27-foot replica of the *Queen Mary* made out of 1,000,000-plus toothpicks. Some of the ships are displayed in dioramas, though most are mounted on pedestals for easy viewing.

201 S. Market St., Sadorus, IL 61872

Phone: (217) 352-1672

Hours: May–November, Saturday 11:30 AM–4 PM or by appointment

Cost: Adults $5, kids $5

Website: www.lincolnshireprop.com/museum

Directions: At the west end of town on Rte. 17 (Market St.).

SHELBYVILLE

➡ Shelbyville claims to be the "City Where the Action Is." No wonder; this is the same town where the household dishwasher was invented in 1886 by local socialite Josephine Cochrane.

THAR THEY BLOW!

Avast ye—if the ship models in Sardorus have ye be itchin' fer a man o' war of yer own, sail up to **Pacific Tall Ships** in Lemont (15200 E. Canal Bank Rd., (800) 690-6601, www.pacifictall-ships.com). These landlubbers have models of all sizes, though some cost a mighty booty—arghhh!

Springfield
Abraham Lincoln's Tomb

Though most days Lincoln's tomb has an aura of solemnity, this memorial has been the site of many strange events over the years, most of them involving the body of the president. When you view Lincoln's sarcophagus today, you're looking at an empty shell; Abe is actually 13 feet below floor level with a six-foot-thick slab of concrete just above his coffin. This is to discourage grave robbers.

Outside the tomb is a bust sculpted by Gutzon Borglum of Mt. Rushmore fame.

One more indignity.

Tradition says you should rub Abe's nose for luck. After several years, his nose became a bright, shining beacon on his dull, bronze face. Caretakers once tried putting Abe on a pedestal out of tourists' reach, but the public demanded that it be lowered, and it was. So rub away—there's plenty of the slain president's good fortune still left in him.

Oak Ridge Cemetery, 1441 N. Monument Ave., Springfield, IL 62702

Phone: (217) 782-2717

Hours: May–August, daily 9 AM–5 PM; September–November and March–April, Tuesday–Saturday 9 AM–5 PM; December–February, Tuesday–Saturday 9 AM–4 PM

Cost: Free

Website: www.state.il.us/hpa/hs/lincoln_tomb.htm

Directions: Two blocks north of Grand Ave.

HONEST ABE IN A SHELL GAME

If you think President Lincoln's assassination was crummy payback from a reunified nation, wait until you hear what happened to the Great Emancipator after he was murdered.

In Washington, Lincoln's blood was drawn and placed in a ceremonial vessel. According to reports, his brain was "scooped out," reflecting the embalming practice of the day. By removing most of the soft, squishy organs from the body, such as the brain, the rest would keep pretty well. This was handy if somebody wanted to view the body later. (Lincoln's son Willie, who died in Washington and whose body was prepared in this manner, was twice disinterred so Abe could gaze at and touch the body.) What exactly happened to Lincoln's brain is not known; it has never been recovered, but you can bet some American family has one heck of a secret heirloom.

Lincoln's body rode to Springfield in the first Pullman sleeping car, stopping in many cities along the way. Willie's body rode along with him. Every year, a ghost of Lincoln's funeral train is reported to travel its original path, draped in black bunting and not making a sound.

By the time the funeral train pulled into Springfield, a $50,000 tomb already had been erected downtown. But Mary Todd threatened to take Abe back to Washington if she didn't get him planted in Oak Ridge, so Lincoln was placed in a temporary vault and the original tomb was dismantled. Abe was transferred to a more permanent, temporary vault in December, along with Willie and Edward, a son who had died in Springfield at age three.

The three Lincolns stayed in the vault until 1871, when they could be moved to the partially completed monument. Just before they were to be placed in the tomb, Lincoln's son Thomas (nicknamed Tad because he had a large head and a wiggly body) died of tuberculosis in Chicago. Thomas was the first Lincoln buried in the Oak Ridge tomb. The monument was dedicated in 1874.

After all the bodies were moved to their new homes, the "Big Jim" Kinealy gang, a band of counterfeiters, tried to steal Abe on Election Day 1876 for a $200,000 ransom. Authorities foiled the plot, but not before the gang yanked Lincoln's casket halfway out of the sarcophagus. They planned to sink the body in a sandbar beneath a bridge on the Sangamon River two miles north of town, then use the ransom to free Benjamin Boyd, their jailed engraver.

The events caused the monument's builders to reconsider their original design. The next time they would bury Abe deeper and make it look as if he was somewhere else. Before the changes could be made, Abe was moved to a mystery location inside the tomb, known only to the "Lincoln Guard of Honor." The public was left to gaze at an empty sarcophagus they thought contained the former president. Lincoln was hidden for 11 years and was shuffled around several times before being buried under the floor with Mary Todd.

In 1899, it was necessary to reconstruct the tomb due to its shoddy original design. Before Abe was buried a third time, his coffin was opened for 23 old friends and associates to confirm that Lincoln was still dead and still there. He was both. Those present claimed Abe had weathered the years well, but had gotten quite stinky. God only knows what he'd have smelled like had his brain been left in.

When repairs were finished in 1901, Lincoln was planted in a reinforced concrete chamber below the sarcophagus with a 20-inch cement slab between the two. Mary Todd Lincoln was reentombed above ground in a wall chamber opposite the president along with their three sons. (Son Robert was never buried with the rest of the family, but in Arlington National Cemetery.)

Lincoln's tomb became a popular tourist destination and soon resembled a sideshow. Caretakers were allowed to charge admission to supplement their meager salaries, and one caretaker, the enterprising former newsman Herbert W. Fay, placed his 30,000-piece collection of Lincoln memorabilia in the monument's rotunda. You could view Abe's vessel of blood (a placard read LINCOLN'S BLOOD, ASK HOW IT CAME HERE), admire bronze statues spruced up with house paint, or get an enterprising local schoolchild to recite the Gettysburg Address for a quarter.

Again, in 1930, repairs were needed. Parts of the external statuary had been nabbed by souvenir hunters, including sabers from the soldiers' hands and telescopes from the sailors', and had to be replaced. The sarcophagus that once held Lincoln's body (up until the counterfeiters tried to nab him) was left outside the tomb where visitors hacked it up for keepsakes. In an attempt to cover their own negligence, tomb caretakers dumped the few remaining fragments between two interior walls where they gathered dust until being uncovered in 1979. The obelisk was reinforced, but not before wind knocked over a 100-foot scaffold holding its three-ton capstone. It nearly smashed through the tomb's roof. Abe, Mary, and the sons were moved to four different mausoleums in an elaborate shell game on the grounds of Oak Ridge during the project's final phases. To discourage vandals, nobody was told they had been moved.

The tomb continues to have its problems. It was desecrated in 1987 by local teenagers, who claimed they had nothing better to do. The kids were caught after police read the vandals' names, which they had spray-painted on the side of the structure.

Several years ago scientists asked to drill into Abe's coffin for tissue samples. They wanted to test his DNA for Marfan syndrome, a genetic disease believed to be responsible for his lanky frame. The request was denied. Conspiracy wackos wondered out loud if the scientists would try to clone him like the dinosaurs in *Jurassic Park*.

A Tomb for Accordions

As you enter Oak Ridge Cemetery you'll immediately spot an impressive crypt dedicated to a remarkable man. No, not Abraham Lincoln. Roy Bertelli—Master of the Accordion! Bertelli bought this plot some time ago, then Oak Ridge had second thoughts (because it was at the first fork in the road) and threatened to take it back. Mr. Accordion took the cemetery to court and won, and then the fun really started.

Bertelli purchased an above-ground sarcophagus and had it etched with a photo of himself as a young man, playing his favorite instrument. A raised headstone with an open accordion marked the other end of the tomb. On sunny days Bertelli would sit atop his tomb, playing away to the amusement of visitors and the annoyance of the owners.

In 2003, Bertelli passed away, and because he was a World War II veteran, he was buried with full honors at nearby Camp Butler. But lest anyone forget his contribution to the art of the squeezebox, his accordions were laid to rest at this Oak Ridge tomb.

Oak Ridge Cemetery, 1441 N. Monument Ave., Springfield, IL 62702

Phone: (217) 782-2717

Hours: May–August, daily 9 AM–5 PM; September–November and March–April, Tuesday–Saturday 9 AM–5 PM; December–February, Tuesday–Saturday 9 AM–4 PM

Cost: Free

Website: www.springfield.il.us/Public%20Works/OakRidgeCemetery.htm

Directions: Two blocks north of N. Grand Ave.

Birthplace of the Corn Dog

Ed Waldmire Jr. first came up with the idea for the corn dog while stationed in Muskogee, Oklahoma, during World War II. There he saw hot dogs baked in cornbread and wondered if there was a way it could be flash-cooked. A few years later, while living in Amarillo, Texas, he perfected a deep-fried recipe he called the Crusty Cur.

Still, Waldmire didn't start selling them to the public until he returned home to Springfield. By then his wife had convinced him to change the name to the Cozy Dog, which he first sold at the Lake Springfield Beach House on June 16, 1946, and later that year at the Illinois State Fair. In 1949 he opened a roadside stand along old Route 66, and they've been sold here ever since. Imitation Cozy Dogs soon followed. The ripoffs were given a

They are cozy!

more generic name—corn dogs—and the name stuck . . . at least outside of Springfield.

The Cozy Dog Inn has a faithful local following, with good reason. Those who did them first still make them best. Several years ago, the Cozy Dog Inn was remodeled to accommodate more customers. It still sits on Old Route 66, an honor it celebrates with a display of 1950s roadside memorabilia.

Cozy Dog Drive In, 2935 S. Sixth St., Springfield, IL 62703

Phone: (217) 525-1992

Hours: Monday–Saturday 8 AM–8 PM

Cost: $1.85 each, plus tax

Website: www.cozydogdrivein.com

Directions: Two blocks north of Stevenson Dr. on Bus. 55.

Giants of Springfield

Much like the village of Crystal Lake (see pages 150–51), Springfield has an unusually large number of giants.

The first Colossus is on the southwest side of town, a familiar Muffler Man (see page 152) statue with a red shirt and black pants. This guy has been named the Lauterbach Giant after the tire and auto repair shop he guards. Back in 2006 a tornado blew his head off, but it was found and reattached. Years ago he held a tire in his right hand, but recently has been waving a jumbo American flag.

1569 Wabash Ave., Springfield, IL 62704

Phone: (217) 546-2600

Hours: Always visible

Cost: Free

Website: www.lauterbachtire.com

Directions: Two blocks east of Chatham Rd.

The second Springfield giant stands above the entryway to Southeast Springfield High School, home of the Spartans. This megamascot started life as a Viking sign outside Barker-Lubin Homebuilders, but he has since been restyled to wear a Spartan tunic. He carries a large sword and a golden shield emblazoned with an S.

Southeast Springfield High School, 2350 E. Ash St., Springfield, IL 62703

Phone: (219) 525-3130

Hours: Always visible

Cost: Free

Website: www.springfield.k12.il.us/schools/southeast

Directions: Four blocks east of Wirt Ave. at Taylor Ave.

The last giant is precisely what you'd expect to see in Springfield: a larger-than-life Abraham Lincoln just inside the main gates of the Illinois State Fair. Technically it's a work of art—*The Rail Splitter*—sculpted by Carl

Rinnus in 1968. It depicts Lincoln as young, skinny, and clean-shaven, swinging an axe and likely scaring the hell out of many young fairgoers.

Illinois State Fair, Gate 1, 801 E. Sangamon Ave., Springfield, IL 62794
Phone: (217) 782-6661
Hours: Always visible
Cost: Free
Website: www.agr.state.il.us/isf
Directions: Two blocks west of Peoria St. (Bus. 55) behind gate 1.

General Santa Anna's Leg and Lincoln Target

When General Antonio de Padua Maria Severino López de Santa Anna y Pérez de Lebrón—let's just call him Santa Anna—was ambushed by the 4th Regiment of the Illinois Volunteer Infantry at the 1847 Battle of Cerro Gordo, he was so surprised that he ran off, leaving a half-eaten chicken dinner and $18,000 in gold. Or rather, he hopped off, because he also left behind his wooden leg. Sergeant John Gill took command of the appendage, which he brought back to display at the Illinois State Fair.

Contrary to what you might have seen on *King of the Hill* (never a good source of historic information), the leg was never captured and repatriated to Mexico, though that country has asked for it back a few times. No doing—finder's keepers. Today you can see it at the Illinois State Military Museum along with artifacts from every conflict in which Illinois soldiers have fought.

While at the museum you can also see a wooden board Abraham Lincoln used on the White House lawn for target practice. On August 18, 1863, the president fired seven shots with a Spencer rifle at 40 yards, and all hit their mark. Not bad!

Illinois State Military Museum, 1301 N. MacArthur Blvd., Springfield, IL 62702
Phone: (217) 761-3910
Hours: Tuesday–Saturday 1–4:30 PM
Cost: Free, but donation suggested
Website: www.springfield-il.com/attract/military.html
Directions: Two blocks north of Grand Ave.

SPRINGFIELD

➡ **The Donner Party** left Springfield for California on April 16, 1846. George Donner's eldest son, William, died before they got going and is buried in Oak Hill Cemetery.

SANTA ANNA'S OTHER LEG

Santa Anna didn't just forget his fancy cork leg with the boot mounted on it; he also forgot his backup peg leg. You can see his spare at **Governor Oglesby's mansion** (421 W. William St., (217) 429-9422, www.oglesbymansion.org) in Decatur. Legend has it Abner Doubleday once used it to hit baseballs.

Taylorville
Lincoln vs. the Pig

For Abraham Lincoln, life as a circuit lawyer wasn't exactly *LA Law* glamorous. Far from it. Lincoln would ride from county seat to county seat in central Illinois, taking cases large and small. The courthouses were often smaller. The original Christian County Courthouse was little more than a farmhouse, and it looked the part; free-roaming pigs would often rummage beneath the floorboards. During one trial they grunted and squealed so loudly that Lincoln made a *writ of quietus* motion, but neither the judge nor the swine upheld his motion.

The Christian County Courthouse has been upgraded since the 1840s, and the pigs have been driven off, but local historians didn't want anyone to forget the original building's role in Lincoln's career. That's why, in 2005, the Siegret family commissioned a bronze sculpture of the young lawyer carrying a long coat over his shoulder. And dodging a pig.

101 S. Main St., Taylorville, IL 62568

No phone

Hours: Always visible

Cost: Free

Directions: At the corner of Washington and Main Cross Sts.

TAYLORVILLE

➡ Oak Hill Cemetery (820 S. Cherokee St., (217) 824-2701, www.taylorville.net/cemetery) in Taylorville has a "devil's chair" that supposedly kills anyone who dares sit in it overnight.

Kewanee
Pluto Model
Woodland Palace

Aledo
A Night Spent in Jail

Dahinda
Sleep in a Barn

Monmouth
Wyatt Earp's Birthplace

Brimfield
Jubilee Rock
Garden

Oquawka
Goodbye, Norma Jean

Abingdon
The Midwest's Tallest Totem Pole

Peoria
Mini Solar System/Maxi Model
Neal Auto Parts Arch
Vanna Whitewall

Pekin
Eyes Cream
Uranus Model

Quincy
Hee Haw Pickup Truck
Jesus in a Tree
Lincoln-Douglas Valentine Museum
Villa Katherine

Mt. Sterling
World's Fattest Dead Man

IOWA

ILLINOIS

MISSOURI

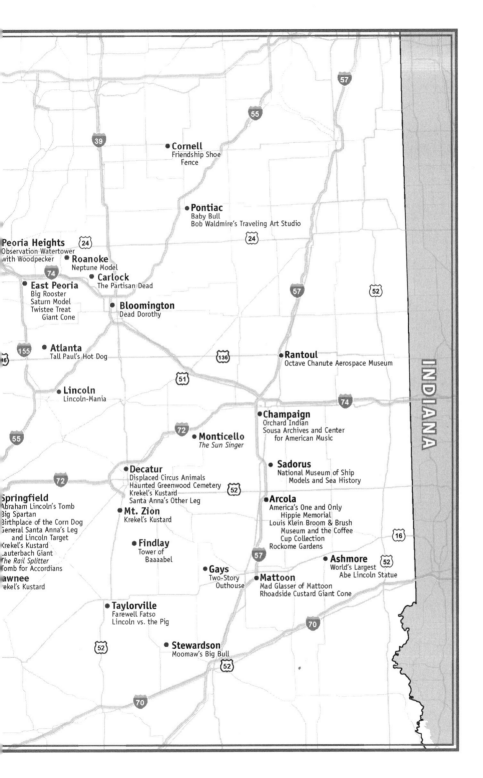

Cornell
Friendship Shoe
Fence

Pontiac
Baby Bull
Bob Waldmire's Traveling Art Studio

Peoria Heights (24)
Observation Watertower
with Woodpecker
Roanoke
Neptune Model
(74)
Carlock
East Peoria   The Partisan Dead
Big Rooster
Saturn Model
Twistee Treat
Giant Cone
Bloomington
Dead Dorothy

(57)   (52)

Atlanta
Tall Paul's Hot Dog
(155)
(136)
Rantoul
Octave Chanute Aerospace Museum

(51)

Lincoln
Lincoln-Mania

(74)

Champaign
Orchard Indian
Sousa Archives and Center
(72)   for American Music
Monticello
The Sun Singer

(55)

Sadorus
National Museum of Ship
Models and Sea History
Decatur
Displaced Circus Animals
(72)   Haunted Greenwood Cemetery   (52)
Krekel's Kustard
Springfield   Santa Anna's Other Leg
Abraham Lincoln's Tomb
Big Spartan   **Arcola**
Birthplace of the Corn Dog   America's One and Only
General Santa Anna's Leg   Hippie Memorial
and Lincoln Target   Louis Klein Broom & Brush
Krekel's Kustard   Museum and the Coffee   (16)
Lauterbach Giant   **Mt. Zion**   Cup Collection
The Rail Splitter   Krekel's Kustard   Rockome Gardens
Tomb for Accordians
Findlay   (57)
awnee   Tower of   **Ashmore**   (52)
ekel's Kustard   Baaaabel   World's Largest
Gays   Abe Lincoln Statue
Two-Story   **Mattoon**
Outhouse   Mad Glasser of Mattoon
Rhoadside Custard Giant Cone
Taylorville
Farewell Fatso
Lincoln vs. the Pig

(70)
(52)
Stewardson
Moomaw's Big Bull
(52)

(70)

INDIANA
(57)
(55)
(39)
(24)
(46)

5

SOUTHERN ILLINOIS

Southern Illinois, often referred to as Little Egypt, is an odd place. It got its name from the Nile-like delta confluence of the Ohio and Mississippi Rivers, but the region has another Egyptian connection. A local man, Russell Burrows, has claimed he found the tombs of Cleopatra, Mark Antony, Ptolemy, and Alexander the Great in a cave near Salem, and he has the artifacts to prove it! But the still-unrevealed "Burrows' Cave" is said to be guarded by several ghosts, so don't even try to find it yourself.

Perhaps all the good-natured use of pyramids and pharaohs by local businesses has opened up a portal to another dimension, allowing devil birds and albino squirrels to enter at will. UFOs and crop circles are not uncommon in this region. And if you're traveling to southern Illinois, you might want to think twice about camping— Bigfoot is no stranger to Little Egypt.

Two Effingham boys first saw the hairy beast in 1912, but it wasn't spotted again until 1941. That year, the Reverend Lepton Harpole was fishing near Mt. Vernon when a "baboon" jumped on him from a tree, knocking off Harpole's hat. As the creature ran away, the good reverend realized it was not a baboon but something much more humanlike.

Sasquatch was sighted three more times, in Chittyville (August 11, 1968); in Shawnee National Forest, where it clawed at Mike Busby before being scared off by a pickup truck (April 10, 1970); and in Cairo (July 25, 1972). Then, in 1974, the monster seemed to settle down around Murphysboro. There, dogs chased it into a barn on the Bullor farm, but it disappeared after the hounds went bonkers. The folks in Murphysboro call their hairy resident the Big Muddy Monster because it hangs out along the Big Muddy River.

But if you think Bigfoot is the only weird thing going on in Little Egypt, think again. There are plenty of bizarre tourist destinations to keep you entertained.

Alto Pass
Bald Knob Cross

When it was built in 1963, Bald Knob Cross claimed the title of North America's Tallest Christian Monument—111 feet tall, 63 feet wide, and able to withstand wind speeds of up to 150 mph. And because it was illuminated at night, it also attracted flying bugs from three different states. Its outer surface was plated in white, porcelain-coated, metal panels, not unlike a giant refrigerator. This eliminated the trouble of having to repaint the cross, and if a big magnetic Jesus were ever found, the owners wouldn't need nails to hang him on it.

Bald Knob Cross was the vision of Wayman Presley and Reverend William Lirely. Each white panel was purchased through contributions, like those of Myrta Clutts. Her prize pig, Betsy, farrowed more than 1,700 piglets, all of which were sold for the Cross Fund. (You can read this touching story on a flyer available in the gift shop.) But such tithing is now in the past. In recent years, the attraction was rehabbed with a $20,000 grant from the state of Illinois—separation of church and state apparently took a backseat to "encouraging tourism."

The best time to visit this mountaintop shrine is on Easter Sunday (6:30 AM), when locals put on a sunrise service and Passion play at an outdoor theater adjoining the cross. If you can't make it, you can always hire Barbara Casey, owner of the gift shop. She has a one-woman puppet show telling the history of Bald Knob Cross and is available for parties and worship services.

3630 Bald Knob Rd., PO Box 35, Alto Pass, IL 62905
Phone: (618) 203-4844
Hours: Daily 8 AM–6 PM
Cost: Free
Website: www.baldknobcross.com
Directions: Follow the signs west out of town from Rte. 127.

Root Beer Saloon

If you like root beer or ice cream and you don't mind a flock of ducks swooping over your head, stop by the Root Beer Saloon for taxidermy and treats. The ducks, which hang from the tin ceiling and appear to be coming

in for a landing on your banana split, are just the beginning. Every square inch of this old general store is covered with antlers and mounted fish and, for some reason, a statue of King Tut. A 14-foot python pelt dresses up the bar that is guarded by an 18-pound lobster (stuffed, though not with crabmeat). The root beer is brewed on the premises, and the food ranges from standard pub fare to the exotic.

#4 Main St., Alto Pass, IL 62905

Phone: (618) 893-1634

Hours: Monday–Friday 11:30 AM–4 PM; Saturday–Sunday 11 AM–5 PM

Cost: Treats, $3–$7; meals, $8–$20

Website: www.rootbeersaloon.com

Directions: At the intersection of Rte. 2 (Main St.) and Lake Dr.

Alton
Elijah Lovejoy, Martyr for Abolition

"As long as I am an American citizen, and as long as American blood runs in these veins, I shall hold myself at liberty to speak, to write, and to publish whatever I please on any subject amenable to the laws of my country for the same." These words were spoken by Reverend Elijah Lovejoy not long before American blood stopped running in his veins.

Reverend Lovejoy was a persistent advocate of abolition. Three times proslavery mobs destroyed the press on which Lovejoy printed his antislavery newspaper, the *Alton Observer*, and each time he replaced it. On November 7, 1837, he was shot while guarding his fourth printing press. He was two days short of his 35th birthday. Lovejoy became a martyr for the abolitionist cause and, in a broader sense, freedom of the press.

A 90-foot monument to Lovejoy now stands in Alton Cemetery, the state's tallest monument to an Illinois resident. The frame from the destroyed printing press, pulled from the Mississippi River muck in 1915, can be seen in the lobby of the *Alton Telegraph* (111 E. Broadway).

Alton City Cemetery, 1205 E. Fifth St., Alton, IL 62002

Phone: (618) 462-1617

Hours: Daily 9 AM–6 PM

Cost: Free

Directions: Three blocks east of Oak St. on Fifth St. at Monument Ave.

The Piasa Bird

The Piasa Bird petroglyph was first documented by Père Marquette in his 1673 diary, but it had been part of the regional mystical heritage for centuries. People believe it was intended to scare travelers along the Mississippi River, to honor a great bird-human battle, or both.

An Illini legend tells of two Piasa (pronounced PIE-saw, which is Illini for "Bird That Devours Man") that lived in a cave along the river. They were not shy about eating an occasional Indian. So Illini warriors, led by Chief Ouatoga, ambushed and killed the flying varmints using Ouatoga as bait. To commemorate the victory, a Piasa Bird was painted on the bluffs. Native Americans canoeing along the river would fire poisoned arrows and later guns at the image.

Stories of a bone-filled cave circulated for years, bolstered by a report from John Russell in March 1836. He claimed to have found a dark recess in the cliffs filled with human skulls and bones. The skeletons were piled so high Russell could not measure their depth.

Keep your eyes peeled for this critter.

Nobody made a clear drawing of the original petroglyph, and descriptions varied. Today's best guess looks like ZZ Top's dragon love child with a squared-off beard, deer antlers, and a tail that wraps back past its head. The bullet-ridden Piasa and the caves on the bluffs were carelessly blasted away by European settlers quarrying for lime in 1846. Local businesses repainted the image in 1925, but it was dynamited in 1950 when McAdams Highway was widened. A Piasa sign was bolted to the cliffs until the 1990s, but now the image has been painted directly onto the rock face. On either side of the Piasa are entrances to caves that were once the gathering place of beer- and devil-worshipping teens. They've since been fenced off and a roadside park has been erected. Bring a bucket of chicken and chow down on the monster's relatives.

Great River Road (Rte. 100), Alton, IL 62002

Phone: (800) 258-6645

Hours: Always visible

Cost: Free

Website: www.altonweb.com/history/piasabird

Directions: On the bluffs along Rte. 100, one mile north of the casino.

DOES THE PIASA STILL LIVE?

Despite the Illini victory over the Piasa Bird, some believe the monster still terrorizes people in the area. Colonel Walter F. Siegmund sighted something odd near Alton on April 4, 1948. He described it as "an enormous bird about the size of a small pursuit plane" flying along the bluffs. Other reports place the Piasa farther north. Two birds with 10-foot wingspans swooped down and carried 10-year-old Marlon Lowe about 35 feet from his Lawndale home on July 25, 1977. His parents frightened the birds away before the 65-pound child became the birds' lunch. The incident so spooked Marlon that his hair turned from red to gray. Three days later, near Lincoln, a farmer saw one of the birds in flight, and on July 30 "Texas John" Huffer of Tuscola took pictures of a Piasa in a local swamp. Finally, a truck driver saw a bird trying to carry a pig over the highway between Delavan and Armington. The bird had an eight-foot wingspan . . . and a heck of an appetite! Skeptics say the birds were just aggressive turkey vultures.

Anna
King Neptune's Grave

Neptune wasn't always a king; royalty was thrust upon him. Parker Neptune was his given name, born in 1941 on the West Frankfort farm of Sherman Boner, named and reared by his daughter Patty. Just a year old, Neptune was drafted in the effort to defeat Adolf Hitler—the Boners donated him for a barbecue to sell war bonds.

Did I forget to mention that Parker Neptune was a pig? Luckily for Neptune, he was rescued by a navy recruiter named Don Lingle. Rather than see the porker turning on a spit, Lingle decided to auction him off instead. Over and over and over again. Nobody ever collected their prize—that was the understanding. So Lingle auctioned Neptune's squeal, he auctioned his bristles, he auctioned every piggy part from snout to tail, and before the war was over Lingle had raised $19 million, much of it earmarked to build the battleship *Illinois*. One million of that came from Illinois governor Dwight Green (with help from Illinois taxpayers).

The setup worked pretty well for Neptune, too. The 700-pound hog became the official mascot of the US Navy and toured the Midwest dressed in a dark blue robe, silver earrings, and a gold crown. On special occasions, Lingle painted his toenails and called him a king. Really.

After the war, Neptune retired to a farm near Anna. He died of pneumonia on May 14, 1950, and was buried with full military honors. Originally interred in King Neptune Park, his grave was later moved to an interstate rest stop, where you can see it today.

Trail of Tears Welcome Center, I-57 Northbound, Anna, IL 92906

Phone: (618) 833-4809

Hours: Always visible

Cost: Free

Directions: North of Exit 31 (Rte. 146).

Belleville

National Shrine of Our Lady of the Snows

If Disney built Catholic shrines, Our Lady of the Snows would be the Magic Kingdom. This place is B-I-G. Two hundred acres big—the largest outdoor Catholic shrine in the United States! Everywhere you turn there's another chapel, prayer bench, or candle-filled grotto. They've also got most of the Bible's memorable scenes carved in marble, tiled in mosaics, or gilded in gold.

Like Disneyland, there's no way to see it all short of a full day, so here are a few highlights to help you bypass the tour groups. First, the Way of the Cross—you can walk it, but the road is there for a reason. Cruise past the stations in the comfort of your vehicle. Each scene is depicted with full-size statues. The speed limit is 25 mph. Next, visit the Lourdes Grotto. Why bother going to France with an exact replica right here? Finally, be sure to check out the Millennium Spire, where you can enter your prayers into a computer and a series of LED lights beams them up to heaven in angel code.

And if you find yourself in Belleville between Thanksgiving and New Year's, come after dark. A million lightbulbs illuminate the shrine's Way of the Lights and blind auto-bound pilgrims on their journey toward the final nativity scene. If the wise men had had this much help finding the baby Jesus, they wouldn't have needed to be so wise.

422 S. DeMazenod Dr., Belleville, IL 62223

Phone: (800) 682-2879 or (618) 397-6700

Hours: Center, daily 7:30 AM–8 PM; shrine, daily 7 AM–10 PM; call ahead at Christmas

Cost: Donations encouraged

Website: www.snows.org

Directions: At the intersection of Rtes. 157 and 15.

SNOWY MARY STOPS BY

There was a time when you could double your excitement on your visit to Our Lady of the Snows. Starting in January 1993, always on the 13th, a man named Ray Doiron would come to the Lourdes Grotto to visit with the Virgin Mary—not the statue, the apparition. While the Shrine did not endorse these heavenly communications, they did not discourage them either.

Doiron claimed that Mary would come to him as he performed the rosary. She was often surrounded by light, making everything around her sparkle, and her robes blew in the wind, not unlike Stevie Nicks. The scent of roses was overpowering. Mary hung out for 45 minutes, speaking slowly so Doiron could remember her message. Though most of her messages were of three types, "Pray, pray, pray," "Look out for Satan," and "The rise of one world government is a prelude to the Rapture," she occasionally tried to explain why there were earthquakes in Japan or floods in the Midwest.

Benton
The Old Franklin County Jail Museum

Most small-town historical museums are dreary collections of postcards, spinning wheels, and farm machinery. The Old Franklin County Jail Museum is not one of them.

Central to the museum is the history surrounding the hanging of Charlie Birger, southern Illinois's most notorious bootlegger. For all his faults as a hoodlum and killer, Birger did some good in the region, not the least of which was to stand up to the KKK-backed law enforcement establishment of the 1920s. Police had been ruthless to immigrant laborers in southern Illinois, so to them, Birger took on the aura of Robin Hood. He was also at the receiving end of the first bomb ever dropped from a plane in the United States. On November 12, 1926, the rival Sheldon gang bombed Birger's hangout in Harrisburg, the Shady Rest, from a biplane. A cockfighting pit was blown to pieces, killing an American eagle and a bulldog but none of Birger's gang.

Birger was arrested for the contract murder of "Fat" Joe Adams, the mayor of West City and a competitive moonshiner. After a lengthy incarceration and trial, Birger was hanged outside the Old Jail on April 19, 1928, before 5,000-plus spectators. It was to be the last public execution in Illinois. Birger hired his own photographer to document the event, and his last words were, "It's a beautiful world."

The noose used to hang Birger is on display at the museum, as is the jail cell in which he spent his final days and a replica of the portable gallows from which he dangled. The jail stayed in use until 1989 and still has original prisoner graffiti.

Also at the museum are several other themed rooms dedicated to local history. In one is the re-created WFRX 1300 radio station of West Frankfort, where a school reporter interviewed George Harrison on the air in 1963. This equipment was the first to broadcast a Beatles single ("From Me to You") in the United States; the band had not yet hit it big here. The museum also has a Coke machine from Main Street in Benton, from which Harrison might have pulled a bottle or two while visiting his sister, Louise, who lived in town.

Last, the museum focuses its attention on several native sons, including John Logan, the Civil War general who founded the Grand Army of the Republic; Doug Collins, former Philadelphia 76er and coach of the Chicago Bulls; and actor John Malkovich.

209 W. Main St., Benton, IL 62812
Phone: (800) 661-9998 or (618) 439-0608
Hours: Monday–Saturday 9 AM–4 PM
Cost: Suggested donation $3 per person
Website: www.historicjail.com
Directions: One block west of the courthouse square on Rte. 14 (W. Main St.).

Cairo
The Hewer

Cairo's statue of *The Hewer* in Halliday Park is thought to be one of the nation's greatest nudes. It was carved by George Grey Barnard in 1906 for the St. Louis World's Fair, and it depicts a young man kneeling on the bank of a river. Once it was described as "a vision of man laboring on the shore of a flood hewing and dragging wood to save the people from death and destruction."

That's all fine and good, but would it hurt to put on a pair of pants?

Put on some pants.

Halliday Park, 950 Washington Ave., Cairo, IL 62914

No phone

Hours: Always visible

Cost: Free

Directions: On Rte. 51 (Washington Ave.) between Ninth and Tenth Sts.

Carbondale
Boo Rochman Memorial Park

Jeremy "Boo" Rochman was a huge Dungeons & Dragons fan, so when he died young in an auto accident his family chose to honor his memory by creating a D&D park in his name. It was completed in 2005 not far from where Rochman crashed. The forested park is privately owned, so it doesn't appear on most maps of Carbondale, and it is maintained by volunteers.

And what a park—giant dragons, wizards hiding behind trees, and a winged Pegasus flying over a flower garden. An enormous wooden castle fills one corner of the property, guarded by trolls and elves and all sorts of bizarre characters. Inside the castle is an elaborate jungle gym of tunnels, stairs, and bridges, most of which are sized for children, not adults. In other words, good luck getting the kids back in the minivan.

31 Homewood Dr., Carbondale, IL 62903

No phone

Hours: Dawn to dusk

Cost: Free, though donations accepted

Directions: At the intersection of Giant City and No Name Rds.

Bucky's Dome

R. Buckminster Fuller had developed and patented the geodesic dome years before joining the faculty of Southern Illinois University in 1959. A year after he arrived, however, he had one built on a quiet residential street and moved in with his wife, Anne Hewlett. It was the first time they'd ever lived inside one of his creations, and it was the only home they ever owned. They would live here a decade before moving out in 1971.

Over time Bucky's Dome home fell into disrepair, but in 2002 a nonprofit was formed to restore the structure. Work progressed until May 8, 2009, when a 700-pound tree branch fell on it during a thunderstorm.

Today it is covered with a large tarp as repairs continue. Come and see it while you still can, or better yet, send a donation its way.

RBF Home, 407 S. Forest Ave., PO Box 1281, Carbondale, IL 62901

Phone: (618) 203-4844

Hours: Daylight

Cost: Free

Website: http://fullerdomehome.org/nfp.html

Directions: One block south of Walnut St. (Rte. 13), two blocks east of Oakland Ave.

Chester
Popeye Town

On January 17, 1929, Elzie Crisler Segar unveiled Popeye, the famous spinach-eating sailor, as a new character in his 10-year-old "Thimble Theatre" comic strip. Popeye was fashioned after Frank "Rocky" Fiegel, a local scrapper on the Mississippi River. Popeye was the captain of a voyage taken by Olive Oyl and her brother, Castor. At the time, Oyl (modeled after rail-thin Chester shopkeeper Dora Paskel) was dating Ham Gravy. Wimpy joined the strip later; he was based on William "Windy Bill" Schuchert, proprietor of the Chester Opera House, where Segar once worked as a projectionist.

In Segar's honor, a six-foot "life-size" bronze Popeye statue was erected in 1977 near the Mississippi River in Segar Park. The statue has been attacked three times by Bluto-ish vandals but has stood its ground. The city has recently embarked on a 16-statue campaign to place Segar's other popular characters all over town. You can now see granite likenesses of Olive Oyl (with Swee' Pea), Bluto, Wimpy, Castor, and the Sea Hag. A new statue is unveiled each year when the town throws its Popeye Picnic on the weekend after Labor Day.

Many Chester establishments have also incorporated Popeye, Olive Oyl, and Wimpy into their names and advertising, and you can buy Popeye-brand canned spinach at many locations around town. The best of the bunch is Spinach Can Collectibles in Wimpy's . . . er . . . Schuchert's old Opera House.

Popeye Statue, Segar Memorial Park, Bridge Bypass Rd. (at bridge), Chester, IL 62233

Olive Oyl and Swee' Pea Statue, Taylor and State Sts. (at courthouse), Chester, IL 62233

Wimpy Statue, 1001 State St. (at Chester Square), Chester, IL 62233

Bluto Statue, Stanwick and Holmes Sts. (at Buena Vista National Bank), Chester, IL 62233

Castor Oyl and Whiffle Hen Statue, 1900 State St. (at Memorial Hospital), Chester, IL 62233

Sea Hag Statue, 2208 State St. (behind McDonald's), Chester, IL 62233

Popeye Mural/Fan Club/Popeye Museum, Spinach Can Collectibles, Chester Opera House, 1001 State St., Chester, IL 62233

Phone: (618) 826-4567

Hours: Monday–Friday 9:30 AM–4:30 PM, Saturday 10 AM–3 PM

Cost: Free

Website: www.popeyethesailor.com, www.popeyepicnic.com/web

Directions: On Chester Square.

He yis what he yis.

Collinsville
Cahokia Mounds

Cahokia Mounds holds the distinction of being this nation's only pre-Columbian urban metropolis. Before St. Louis became the Gateway to the West, Cahokia (just across the river) was the gateway to the north. It was the trade hub in the Mississippi Valley starting around 700 AD until its inhabitants, the Hopewell culture, vacated the site around 1400 AD. During those 700 years they moved a lot of dirt. More than 120 mounds once covered the region, though only 109 remain. Some of the mounds were destroyed by railroad engineers looking for dirt for train beds.

The focal point of Cahokia is Monk's Mound. It was named for French Trappist monks who built a monastery on top of it in the 1700s. It stands 100 feet tall and covers 14 acres—only two pyramids in Mexico are larger. A large stone structure is believed to be at the center of Monk's Mound, though researchers are baffled as to how it got there. While drilling a drainage hole into the mound in 1998, a crew hit a large rock where no stone was supposed to be. Could the Hopewell culture have been masons? Until recently, archeologists believed not. We may never know what this rock is, for there are no plans to excavate the mound.

As impressive as Monk's Mound is, Mound 72 is cooler. Whoever was buried in Mound 72 was a mighty Big Cheese. The guy was laid out in a robe of 36,000 seashells with 400 arrowheads and was "accompanied" by 53 female and 4 male sacrifices, all of them missing their hands and heads! Sadly, the Interpretive Center plays down these tales of human sacrifice. Perhaps the curators need to do a little market research. Ask 100 visitors which is more interesting, a pile of dirt or decapitated human offerings? Isn't it obvious?

The entire site only hints at the size of the city that once stood here since all the wooden shelters on and around the mounds have long since disintegrated. If your heart can survive it, climb to the top of Monk's Mound and take in the landscape.

7850 Collinsville Rd., Collinsville, IL 62234
Phone: (618) 346-5160
Hours: Museum, May–October, daily 9 AM–5 PM, November–April, Wednesday–Sunday 9 AM–5 PM; park, daily 8 AM–dusk
Cost: Museum, adults $4, kids $2; free parking
Website: http://cahokiamounds.org
Directions: Exit 24 from I-255 and turn west on Collinsville Rd.

Many tomatoes gave their lives.

World's Largest Catsup Bottle

Towering above the former G. S. Suppiger factory, bottler of Brooks catsup, the World's Largest Catsup Bottle seems lonely without the World's Largest Mustard Bottle by its side. The 70-foot-tall conical tank, built in 1949, is roughly 25 feet wide at the base and tapers up to an eight-foot cap. It sits atop a 100-foot pedestal and can hold about 100,000 gallons . . . of water. If it were filled with catsup, this tower could satisfy about 26 million burger eaters with a teaspoon each.

The bottle's fate was in danger in 1993 when the plant was sold, but the citizens of Collinsville rallied and restored the landmark in 1995. Today, the locals occasionally celebrate Catsup Bottle Celebration Day to raise money for the tower's upkeep and to sing the praises of catsup. Capping the day, children dress up in bottle-shaped costumes and march in the Catsup Parade. With all this enthusiasm, is another condiment tower in the works? Not likely. Brooks Foods has long since relocated to Indiana.

800 S. Morrison, Collinsville, IL 62234

Phone: (618) 344-8775

Hours: Always visible

Cost: Free

Website: www.catsupbottle.com, www.catsupbottlefestival.com

Directions: On Morrison Rd. (Rte. 159) south of downtown.

Effingham
The Cross at the Crossroads

The Cross at the Crossroads is difficult to miss, situated as it is at the intersection of I-57 and I-70 where some 50,000 vehicles pass by each day. It stands 198 feet tall, is 113 feet wide, and can withstand 145-mph winds. And if you're coming through Effingham in the middle of the night, no need to worry—it's bathed in floodlights.

Getting to the cross, on the other hand, is a bit trickier, as it is tucked away behind an industrial park where many of the roads are cut off by the Little Wabash River and those dang interstates. But have faith, driver, and ye shall find it. Up close it looks more like a farm's machine shed on end, and seems to have been built from the same material. Ten granite books encircle the base, each one opened to a different commandment. Push the nearby buttons to hear 10 corresponding sermonettes. There's also a small chapel from which to view the cross in bad weather. The Cross Foundation hosts events such as the Blessing of the Bikes, the Blessing of the Corvettes, and plenty of weddings.

The Cross Foundation, W. Knagge St., PO Box 1103, Effingham, IL 62401

Phone: (217) 347-2846

Hours: Always visible; chapel, daily 10 AM–5 PM (7 PM in summer)

Cost: Free

Website: www.crossusa.org

Directions: Eastbound on Fayette Ave. off I-57/70 at Exit 159, turn south on Raney St., go over the overpass, and turn right on Knagge St.

Eldorado, Metropolis, Carmi
Big Johns

Big John statues were once commonplace in southern Illinois. These three-story bag boys—men, actually—stood outside Big John Super Food stores, a sack of groceries in one arm and two in the other. But because of a combination of vandals, pranksters, and (worst of all) those who claim to have "taste," only a few of the statues remain. Two still guard Big John supermarkets, one in Eldorado and the other in Metropolis. A third has switched jobs and now works for a deli in Carmi. Maybe they had better benefits.

Big John Super Foods Store, 1105 US Hwy. 45, Eldorado, IL 62930

Phone: (618) 273-9811

Hours: Always visible

Cost: Free

Directions: At the intersection of Rtes. 45 and 142.

Big John Super Foods Store, 1200 E. Fifth St., Metropolis, IL 92960

Phone: (618) 524-4096

Hours: Always visible

Cost: Free

Website: http://bigjohngrocery.com

Directions: Just west of where Rte. 45 bends onto Fifth St.

Little Giant Deli, 1347 State Hwy. 1, Carmi, IL 62821

Phone: (618) 382-3347

Hours: Always visible

Cost: Free

Directions: On Main St. (Rte. 1) on the southwest side of town.

Elsah

Mistake House

Barely larger than a two-car garage, the Mistake House on the campus of Principia College is anything but a mistake. The brainchild of Bernard Maybeck, it was originally called the Sample House because it was used to test materials and methods that would be incorporated into other college buildings. On this 1931 structure you can see poured concrete, a thatched roof, a terra-cotta tiled roof, brick walls, half-timbers, a chimney, a gabled second floor . . . you name it, it's there.

Driving through Principia College, you'll see many of the Mistake House's features in practice. Principia is one of the most beautiful college campuses in the state and would be worth a visit even if the Mistake House weren't there.

Principia College, Elsah, IL 62028

Phone: (618) 374-2131

Hours: Campus tours 2 PM

Cost: Free

Website: www.principia.edu

Directions: Adjacent to the chapel along the bluff.

Flora
Little Toot Railroad Company

Gaylon Borders had a dream: he wanted his own railroad. Nothing big, just an engine and tender, a few passenger cars, and a caboose. So in 1958 he ordered one out of a catalog from Pennsylvania. What he bought would become the Little Toot Railroad, a miniature steam locomotive that could pull a dozen or so passengers around Charley Brown Park. Sadly, Borders passed away in 1965, and his coal-burning baby was sold off two years later. It found a home in Centralia and later Peoria, but was shipped to Reedley, California, in 1993. Then, in 1998, the folks of Flora brought it back to its original home, where you'll find it today.

Your ride on the Little Toot starts at a small depot platform, covers a mile of track crossing three wooden trestles (one 15 feet high), and brings you back to where you started . . . a perfect analogy for the life of this little chugger that could.

Charley Brown Park, RR2, Flora, IL 62839

Phone: (618) 662-8040

Hours: May–September, Friday 11 AM–6 PM, Saturday 10 AM–6 PM, Sunday noon–4 PM, Monday 11 AM–4 PM

Cost: 1 trip $4, 2 trips $6, 12 trips $30

Website: www.littletootrailroad.com

Directions: Two miles west of town on North Ave. (Old Rte. 50).

Grafton
Fin Inn

If you're the type of carnivore who does not suffer pangs of guilt while chowing down on our finned, feathered, and furry friends, stop on by the Fin Inn. This family-owned establishment specializes in fish dinners that you enjoy while your meal's still-living brethren glare at you from their boothside aquariums.

The Fin Inn opened in 1981, and each and every stone in the place was laid by the man who came up with the idea, James Seib. The restaurant has four 2,000-gallon tanks filled with Mississippi River species—both fish and turtles—giving you the impression you're diving in the Big Muddy (though they're much cleaner than the real thing).

1000 W. Main St., Grafton, IL 62037

Phone: (618) 786-2030

Hours: Summer, daily 11 AM–9 PM; winter, daily 11 AM–8 PM

Cost: Meals, $6–$13

Website: www.fininn.com

Directions: Two blocks east of Springfield St.

Livingston
Pink Elephant Antique Mall

As roadside attention-getters go, it's hard to miss a giant pink elephant. Harder still a bright green UFO or a two-story, half-nekkid guy in board shorts. But put them all together, add a gigantic cone-shaped ice cream stand and a Harley-Davidson "Muffler Man" (see page 152), and you have Livingston's Pink Elephant Antique Mall.

The Pink Elephant is housed in the town's old high school, and it has enough old junk on three levels to keep you browsing for hours, if that's your thing. But if it's weird stuff you're after, all the statues are outside and free to view.

908 Veterans Memorial Dr., Livingston, IL 92074

Phone: (618) 637-2366

Hours: Always visible; store, daily 9:30 AM–5 PM

Cost: Free

Directions: On the south end of town along the west-side frontage road.

It's hard to miss.

Makanda
Boomer's Grave

Boomer was a faithful hound dog, but not very bright. This three-legged pooch was the trusted pet of a local train engineer back in the 1850s. Boomer loved to race locomotives, and oftentimes he won. That says either a lot for Boomer or not much for early locomotives.

Then, on September 2, 1859, Boomer ran barking alongside his master's train, trying to warn him to put out a hotbox fire. The dog was so intent on saving the engine that he did not see an upcoming bridge abutment. He ran headlong into the iron bridge and was killed instantly.

Boomer's body was laid to rest beside the railroad tracks by the man he saved. Today, the monument sits next to a basketball court, 300 feet from the deadly abutment. In the dog's honor, a dormitory at nearby Southern Illinois University was named Boomer Hall.

Railroad Depot, Makanda Rd., Makanda, IL 62958
No phone
Hours: Always visible
Cost: Free
Directions: Just east of the railroad tracks, south of the depot.

Dave's Secret Garden in the Valley of the Arts

Makanda is one of those towns where it looks as if time stopped around 1967. A strip of storefronts along an old boardwalk sells beads, incense, pottery, art, T-shirts, and ice cream—one block long, one side of the street, that's the entire business district. Nobody's in any hurry, and neither should you be.

All this is not to say that nothing interesting ever happens in Makanda. Check out the last door on the right, which opens into the RainMaker Art studio of copper and bronze artist Dave Dardis. Dardis isn't just a metalsmith; he's a stonemason and landscaper who has created an elaborate environment behind the boardwalk shops—Dave's Secret Garden in the Valley of the Arts. Stone towers, reflecting pools (with a mini mermaid!), bridges, and pathways ramble up the hill covered in statuary, flowers, and reclaimed objects. Visitors are invited to enjoy the garden, set a spell, and soak up some of the Makanda hippie vibe. The secret's out.

RainMaker Art, Makanda Rd., Makanda, IL 62958
Phone: (618) 457-6282
Hours: Always visible
Cost: Free
Website: www.davedardis.com
Directions: Behind the only shops in town.

Martinsville
Moonshine Burgers

The first time you drive out to Moonshine, population 2, on the some-times-paved-but-more-often-not single-lane roads of southeast Illinois, you'll wonder, Are the burgers really that good? Then you'll step into the century-old general store, place your order, receive a burger almost imme-diately, and look for a seat in one of the two old pews lining either side of the room. Then you'll bite into your greasy quarry and you'll have your answer: Ohhhh, yeahhhhhh!

Who knows the secret of the Moonshine Store's success, and why hun-dreds and sometimes thousands of people make the trek every day? Helen and Roy Tuttle know, that's who! The couple—the only residents in town—bought the store in 1982, and its reputation has grown ever since. Roy flips the patties and Helen handles the rest, and she runs a tight ship. GRILL CLOSED SHARPLY AT 12:30 PM proclaims a sign, and you should plan your visit with this in mind.

The Tuttles show no sign of slowing, and they are always out to break their one-day record—currently 2,068 burgers served on April 9, 2011, during the Terry Hammond Memorial Moonshine Lunch Run, a Moon-shine burger and motorcycle lover's road rally.

Moonshine Store, 6017 E. 300th Rd., Martinsville, IL 62442
Phone: (618) 569-9200
Hours: Monday–Saturday, 6 AM–1 PM
Cost: $3.50 for a burger, $3.75 for a cheeseburger
Website: www.themoonshinestore.com
Directions: Twelve miles south of Martinsville; get a detailed map.

McLEANSBORO

➡ A headless horseman rides along Lakey's Creek in McLeansboro. It is the ghost of Mr. Lakey, a settler who was beheaded by bandits in the 1840s.

Metropolis
Americana Hollywood Museum

Visiting the Americana Hollywood Museum is like stepping into an episode of *Hoarders*, except that everything you see is clean and in some sort of kooky order. "Keep to the right," the ticket taker says, and you'd best heed the advice or you may never find your way back out. Room after room is crammed rug to rafters with action figures, collector plates, Happy Meal toys, record albums, licensed trinkets—basically anything you could plaster the image of a show business legend on and sell through the back of a magazine.

The rooms run one into the next, each dedicated to a different star or theme—the Robot Room, the Elvis Room, the Horror Room, the James Dean Room, the Houdini Room, the Hendrix Room, the Tarzan Room—on and on and on. If you were hoping to see movie props, this isn't the place, though for some reason they do have a large collection of costumes once worn by Pamela Anderson, a few pulled over big-busted mannequins.

If you ever do return to the sunlight, have your picture taken on one of the "movie sets" on the patio out front. This being Metropolis, they've got several Superman-inspired sets, including a large contraption with liquid kryptonite and the largest glowing green boulder you'll ever find. Hey—whose side are they on!?

Americana Hollywood Museum, Ferry and Third Sts., Metropolis, IL 62960

Phone: (618) 524-5518

Hours: Daily 9 AM–5 PM

Cost: Adults $5, kids (5 and under) free

Website: http://store.supermansuperstore.com/americana-hollywood.html

Directions: Two blocks southeast of the town square.

Superman's Hometown

Any true Superfan knows Superman hailed from Smallville, not Metropolis, but the Metropolis Chamber of Commerce didn't let that detail get in its way. After all, they are the only town named Metropolis in the nation (established 1839), at least according to the US Postal Service. There are plenty of Smallvilles.

During the 1970s, town leaders transformed this sleepy river burg into the Man of Steel's hometown. Today, Superman's image is on street signs

The Man of Steel (of bronze).

(one is Lois Lane), stop signs, and telephone booths surrounding the town square. And the local paper? The *Metropolis Planet*!

The town's first Superman statue, made of fiberglass, was a bit misshapen, and somebody shot its chest with a speeding bullet. A new bronze (not steel?) Superman was commissioned in 1992 and erected next to the courthouse a year later. A storefront Super Museum opened just off the

square, the impressive collection of Jim Hambrick; it houses one of George Reeves's original TV costumes, a kryptonite crystal from the 1978 movie, and 20,000 other pieces of Super Junk.

Every June the town throws a Superman Celebration, during which actors who have appeared in the TV show or movies sign autographs for the non-Super mortals. One crowd favorite, Noel Neill, who portrayed Lois Lane on the TV series, was honored with her own statue in 2010.

Superman Statue, 1 Superman Square, Metropolis, IL 62960

Phone: (877) 424-5025

Hours: Always visible

Cost: Free

Website: www.metropolistourism.com, www.metropolisplanet.com

Directions: On the north side of the town square at Market St.

Lois Lane/Noel Neill Statue, Market and W. Eighth Sts., Metropolis, IL 62960

No phone

Hours: Always visible

Cost: Free

Directions: Three blocks north of the Superman statue.

Super Museum, 517 Market St., Metropolis, IL 62960

Phone: (618) 524-5518

Hours: Daily 9 AM–5 PM

Cost: Adults $5, kids (5 and under) free

Website: www.supermuseum.com

Directions: Just north of the town square.

Mt. Olive
Mother Jones's Grave

Her name was Mary Harris, but most called her Mother Jones, the "most dangerous woman in America." Mother Jones was a labor organizer who got her start in Chicago after the Great Fire of 1871. She was already in her 40s, but she had 60 good years ahead of her. In 1898, Mother Jones spoke for the rights of miners who were battling with coal companies in Virden, Illinois. Before the strike ended, 13 were dead.

Four of those murdered were buried in the Union Miners Cemetery in Mt. Olive. After Mother Jones died at the age of 100 on November 30,

1930, she was laid to rest here, too. This was her wish: "I hope it will be my consolation when I pass away to feel I sleep under the clay with those brave boys." A bronze portrait of Mother Jones adorns a 22-foot-high monument, erected in 1936, that looks far from proletarian.

Union Miners Cemetery, North Lake Ave., Mt. Olive, IL 62069

No phone

Hours: Daily 9 AM–5 PM

Cost: Free

Website: www.illinoislaborhistory.org/union-miners-cemetary.html

Directions: Two miles north of town on old Rte. 66 (Lake Ave.).

Mt. Vernon
Mini Washington Monument

If you're driving southbound on I-57/64 through Mt. Vernon, you'll no doubt spot the Washington Monument. It's even illuminated at night for you drive-till-you-droppers.

What? You say the actual monument it's based on isn't even at the president's Virginia estate? So why is it in Mt. Vernon? Aren't you the stickler! If you want to get picky, smarty-pants, this Illinois replica is also made of painted plywood rather than marble and is only 40 feet tall instead of 555 feet.

But it all looks the same at 75 mph, my friend.

600 Potomac Blvd., Mt. Vernon, IL 62864

No phone

Hours: Always visible

Cost: Free

Directions: Broadway St. (Rte. 15) westbound from I-57/64, then north two blocks on Potomac Blvd.

Olney
White Squirrel Town

Strange as it sounds, most of the gray squirrels in this small town are albinos . . . and the locals want to keep it that way! The first white squirrels were brought to town in 1902 by William Stroup and/or George Ridgely (there's a dispute), and there was a population explosion. Olney soon dubbed itself "Home of the White Squirrels." Brown squirrels were rounded up and

transported to other communities in an ongoing effort to boost Olney's albino population.

In some ways, these rodents rule over the folks of Olney, rather than the other way around. By law, white squirrels have the right-of-way on all local roads. If you run over one, it'll cost you $25, and if you have a cat, you must keep it on a leash when outdoors. The police department's patches have a white silhouette on them. Say . . . who's in charge here?

The number of white squirrels has diminished in recent years. Some blame inbreeding. Others blame human encroachment and interaction. If you're out squirrel watching, look closely; if the critter you spot doesn't move, it's probably one of the many white squirrel lawn ornaments used to replace the vanishing breed.

City Park, 584 N. West St. (Rte. 130), Olney, IL 62450

Phone: (618) 392-2241

Hours: Daily 8 AM–10 PM

Cost: Free

Website: www.ci.olney.il.us/Visitors/WhiteSquirrel.htm

Directions: All over town, but mainly in City Park.

Salem
Pollard's Collection

When you get to talking with Richard Pollard—and you most definitely should—you get the impression that his used-car business is just a hobby, whereas his real occupation is to create corny visual puns from old junk and the cars he couldn't sell. In other words, he's a used-car salesman whose company you'll actually enjoy. You have to go into Pollard's backyard to see it, but you're more than welcome to explore.

He's got a tree filled with shoes and another decorated with credit cards. What's that Jet Ski doing up in the branches? FLOOD OF 93, the sign explains. A small airplane has crashed nose down in a clearing, though it barely looks dented. Luckily it just missed Pollard's riding lawnmower–toilet–bathtub and his giant Volkswagen ladybug. How did a tree grow through the hood of that '57 Chevy? Pollard's not telling, but he does seem to be laughing under his breath. On and on it goes, back past a chrome-filled garden—a "bumper crop"—and off into the woods. Pollard may be in his golden years, but he's just getting started.

The Volkswagen ladybug.

Pollard Motor Sales, 1860 N. Broadway Ave., Salem, IL 62881

Phone: (618) 548-2388

Hours: Daily 9 AM–5 PM

Cost: Free

Directions: On Rte. 37 (Broadway Ave.) north of Hardacre Rd.

Staunton
Henry's Ra66it Ranch

Rich and Linda Henry love rabbits, and it shows. In 1995 they converted an old gas station on old Route 66 into Henry's Ra66it Ranch, a bunny hutch–gift shop–tourist information center, and hung out a sign announcing HARE IT IS.

The Caddy-Rabby Ranch.

Yes, the puns multiply like, well, you know what here on the ranch. In 2007 the Henrys built an homage to another Route 66 attraction, Amarillo's *Cadillac Ranch*, only they used eight Volkswagen Rabbits and titled it the *Caddy-Rabby Ranch*. And when any of the dozen bunnies they own go to that great carrot patch in the sky, they're given a proper burial along the Tale of Ears out back. If the hare on the back of your neck isn't already on end, feel free to pose for a photo atop Bernie, the Henrys' giant saddled fiberglass rabbit.

1107 Historic Route 66, Staunton, IL 62088

Phone: (618) 635-5655

Hours: Monday–Saturday 9 AM–4 PM

Cost: Free

Website: www.henrysroute66.com

Directions: One block west of Bentrup Rd. at Henry St.

TAMAROA

→ A UFO hovering over Tamaroa on November 14, 1957, caused power outages throughout the area.

Vandalia
Coin-Operated Fire-Breathing Dragon

Not every True Value hardware store has its own dragon. In fact, none of them do except Walt Barenfanger's store in Vandalia. Berenfanger also owns the ESC Construction Company, and back in 1999 business was slow, so he asked his welder, Paul Schaub, if he could build a roadside monster to attract customers. Forty feet long. With glowing red eyes! And he wanted it to spit fire!

Schaub did just that, using four tons of recycled metal wrapped around a large tank of propane. Today you can purchase a one-dollar token at the True Value (or the adjacent LoMac's Liquor Store) that will make the silver, winged creature belch a hefty flame. Just know it doesn't last long, so have your camera ready. If you want to scare truckers passing by on I-70, fire it up at night.

2024 Progress West Dr., Vandalia, IL 62471
Phone: (618) 283-9700
Hours: Always visible
Cost: Free; flames, $1
Website: www.kaskaskiadragon.com
Directions: Rte. 51 exit south from I-70, then four blocks west on the frontage road (Veterans Ave.).

Drop in a dollar and stand back.

Yale

Mug Tree

Have you grown tired of your old coffee mug? Does that old carafe not fit into the cup holder of your new car? Sure, you could stop by the Dollar Store and pick up a new one, but why not drive out to the middle of nowhere and save a buck?

Established in 2009, the Mug Tree has about a hundred mugs hanging on its fat trunk. As trees go, it's more of a very tall stump—no branches or leaves will shade your visit—though a small shed has been built on top. Nobody knows why. Bring an old mug and swap it for a better model. And be sure to sign the guestbook; it's in a mailbox nailed to the trunk.

Route 49, Yale, IL 62481

No phone

Hours: Always visible

Cost: Free, or 1 mug

Directions: One mile south of town.

We're as confused as you are.

Mt. Olive
Mother Jones's Grave

Grafton
Fin Inn

Elsah
Mistake House

Staunton
Henry's Ra66it Ranch

Livingston
Pink Elephant Antique Store

Alton
Deaf Bill, the Mummy
Elijah Lovejoy, Martyr for Abolition
The Piasa Bird
World's Tallest (Dead) Man

Granite City
Holt Shoe Shop

Collinsville
Cahokia Mounds
World's Largest Catsup Bottle

Belleville
National Shrine of
Our Lady of the Snows

ILLINOIS

Chester
Popeye Town

Carbondale
Boo Rochman Memorial Park
Bucky's Dome

Makanda
Boomer's Grave
Dave's Secret Garden in the Valley
of the Arts

Alto Pass
Bald Knob Cross
Root Beer Saloon

Anna
King Netpu
Grave

MISSOURI

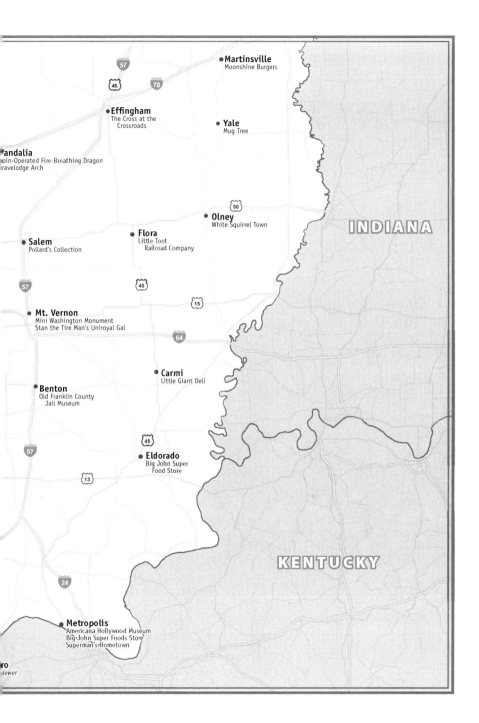

Martinsville
Moonshine Burgers

Effingham
The Cross at the
Crossroads

Yale
Mug Tree

Vandalia
Coin-Operated Fire-Breathing Dragon
Travelodge Arch

Olney
White Squirrel Town

Flora
Little Toot
Railroad Company

Salem
Pollard's Collection

Mt. Vernon
Mini Washington Monument
Stan the Tire Man's Uniroyal Gal

Carmi
Little Giant Deli

Benton
Old Franklin County
Jail Museum

Eldorado
Big John Super
Food Store

Metropolis
Americana Hollywood Museum
Big John Super Foods Store
Superman's Hometown

Cairo
Hewer

INDIANA

KENTUCKY

6

THEME TOURS

Oddball spots must be experienced to be appreciated—armchair travel is no way to spend your vacation. This book is not intended to be a passive experience, so get up, gas up, and go.

If you plan your trip efficiently, you can visit an oddball spot every half hour or so, making it easy to visit a dozen sites in a single day. Questions of "Are we there yet?" will be replaced by more engaging dialogue, such as "What the hell is that?" and "Do you think that person is crazy?" Imagine the time you'll have!

And if you're creative, you can map your trip around a theme. That's what this chapter is all about: theme tours. The first, the Dead Circus Sideshow Tour, is a statewide trek touching the final resting places of Illinois's strangest deceased citizens. The second, the Mob Mania Tour, is a listing of Chicago-area gangster death sites. Pick your favorite crimes, grab a metro-area map, and away you go. Both are perfect for a Sunday drive!

The Dead Circus Sideshow Tour

According to the Illinois Bureau of Tourism, during any weekend in this state you're "A Million Miles from Monday," but oddly enough, you're barely 50 miles from the closest grave of a dead circus-sideshow performer or somebody who might have been one. The Fat Man, the Tall Man, the Devil Baby, the Deli-Sliced Duo—they're all here!

Hard to believe? Not really. Illinois has a long sideshow history. Chicago's first public performance was a freak show; in 1834, a "Mr. Bowers" ate burning sealing wax and dropped molten lead on his tongue to the delight of the early settlers. He followed it with a ventriloquist act. Hucksters begged Mrs. O'Leary to take part in a touring sideshow after her cow burned down the city, but she turned them all down, dozens of them.

The Columbian Exposition had the Streets of Cairo, where men charmed snakes and Little Egypt danced the hootchie kootchie, and the 1933 Century of Progress had a 72-resident Midget Village.

So why shouldn't you join in the fun just because these performers are all dead? Make a weekend of it: the Dead Circus Sideshow Tour! Here's how:

Start your journey downstate in Alton, home of . . .

The World's Tallest (Dead) Man

Harold and Addie Wadlow knew they had a special child. When young Robert entered kindergarten in 1923, he was 5 feet 6.5 inches tall and wore the clothes of a 17-year-old. By the fifth grade he was 6 feet 5 inches, and Harold decided, at long last, to bring his son in for his first checkup. A doctor at Barnes Hospital in St. Louis diagnosed the problem: Robert had an overactive pituitary gland, and there was no known way to correct the problem, at least not at the time.

Wadlow continued to grow. At age 13, he was declared the World's Tallest Boy Scout at 7 feet 4 inches, and by his 1936 high school graduation he had reached 8 feet 3.5 inches. He initially resisted the temptation to become a full-time sideshow attraction and enrolled at Shurtleff College, but he withdrew after one year. He then signed up for a six-week stint with Ringling Brothers Circus; his "act" consisted of walking out and standing in the center ring for a few minutes. He also made a good-will tour for the International Shoe Company, which provided him with free shoes, size 37 ½ AA.

People everywhere loved him. An Indian tribe in Minnesota "adopted" Wadlow and named him Tall Pine. Folks around Alton dubbed him the "Gentle Giant" for his quiet, humble demeanor. But sometimes his patience was challenged, for children were known to kick him in the shins to see if he was standing on stilts.

Wadlow never stopped growing, and it led to his demise. While making an appearance at the Lumberman's Festival in Manistee, Michigan, a misadjusted leg brace rubbed his ankle, causing a blister that became infected. On July 15, 1940, at the age of 22, Wadlow died from a fever brought on by that injury. At the time he was 8 feet 11.1 inches tall and weighed 491 pounds—a world record!

The 6-foot-3-inch author with the Gentle Giant.

Thousands of Alton residents turned out for Wadlow's funeral. His 10-foot casket took twelve pallbearers to carry to the Upper Alton Cemetery (2090 Oakwood Ave.). Wadlow was sealed in a sarcophagus and

cement was poured over it so that people would be unable to steal his body. An honor guard from the Order of DeMolay stood over the grave until the cement hardened.

Wadlow has not been forgotten in Alton. Quite the contrary; this town is wacko for Wadlow. In his honor, citizens erected a life-sized bronze statue in a small park across from their history museum, and they recently added a Wadlow-sized bronze La-Z-Boy. Inside the museum, you can purchase 18.5-inch construction-paper footprints that have Robert's measurements printed on them, and you can see a pair of his enormous shoes.

Alton Museum of History and Art, Loomis Hall, 2809 College Ave., Alton, IL 62002

Phone: (618) 462-2763

Hours: Statue, always visible; museum, Wednesday–Saturday 10 AM–4 PM

Cost: Adults $3, kids (4–12) $1

Website: www.altonmuseum.com/html/robert_wadlow.html, www.altonweb.com/history/wadlow

Directions: On Route 140 (College Ave.); Wadlow's statue is across the street.

BIG SHOES EVERYWHERE

If you'd like to see a pair of Wadlow's giant shoes and can't make it to Alton, there are a few others on display around Illinois. One pair is at the **Square Deal Shoe Store** (1516 Miner St., (847) 824-5262) in Des Plaines. Another can be seen at— where else?—**Feet First** in North Chicago (see page 166). The **Holt Shoe Shop** (2721 Madison Ave., (618) 876-0120) in Granite City has a pair, too.

Alton was long home to another sideshow attraction of sorts.

Deaf Bill, the Mummy

Around the turn of the last century, William Lee was a well-known figure in these parts. Part river preacher, part brawler, and full-time drunk, he was known to walk into services, take the podium, and give his own slurred sermons. If anyone complained, he probably never heard it; Lee's

nickname was Deaf Bill because, well, he was nearly deaf. When all the hard livin' started to catch up with him, he was admitted to the Madison County Poor Farm (333 S. Main St.) in Edwardsville, where he died on November 13, 1915. Because nobody knew his next of kin, his body was embalmed using high-powered chemicals to keep him around for a while. And the body did go unclaimed . . . for almost 80 years.

Now stuck with him, the funeral home couldn't just leave Deaf Bill lying around, so they propped him up in a closet, clad in only a loincloth and a bushy mustache. Visitors were allowed to take a peek at him, and he became a bit of an Alton legend. But that's where the exploitation ended—the owners reportedly turned down a $2,500 offer to take Deaf Bill on tour with a sideshow.

In 1996 the Burke Funeral Home merged with Fine and Quinn Funeral Home and the new director, Brian Fine, decided it was time for Deaf Bill to get a proper burial. Researchers found a grave they believed held Lee's younger brother in the St. Francis of Assisi Cemetery in Portage des Sioux, Missouri, just across the Mississippi River. On June 24, 1996, Lee was laid to rest beside him in a donated tux.

Burke-Fine Funeral Home, 727 Langdon St., Alton, IL 62002
Phone: (618) 462-9296
Hours: Always visible
Cost: Free
Website: www.finefunerals.com/Home.html
Directions: Two blocks west of Liberty St. at Seventh St.

St. Francis of Assisi Cemetery, Fourth and Drummond Sts., Portage des Sioux, MO 63373
No phone
Hours: Always visible
Cost: Free
Directions: North of Portage Rd. on the west end of town.

From Alton, head northeast to Decatur, a watering hole for . . .

Displaced Circus Animals

There's no guarantee the free-roaming circus animals spotted in and around Decatur are dead, but considering the bitter winters, it's a safe bet. Still, keep your car windows rolled up and your picnic basket in the trunk—this town is a genuine Lion Country Safari!

In July 1917, while Thomas Gulliet picked flowers along the Sangamon River, he was mauled by an adult African lion. Four people riding in a car were jumped by the same cat later in the month. More than 300 Decaturites formed a posse and scoured the countryside, but Nellie the Lion (as named by the press) was never captured. How did she get to Decatur in the first place? Nobody knew.

Another cat, a panther, stuck around a little longer. It was first spotted, and fired upon, on October 25, 1955. It returned a decade later on June 25, 1965, to chase a woman's car. Several days later it stole the sack lunches of three children picnicking in Lincoln Park (Lincoln Park Dr. and Cree St.). In June 1967, the cat was blamed for killing 20 local sheep. It was also spotted tearing up an electric fence near the Macon Seed Company.

And how about crocodiles? Three have been nabbed swimming in Lake Decatur, one each in 1937, 1966, and 1971. A fourth found its way into town and was captured at 895 West Eldorado Street in 1967. If you want to see these critters, keep your eyes peeled for residents sporting fancy handbags and boots.

Finally, a kangaroo was sighted by Rosemary Hopwood on July 14, 1975. It was hopping down Route 128. Kangaroos are less dangerous than large felines and crocodiles, but you should never challenge them to a boxing match.

So let this be a warning to those traveling with small pets: pass up Decatur if you plan to walk little Fifi.

Decatur Area Convention and Visitors Bureau, 202 E. North St., Decatur, IL 62523

Phone: (800) 331-4479

Hours: Always possible

Cost: Free

Website: www.decaturcvb.com

Directions: All over town.

Next stop? Chicago. The Hog Butcher Capital of the World put its cleavers into service to create one of the city's weirdest attractions . . .

The Deli-Sliced Duo

They're gruesome, gray, and gag inspiring: the Deli-Sliced Duo or, as I prefer to call them, Mr. and Ms. Carver, star attractions at the Museum

of Science and Industry. As disturbing as it sounds, somebody once ran two cadavers through a deli slicer set on "extra thick," all in the name of science. Who says biology is dull?

The male was cut into inch-thick slabs horizontally, while the female was sliced vertically from head to toe in profile. The cross sections are attractively presented between panes of glass so they can be viewed from either side, a complete set of anatomically correct stained glass windows.

Several of the displays could benefit from a formaldehyde fill-up as the level of the suspending liquid has dropped, but that's a minor complaint. Whatever the Carvers' condition, it's important to appreciate the Museum of Science and Industry's efforts to expose you to what you may never have wanted to see.

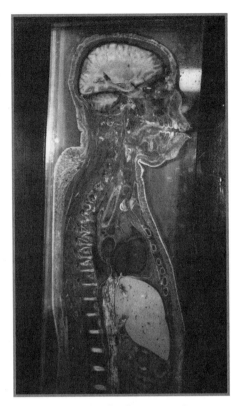

Never play with a food processor!
Photo by author, courtesy the Museum of Science and Industry, Chicago

Museum of Science and Industry, 5700 S. Lake Shore Dr., Chicago, IL 60637
Phone: (773) 684-1414
Hours: June–August, daily 9:30 AM–5:30 PM; September–May, daily 9:30 AM–4 PM
Cost: Adults $15, seniors (65+) $14, kids (3–11) $10; check website for free days
Website: www.msichicago.org
Directions: At the north end of Jackson Park, off Lake Shore Dr. at 57th St. The couple is displayed in the Green Stairwell.

Sometimes sideshows aren't found at the circus but at the ballpark. Consider the short career of Eddie Gaedel, who is buried in Evergreen Park:

Eddie Gaedel, Number ⅛

On August 19, 1951, during the between-games break of a St. Louis Browns–Detroit Tigers doubleheader, a giant cake was pulled onto the infield to honor the 50th anniversary of the American League. To almost everyone's surprise, a three-foot-seven-inch man popped out—Eddie Gaedel—and he was wearing a Browns uniform, number ⅛.

It was the kind of stunt fans had come to expect from owner Bill Veeck, but what they didn't know was that Gaedel had signed onto the team a few days earlier. During the first inning of the second game, Gaedel was sent in as a pinch hitter, and the crowd went crazy. So did the umpire, but Browns manager Zack Taylor had Gaedel's contract ready for inspection. Everything was in order, and the game resumed.

Eddie Gaedel had been instructed not to swing, as there was no way pitcher Bob Cain could throw a strike through his inch-and-a-half strike zone; the Tigers would have to walk him. Cain (who was laughing) attempted to on the first two pitches, but threw high. He didn't even try on the next two pitches; Gaedel started off down the first base line, stopping twice to bow to the fans. He was replaced by a pinch runner at first, and his baseball career was over with an on-base percentage of 1.000. Not bad!

The president of the American League was not as amused as, well, everybody else in the universe, and he ordered Gaedel's career stats to be permanently scrubbed from the league's official record books. A year later they were restored, and today Gaedel's autograph is worth more to collectors than Babe Ruth's.

St. Mary Cemetery, 87th St. and Hamlin Ave., Evergreen Park, IL 60652
Phone: (708) 422-8720
Hours: Daily 9 AM–5 PM
Cost: Free
Directions: East of Pulaski Rd. on 87th St.

Another Chicago oddity who was once a sideshow all by himself but has since been overshadowed by Nobel Peace Prize enthusiasts and other do-gooders is . . .

The Devil Baby

Back in 1913, a pious Italian girl married an atheist who cursed the portrait of Jesus she had hung on their wall. "I'd rather have the Devil live here than have that picture hang on our wall!" he screamed, or something similar.

He's baaaaaaack!

He got his wish. When the baby was born it had cloven feet, scales, and horns and could talk and smoke cigars. Not knowing what to do, the woman brought the baby to Hull House and turned it over to Jane Addams, the living saint of the West Side downtrodden.

Jane cared for the Devil Baby as if it were her own . . . that is, if she would have locked her own child up in the attic for the rest of its natural life! Then word got around Chicago that the Devil Baby could be viewed for 25 cents. A quarter was a lot of money at the time but well worth it. Addams described in her Hull House memoirs how she turned away dozens of visitors each day. "There's no Devil Baby here," she'd tell the disappointed Satan seekers.

Likely story. Addams's denials weren't enough to counteract numerous sightings of an adult Devil seen driving around Chicago in a red convertible for years to come, nor the eerie face spotted peering out of Hull House's attic windows at night. Hollywood even used the Hull House Devil Baby as the inspiration for *Rosemary's Baby*.

The staff at the Hull House Museum sometimes bristle when asked about the Devil Baby. They try to focus your attention on Addams's other accomplishments, such as her 1931 Nobel Peace Prize for founding the

Women's International League for Peace and Freedom, her pivotal role in the creation of the NAACP, or her receiving the first female honorary doctorate from Yale. Blah, blah, blah. Just tell us where Satan's Child is, thank you very much!

Jane Addams Hull House, 800 S. Halsted St., Chicago, IL 60607
Phone: (312) 413-5353
Hours: Tuesday–Friday 10 AM–4 PM, Sunday noon–4 PM
Cost: Suggested $5 donation
Website: www.uic.edu/jaddams/hull/hull_house.html
Directions: One block south of the Eisenhower Expy. on the east side of the UIC campus.

Who better to haul around a bunch of dead sideshow performers than a bunch of dead circus roadies? You'll find them in Forest Park at . . .

Showman's Rest

A train carrying the Hagenback-Wallace traveling circus was rammed by an empty troop train near Ivanhoe, Indiana, on June 22, 1918. Many carnies and performers perished in the resulting blaze, and bodies were difficult to identify. Rather than ship all 86 victims back to their hometowns (which weren't often known), the owners buried 56 in a large plot called Showman's Rest in Forest Park. The special section had been set aside in 1913 by Buffalo Bill Cody and the Showmen's League of America.

Granite elephants guard the dead here, their trunks lowered as a sign of respect. Many of the gravestones indicate only the victims' professions or nicknames, such as "4-Horse Driver" and "Baldy." Also buried here was Edward Kann, the Fat Man, who took up two plots. Today the section contains other performers who did not die in the crash but still gave their lives to the circus.

Legend has it that you can hear the painful cry of ghost elephants here at night, but none were buried at Woodlawn, nor were any killed in the Ivanhoe wreck. More likely, the trumpeting pachyderms are wafting over from the nearby Brookfield Zoo.

Woodlawn Cemetery, 7600 W. Cermak Rd., Forest Park, IL 60130
Phone: (708) 442-8500
Hours: Daily 9 AM–5 PM
Cost: Free
Website: www.woodlawncemeteryofchicago.com
Directions: To the west of the main entrance off Cermak Rd., two blocks west of Harlem Ave.

If you had your heart set on a dead elephant, head west out of the Windy City to Oquawka, where you can say . . .

Good-bye, Norma Jean

. . . Norma Jean the Elephant, that is. This poor creature, star of the Clark and Walters Circus, was chained to the tallest tree on the block on the night of July 17, 1972. Lightning struck, and she was killed instantly.

Good-bye, Norma Jean.

Norma Jean's handler, Larry "Possum Red" Harsh, unable to move her 6,500-pound carcass, buried her where she dropped. Two years later, a memorial wall topped with a small bronze elephant was built to mark her final resting place.

Norma Jean Monument, Fifth St. and Mercer St., Oquawka, IL 61469

No phone

Hours: Always visible

Cost: Free

Website: www.oquawka.info/sightseeing.html

Directions: On Fifth St. between Mercer and Clay Sts.

. . . or you can always head south to Taylorville, where you can say . . .

Farewell Fatso

Yes, Fatso had a name—Kay—but in our body-conscious world she was given a cruel nickname. That and far too much popcorn and cotton candy. Kay was the star attraction of the Carson and Barnes Circus and she was certainly big, but then again most elephants are. That didn't prevent her from living to the age of 58.

But when the circus was visiting Taylorville on October 21, 1994, she collapsed backstage while waiting to take her spot in the center ring. Kidney failure, the vet said, followed by, "You better get her buried somewhere soon." Her body was loaded on a flatbed truck and taken to the farm of Jerry Breuel. There she was interred in a 20-foot-deep hole, and a headstone was placed over her grave. Plans for a small park around the marker are in the works.

N. 1250 East Rd., Taylorville, IL 62568

Hours: Always visible

Cost: Free

Directions: One mile south of town on Shumway St. (N. 1250 East Rd.), turn right onto the first gravel road after passing over the bridge.

A man weighing not quite as much received slightly better funeral arrangements when he was planted in an oversized coffin south of Mt. Sterling.

The World's Fattest (Dead) Man

Robert Earl Hughes was born in Lewis County, Missouri, on June 4, 1926, weighing in at nine pounds. Before he turned a year old, his family moved to Fishhook, Illinois, where he contracted a case of whooping cough that apparently damaged his pituitary gland. On his sixth birthday he tipped the scales at 203 pounds. By his early 30s he had maxed out at 1,069 pounds, earning the title of the World's Fattest Man. His upper arms were 40 inches in circumference, his chest was 122 inches, and his waist 124 inches.

Double-wide grave.

Hughes used his weight to earn money at personal appearances, but his girth became a liability when he contracted the measles and could not fit through the doors of Indiana's Bremen Hospital. On July 10, 1958, he passed away in his travel van in the hospital parking lot.

His 1,041-pound body was returned to the family plot in Brown County. The burial became its own sideshow when the piano-crate-sized coffin was opened for everyone to get one last gawking look. A few enterprising folk sold souvenir photos. A crane lowered Hughes to his final resting place. His gravestone gives a scant record of the local boy who made it big . . . really, really big. Another monument was erected a few years back in the community of Fishhook, where his family sharecropped.

Benville Cemetery, County Road 6, Mt. Sterling, IL 62353

No phone

Hours: Dawn to dusk

Cost: Free

Directions: At the first fork in the road heading east out of Siloam Springs State Park.

Hughes Monument, Perry–Fishhook Rd., Fishhook, IL 62353

No phone

Hours: Always visible

Cost: Free

Directions: At the only intersection in town.

The Mob Mania Tour

Ask anyone, anywhere, to play a game of word association, and throw out the name Chicago. You'll invariably get a response like "Gangsters!" or "Bang! Bang!" The response is the same, from Venetian gondoliers to Himalayan sherpas. Why else would Europeans propose that EuroDisney's Main Street be fashioned after 1920s Chicago, complete with machine gun–toting mobsters? (Disney's corporate offices killed the idea faster than Capone rubbed out a rat.)

It's not as if Chicago didn't earn its reputation. During the early part of the 20th century there were more than a thousand gangland hits in Chicago, but only four were successfully prosecuted. One intersection in the "Little Hell" neighborhood, Deadman's Corner at Oak Street and Cleveland Avenue, saw 42 unsolved murders between 1910 and 1911. Face it: Chicago and the Mob have received a tommy gun wedding, and nothing the city does will change that.

City Hall has been almost rabid in its anti-Mob tourist policy. For years, mayor Richard J. Daley blocked the shooting of movies that put Chicago in a bad light with respect to gangsters. Capone's Chicago, a multimedia show narrated by a robotic Scarface, went out of business after being ignored by the city's tourism establishment. And Untouchable Tours gets no mention in city-funded promotional material, though the Hard Rock Cafe gets a spot. Is that fair?

It takes a dedicated traveler to find the crime sites that made Chicago world famous. Most buildings associated with Capone have met the wrecking ball. You won't find memorial plaques. You won't see a machine gun on the city seal. When it comes to the Mob, you're on your own.

DEEP THOUGHTS FROM AL CAPONE

➡ "You can get much farther with a smile, a kind word, and a gun than you can with a smile and a kind word."

➡ "I've given the public what the public wants. I never had to send out high-pressure salesmen. I could never meet the demand."

➡ "They blamed everything but the Chicago Fire on me."

Big Jim Hits the Floor

Before there was Al Capone, there was "Big Jim" Colosimo. Big Jim was the Chicago connection for "Little John" Torrio, a powerful New York mobster (and Colosimo's nephew). Colosimo ran the operations out of his South Side drinking establishment, Colosimo's Restaurant. Mob ties aside, it was a wonderful place: a converted warehouse with green velvet wallpaper, clouds and angels flying high overhead, and a hydraulic stage to raise the dancers up where you could see them. But it all went bye-bye when Big Jim hit the floor.

Colosimo was executed on May 11, 1920, in a hit ordered by Torrio. Little John felt Big Jim was spending too little time on the family business and too much time with his new bride, 19-year-old nightclub singer Dale Winter. It probably didn't help that Big Jim had tossed aside his first wife, cathouse madam Victoria Moresco, who happened to be Torrio's cousin. The hit took place at Colosimo's Restaurant; Torrio told Big Jim to wait for a booze shipment, and Frankie Yale (reportedly, though some think it was Al Capone) showed up instead. Big Jim was shot twice, once behind the right ear.

Big Jim was denied a religious burial by the Catholic Church because of his recent divorce, not because he was a murderer, pimp, extortionist, and thief.

Colosimo's Restaurant, 2126 S. Wabash Ave., Chicago, IL 60616
No phone
Hours: Destroyed
Cost: Free
Directions: One block east of State St. and one block north of Cermak Rd.

Al Capone's Home and Businesses

With Big Jim out of the way, leadership of the Chicago Outfit was wide open. Torrio moved Capone to Chicago, where Al was soon "managing" the Four Deuces, a brothel just a few doors down from Colosimo's Restaurant. Capone was in charge of beating up and torturing snitches in the basement, known as the Vault. Eventually Torrio would give Capone a controlling share in the Four Deuces.

Four Deuces Brothel, 2222 S. Wabash Ave., Chicago, IL 60616
No phone
Hours: Demolished
Cost: Free
Directions: One block south of Cermak Rd., one block east of State St.

A man's home is his fortress.

Capone had a bungalow built on the South Side where he ended up living for 11 years, from 1922 to 1933. Its commonplace exterior doesn't hint at its fortresslike amenities, such as solid cement walls and steel doors. If, as his business card claimed, he was a "Second-Hand Furniture Dealer," he sure was security conscious.

Capone Home, 7244 S. Prairie Ave., Chicago, IL 60619

Private phone

Hours: Always visible

Cost: Free

Directions: Four blocks east of State St. at 72nd St.

Al opened an office on two floors of the Metropole Hotel, across the street from the Four Deuces, and kept regular business hours on Sundays. Capone had a corner suite on the fourth floor, and to be on the safe side his high-backed chair was bulletproofed. By 1925, at age 26, he was running a 1,000-person operation and earning $300,000 a week. That was a lot of money back then.

The city of Chicago demolished the Metropole just before the 1968 Democratic Convention. Some people tried to get Capone's Prairie Ave-

nue home designated a national historic landmark, but the city and Italian American groups put the kibosh on that. The Sons of Italy claimed that naming Capone's home as historic would "assist in the stereotyping and defamation of all Italian Americans," or at least the ones who were not Mob members already.

Metropole Hotel, 2300 S. Michigan Ave., Chicago, IL 60616
No phone
Hours: Demolished
Cost: Free
Directions: Two blocks east of State St., one block south of Cermak Rd.

Al Capone's Suburban Headquarters

Most city folk reach a point when the rat race starts to get to them and they move to the suburbs. Al Capone was no exception. When the mayor turned up the heat in 1923, the Mob moved to Cicero. Scarface took up residence in the Hawthorne Inn while still keeping his place on the South Side. Capone's brother Ralph ran the Cotton Club (5342 W. 22nd St.), four blocks away.

The Hawthorne Inn wasn't exactly quieter than the city—Hymie Weiss's crew shot the place up with 1,000-plus rounds on September 20, 1926—but at least Al could find parking. Capone controlled the Hawthorne Racecourse and bought a controlling interest in the Cicero newspaper, the *Cicero Tribune*, after crusading editor Robert St. John called for the Mob to get out of town. St. John resigned after he learned of his new boss's identity.

But not all was perfect in suburbia. Al's brother Frank was accidentally shot and killed by undercover officers near the Cotton Club. The police were trying to prevent ballot stuffing in Cicero's 1924 election, as if that was even possible.

Capone moved his operations back to Chicago in 1927 after the election of Republican William "Big Bill" Thompson, Chicago's most crooked mayor. The Hawthorne Inn was later renamed the Towne Hotel, which burned down on February 17, 1970.

Hawthorne Inn, 4833 W. Cermak Rd., Cicero, IL 60804
No phone
Hours: Gone
Cost: Free
Directions: One block west of Cicero Ave. on Cermak Rd. (22nd St.).

Geraldo Goes Digging

Al Capone set up his new Chicago offices on the fourth floor, suite 430, of the Lexington Hotel, where he worked until the day he was indicted on tax charges. Rumor had it the mobster had buried loot in the Lexington's basement, bricked in behind a false wall. Everyone in Chicago knew the rumor, including the Mob, yet Geraldo Rivera thought he'd be the one to crack the mystery.

Geraldo chose to open the vault on a two-hour live TV special on April 21, 1986. He sang "Chicago," fired a Thompson submachine gun, and detonated sticks of dynamite. After an hour and a half of this tedious buildup, a minibulldozer crashed through the basement wall. Geraldo rushed in, cameras rolling, to find only a couple of empty bottles. No loot, no skeletons, no aged whiskey. It almost ruined his career, but sadly it didn't. The city later demolished the Lexington in the months leading up to the 1996 Democratic National Convention.

Lexington Hotel, 2135 S. Michigan Ave., Chicago, IL 60616

No phone

Hours: Demolished

Cost: Free

Directions: At the northeast corner of Cermak Rd. and Michigan Ave.

St. Valentine's Day Massacre

Al Capone picked a memorable day in 1929 to gun down seven of George "Bugs" Moran's men. He had hoped to get Bugs, too, but, as Elmer Fudd knows, that ain't easy.

While dressed as policemen, four of Capone's men raided Moran's liquor warehouse at the SMC Cartage Company on Clark Street. Moran's hoods thought it was a real bust and stood up against the wall as ordered. Seventy-something rat-a-tat-tats later, five thugs, a dentist, and a mechanic were dead, or nearly so. The only survivor, Frank Gusenberg, claimed, "Nobody shot me," to the first police on the scene, then died from his non–bullet holes. Moran was almost one of the victims, but when he saw the (fake) police cruiser drive up, he headed in the other direction.

At the time all this was happening, Capone was busy making himself overly visible, and therefore incredibly guilty, in Miami. Bugs Moran knew better: "Only Capone kills like that."

Rat-a-tat-tat! Happy Valentine's Day!

The city tore down the garage in 1967, and 417 of the bullet-ridden bricks were sold to a Canadian developer. He had them installed in the men's bathroom of the Banjo Palace karaoke bar in Vancouver. When the place closed, individual bricks were offered online for $1,000 each. The price seemed a bit high; no bricks were sold.

Today, the massacre site is a parking lot. Some claim to hear moans near the murder location. Others say dogs won't go near it, or freak out if they do.

SMC Cartage Company, 2122 N. Clark St., Chicago, IL 60614

No phone

Hours: None (torn down; now a private parking lot)

Cost: Free

Directions: One block north of Armitage Ave., just west of Lincoln Park.

Al Capone's Grave, Julia the Uncorruptable, and the Whirling DiSalvos

The end for Al Capone was far from glamorous. After being convicted of income tax evasion on October 17, 1931, Capone was sentenced to 11 years

in federal prison. He served time in Atlanta, Georgia, and Alcatraz, where other mobsters referred to him as the "Wop with the Mop." Capone was released in 1939, partially paralyzed from advanced syphilis, and went off to Miami to die. His final days were spent fishing off his dock and drooling into his bathrobe.

Scarface was originally buried on the South Side at Mount Olivet Cemetery (2755 W. 111th St., the same cemetery that holds Mrs. O'Leary), where a monument still stands, but his body was moved to Hillside in 1950 to discourage body snatchers. At his family plot at Mount Carmel, only his headstone has been stolen . . . twice. Scarface's fans often leave offerings at his grave, such as coins, cigars, and cans of nonbootleg beer.

While you're at Mount Carmel, look for the nearby grave of Julia Buccola Petta, a woman who died in childbirth in 1921. Her monument is topped with a bride in a wedding dress and has a picture of Petta in her coffin. If you can't read Italian, the caption says the photo was taken six years after her death. Julia was dug up at her mother Filomena's request after she had strange dreams of Julia being buried alive. Julia was indeed dead, but she had not rotted at all! (The child who had died and been buried with her had decomposed.) Some claim you can smell the scent of roses near her grave, even in the dead of winter, proof of her "uncorruptability."

Another strange plot at Mount Carmel is that of the DiSalvo family. Life-sized reproductions of Angelo and Rosa DiSalvo and their three children were carved in marble—nothing particularly weird there—but then the whole tableau was mounted on a spinning turntable. Visitors can turn the monument to face any direction they please, which is perfect for photographers.

Mount Carmel Cemetery, 1400 S. Wolf Rd., Hillside, IL 60162

Phone: (630) 449-8300

Hours: Daily 9 AM–5 PM

Cost: Free

Website: www.catholiccemeterieschicago.org/locations.php?id=11

Directions: West of Wolf Rd., north of Roosevelt Rd.; Capone, turn right from Roosevelt Rd. gate, six markers down on the right, behind shrubs (Section 35); Julia, Section A; DiSalvo family, Section 19.

OTHER GANGSTERS BURIED IN MOUNT CARMEL

⇒ **Angelo "Bloody Angelo" Genna:** Hit man for the Genna bootleg gang. Dion O'Banion's henchmen (led by Bugs Moran) shotgunned Genna on May 25, 1925, as he drove out to Oak Park, looking to buy a home. Genna ran into a lamppost on the corner of Ogden and Hudson Avenues (which crossed at the time) and bled to death at the scene.

⇒ **Antonio "Tony the Gent" Genna:** Advisor to the Genna bootleg gang. Tony was shot five times in the back on July 8, 1925, while talking to Giuseppe "The Cavalier" Nerone outside a grocery store.

⇒ **Mike "The Devil" Genna:** Hit man for the Genna bootleg gang. The Devil was shot by police on Western Avenue during a high-speed chase. He died after kicking the ambulance attendant who was trying to stop the bleeding from Genna's femoral artery.

⇒ **Sam "Mooney" Giancana:** Head of the Chicago Outfit from 1957 to 1966. Linked by some to the assassination of JFK, Giancana was shot in the back of the head on June 19, 1975, while cooking sausages in the basement of his Oak Park home (1147 S. Wenonah Ave.).

⇒ **Jake Lingle:** Corrupt *Chicago Tribune* reporter. Lingle was executed near the Randolph Street Station (in the pedway beneath Michigan Ave.).

⇒ **Antonio "The Scourge" Lombardo:** Capone's pick for the head of the Unione Siciliana. Lombardo was killed in one of the Mob's boldest hits: in broad daylight at the corner of Dearborn and Madison Streets on September 7, 1928. The rush-hour crowd allowed his killers to move in and kill him at point-blank range.

- ➡ **"Machine Gun" Jack McGurn:** Coordinator of the Valentine's Day Massacre for Al Capone. McGurn was killed on Valentine's Day in 1936 as payback. It happened at the Avenue Recreation Rooms (805 N. Milwaukee Ave.). A valentine card was left on his chest that read, "You've lost your job/You've lost your dough/Your jewels and handsome houses/But things could be worse, you know/You haven't lost your trousers."

- ➡ **Frank "The Enforcer" Nitti:** Replaced Capone as head of the Chicago Mob. Nitti shot himself along the railroad tracks near Harlem and Cermak Avenues in North Riverside on March 19, 1943.

- ➡ **Dion "Deanie" O'Banion:** Rival of Capone's. Deanie was gunned down on November 10, 1924, in his Schofield's Flower Shop (738 N. State St.) across the street from Chicago's Holy Name Cathedral.

- ➡ **Earl "Hymie" Weiss:** Tried to kill Al Capone three times. Hymie was shot on the steps of Holy Name Cathedral (735 N. State St.) on October 11, 1926. There's still a bullet hole in the cornerstone.

The Al Capone Experience

Since the repeal of Prohibition, things haven't been the same for the Mob. Sure, there's gambling and prostitution and drugs and fixed contracts from friends at City Hall, but the glamour is all gone. Well, almost all gone. If you want the experience of drinking in a 1920s roadhouse, head out to Al Capone's Hideaway in St. Charles. Regardless of the name, this place never was Al Capone's hideaway, though it does try to faithfully re-create a joint of the era . . . minus the possibility that G-men will kick in the door and haul you away in a paddy wagon. During Prohibition this place was a speakeasy, but the Mob wasn't involved; rival gangs suspected the others were supplying the booze served here, but its owners were bootleggers who had a still behind their chicken coop out back.

Today the main floor is a restaurant while the speakeasy, where you can hear live jazz on Saturday nights, is upstairs. And the Hideaway is just one part of a larger enterprise that includes products such as Bootleggers Cigars, Tommy Guns Vodka, and Al Capone's Warehouse, an online store hawking all things gangster.

Al Capone's Hideaway & Steak House, 35W337 Riverside Dr., St. Charles, IL 60174

Phone: (888) SCARFACE

Hours: Monday–Friday 5–10 PM, Saturday 4–11 PM, Sunday 4–9 PM

Cost: Meals $8–$20

Website: www.al-capone.com

Directions: West off Rte. 25 to Weber Rd., then north and follow the signs.

Untouchable Tours

If you want to see Mob sites but are not good with maps—and you're not self-conscious about riding around in a black bus filled with bullet holes—let Untouchable Tours do the work for you. Far from a stuffy, academic guided tour, Untouchables is a two-hour, nonstop show on wheels, complete with sing-alongs, fake gunfire, raffles, and a few surprises.

Before departing, you're advised to behave by the costumed driver and tour guide, and since they're the ones with the fake guns, you listen.

Get on the bus . . . or else!

The bus rolls along past 17 different sites while the thugs relay all the gory details interspersed with vaudeville banter. Between sights you're treated to Italian opera, card tricks, and a "reenactment" of the Great Chicago Fire, and you're given pointers on dodging bullets.

"Southside" Alton Craig has been running the tours for 20 years, and interest shows no sign of waning. It's the perfect afternoon diversion for out-of-towners and is even appreciated by those not on the tour; you'll see bystanders on the sidewalk getting into the act by laughing, pointing, and machine-gunning the bus through participatory mime. It's all part of the fun, and, let's face it, gangsters are F-U-N!

Tour Departure Site, 600 N. Clark St., Chicago, IL 60643

Phone: (773) 881-1195

Hours: Check website

Cost: Adults $30 per person

Website: www.gangstertour.com

Directions: Bus departs from Ohio and Clark Sts., next to the McDonald's.

Tommy Gun's Garage

Untouchable Tours might not be your thing. Perhaps you like the style of the Mob era but think it should be set to music. You do have an option: Tommy Gun's Garage. This gangster dinner theater lays on the atmosphere pretty thick, from the moment "Gloves" meets you at the door with machine gun in hand and asks for the password. Have no fear—as long as you have a valid ticket, you'll be admitted. Your waitstaff will engage in speakeasy shtick as you order "Frankie's Feast" (pork chops), Big Jim Colosimo (lasagna), or Don't Call Me Chicken (turns out it's chicken). Once you've been served, the show begins, complete with vaudeville banter, dancing flappers, and even a little gunfire. But be forewarned, this is interactive dinner theater, so you might be pulled up onstage.

Be sure to bring your camera—Tommy Gun's has a 1928 Model A Ford and a re-created St. Valentine's Day Massacre wall where you can pose either pre- or post-machine-gunning. Every February 14 they faithfully re-create the murders in a special show for hopeless romantics. This place hosts a lot of corporate outings and tour groups, but they also see the occasional school field trip. Crime doesn't pay, kiddos, though crime theater apparently does.

2114 S. Wabash Ave., Chicago, IL 60616

Phone: (800) 461-0178 or (773) RAT-A-TAT

Hours: Check website

Cost: $60–$70 per person

Website: www.tommygunsgarage.com

Directions: One block north of Cermak Rd., one block west of Michigan Ave.

Jack Ruby's Grave

Long before he became an assassin's assassin, Jack Ruby was a small-time hustler in Chicago. He changed his name from Jack Rubenstein to "fit in" better with Capone's crowd. Ruby's primary activity was to run numbers for the South Side Mob.

Ruby went on to, if not greater, perhaps more notorious endeavors. Millions watched him kill Lee Harvey Oswald on live TV, supposedly to spare Jackie the agony of recounting her husband's murder. He died of cancer while awaiting execution, cancer that Oliver Stone types think was induced to ensure his silence.

Well, silent he is, six feet under in his old hometown. You can also find Gene Siskel in this same cemetery, as well as the founder of the Harlem Globetrotters, Abe Saperstein.

Westlawn Cemetery, 7801 W. Montrose Ave., Chicago, IL 60634

Phone: (773) 625-8600

Hours: Daily 9 AM–5 PM

Cost: Free

Website: http://westlawnjewishfunerals.com

Directions: Six blocks west of Harlem.

John Dillinger Death Site

Public Enemy #1 finally bought the farm on July 22, 1934, after sitting through the movie *Manhattan Melodrama* with Polly Hamilton, his girlfriend, and her friend Anna Sage. Dillinger had recently undergone plastic surgery and was living with Hamilton under the alias Jimmy Lawrence at 2420 North Halsted Street. Hamilton later claimed she thought he worked at the Chicago Board of Trade.

Sage, a brothel madam and Romanian immigrant who feared deportation, ratted on Dillinger to Melvin Purvis's FBI team as a way to curry favor

with the feds. (It didn't work; they deported her after Dillinger was dead.) She informed the team that her trio would be at the Biograph Theater that night; when they exited, 16 agents moved in. Dillinger made a run for the alley to the south. Three bullets hit Dillinger in the back, head, and side, killing him immediately. Two moviegoers were also shot, though neither seriously.

Rumors circulated that a woman dressed in red had fingered Dillinger. However, Sage was wearing an orange skirt and Hamilton had on a tan ensemble. Nevertheless, the story of the Woman in Red continues.

Crowds flocked to daub some of Dillinger's blood off the street. A helpful bystander mixed soda water from a nearby bar with the blood to make it go further for the handkerchief-toting ghouls. In the following weeks, many more bloodied handkerchiefs were sold around Chicago than could have ever been dipped in the blood.

Dillinger's body was placed on public view at the Cook County Morgue, where 15,000 filed past his body. A photo taken that night was the origin of the 14-inch penis (20 inches erect) rumor. Rigor mortis had caused his arm, not his penis, to push up the sheet around his groin. Some news photographs were altered for modesty's sake.

Several students from a "college of embalming" stopped by the morgue to make a death mask, but FBI agents confiscated the cast when they realized the group had no credentials. Dillinger's brain was removed and reportedly sent to Northwestern University for study. From there it ended up on a shelf in Kearney, Nebraska, or in the hands of Jimmy Hoffa, depending on whom you believe. Dillinger's brain was definitely missing before his body arrived in Indiana. The family threatened to sue, but the FBI assured them it had been put to good use in a "scientific study."

The Biograph's exterior looks much like it did when Dillinger was shot, though the interior is now a live theater. Some have claimed you can still see his ghost on the anniversary of his death in the alley just south of the entrance, today known as Dillinger's Alley.

Victory Gardens Biograph Theater, 2433 N. Lincoln Ave., Chicago, IL 60614
Phone: (773) 549-5788
Hours: Always visible
Cost: Free
Website: www.victorygardens.org
Directions: One block north of Fullerton Ave., west of Halsted St.

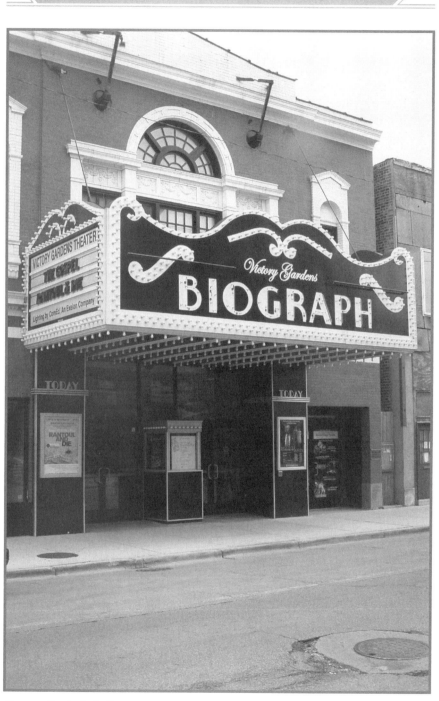

Beware the Lady in Orange.

WAS THAT REALLY DILLINGER?

Some conspiracy theorists believe that Dillinger was not gunned down outside the Biograph, but the victim was instead small-time Wisconsin thug Jimmy Lawrence. Consider that Dillinger's autopsy wasn't released until 30 years after his death, perhaps for good reason:

→ The body at the morgue was shorter and heavier than Dillinger's body.

→ The body at the morgue had brown eyes, but Dillinger's were blue.

→ The body's heart showed damage from rheumatic fever, though Dillinger never had the disease.

→ Two of Dillinger's telltale scars had mysteriously vanished from his body.

The real Jimmy Lawrence disappeared, coincidentally, the day of Dillinger's shooting. Could Anna Sage have arranged a date with Lawrence to give Dillinger an out? J. Edgar Hoover or his agents might have been too embarrassed to admit they had made a terrible mistake, so they perpetrated an elaborate hoax.

So where did Dillinger end up, if in fact he survived? The most popular legend says he married and moved to Oregon where he died or disappeared sometime during the 1940s.

John Dillinger Museum

True, this destination isn't in Illinois, but it might as well be—it's just over the border, and nobody on a Mob Mania Tour should pass it up on a technicality. Sponsored by the Lake County Convention and Visitors Bureau, this fascinating hands-on collection is probably the most entertaining museum around. Surprisingly, the curators are not shy about their county's associa-

tion with the most embarrassing tale in the Dillinger saga, the Crown Point jailbreak, but give accurate and complete information, even if it hurts.

The museum is arranged chronologically according to Dillinger's life. You start by visiting John's early years on the farm, then BAM! you're in prison. The small cell and looped recording of an angry guard have a distinctly Oz-like feel. Judge for yourself whether Dillinger's sentence fit the Mooresville crime with an interactive game. Once in prison, see the faces of the Terror Gang formed in Michigan City.

Next, follow the gang's crime spree as a witness to the East Chicago holdup—see how many details you can remember after staring down the barrel of a gun. Check out the 1933 Essex Terraplane, Dillinger's getaway car of choice. And see a replica of the wooden gun that fooled Crown Point officials. (The original gun is part of the museum's collection but is too valuable to put on display.)

Do you think a life of crime might be a glamorous career option? Think again—the next exhibit is an FBI lab where you are fingerprinted and booked. View the aftermath of the Little Bohemia shootout, and the bloody end for Dillinger and the gang. The final, shocking displays include Dillinger's "pants of death," a bleeding wax dummy of him on the Cook County Morgue's autopsy slab, and the undertaker's basket used to transport his body.

Scattered throughout the museum are dummies of other Depression-era hoodlums, including Pretty Boy Floyd, Baby Face Nelson, Ma Barker, and Bonnie and Clyde, all of whom would die of acute lead poisoning.

7770 Corinne Dr., Hammond, IN 46323
Phone: (219) 989-7979
Hours: Daily 10 AM–4 PM
Cost: Adults $4, seniors (55+) $3, kids (6–12) $2
Website: www.dillingermuseum.com
Directions: Take the Kennedy Ave. exit south from I-80/94, turn right at the first light.

Baby Face Nelson's Final Shootout, Death Site, and Grave

George "Baby Face" Nelson became Public Enemy #1 after his former gangmate Dillinger was killed outside the Biograph Theater. His ranking on the FBI list didn't last very long. Nelson, his wife, Helen, and fellow criminal John Paul Chase were ambushed by agents near Lake Geneva, Wisconsin, on November 27, 1934. They escaped and were chased into Illinois, exchanging gunfire with police as they fled toward Chicago at high speeds.

Near Barrington, Nelson's fuel pump was shot out, and he turned his car into the entrance to what is now Langendorf Park. The G-men skidded past the road, stopped, hopped out of their car, and were promptly gunned down by the gangsters. FBI agents Herman Hollis (the agent who had shot John Dillinger four months earlier) and Samuel Cowley were killed, but not before pumping seventeen rounds into Nelson. Chase loaded Nelson's body into the FBI car and escaped with Nelson's wife.

A stone monument to the two slain FBI agents, and another who Nelson had killed the previous April in Koerner's Corners, Wisconsin, stands near the site of the shootout.

Langendorf Park, 235 Lions Dr., Barrington, IL 60010
Phone: (847) 381-0687
Hours: Always visible
Cost: Free
Directions: South of Rte. 14, three blocks east of Rte. 59.

Nelson was likely killed in Barrington, but his body didn't turn up until the following day, miles away near a cemetery in Skokie. His nude body was wrapped in a blanket and dumped in a ditch adjoining St. Paul's Cemetery. Helen Gillis and John Paul Chase abandoned the FBI car in Winnetka, then fled in opposite directions.

5400 W. Conrad St., Skokie, IL 60077
No phone
Hours: Always visible
Cost: Free
Directions: Adjacent to St. Paul's Cemetery on the southwest corner of Conrad St. and Long Ave., three blocks south of Dempster St., one block west of Lockwood Ave.

St. Paul's felt no special obligation to bury Nelson just because he was dumped there. Nelson was instead buried in St. Joseph's Cemetery in River Grove under his birth name, Lester Gillis. Helen Gillis was apprehended in Michigan, and Chase was picked up in California.

St. Joseph's Cemetery, 3100 N. Thatcher, River Grove, IL 60171
Phone: (708) 453-0184
Hours: Daily 9 AM–5 PM
Cost: Free
Website: www.catholiccemeterieschicago.org/locations.php?id=29
Directions: At the intersection of Thatcher/Cumberland Ave. and Belmont Ave.

7

EPiLOGUE

s you can imagine, many forces work against the survival of roadside oddities: pissed-off neighbors, competing attractions, culture Nazis, Mother Nature, the Grim Reaper, and simple, basic economics.

Some sites were always fleeting blips on the tourism radar, destined for destruction before they were even opened. Most of Chicago's 1893 Columbian Exposition buildings were built of plaster. They included the Panorama of Kilauea, an erupting Hawaiian volcano with simulated lava, an electrified Egyptian Temple, a Mammoth Crystal Cave, the world's first Ferris wheel, and a lagoon filled with Venetian gondolas, Viking war ships, and a replica of Columbus's *Santa Maria*. The plaster lasted long enough to burn up in a mysteriously convenient conflagration on January 8, 1894, at the end of the Expo.

The 1933 Century of Progress was equally fleeting. Madame Tussaud animated her Torture Chamber so visitors could witness people being stretched, roasted, and hacked to pieces. P. T. Barnum's American Museum re-created Barnum, Tom Thumb, the Fat Lady, and the original Siamese Twins with freakish robots. The 23-story Sky Ride took you up to see the Loop skyline in an RV-sized rocket belching simulated exhaust! But it was all torn down to make way for Meigs Field, a dinky airport that served literally dozens of airplanes a day. Mayor Daley eventually bulldozed the worthless airport in the middle of the night in 2003. What a waste.

Many roadside attractions survive only on the health and good fortune of their proprietors. Norvina Thatch built a Whirligig Garden in Future City, just north of Cairo, but it was torn down shortly after Thatch died. Similar was the fate of Aldo Piacenza's Birdhouse Garden in Highwood, but instead of bulldozers, his elaborate creations were cleared by folk art dealers and collectors.

Other places just go out of business. You used to be able to take a gondola ride on the Des Plaines River after enjoying a dinner at Wheeling's Villa Venice. No more. Do you like airline food but can't stand flying? If Chicago's Ski-Hi Drive-In were still open, you'd be able to dine in the fuselage of an airliner atop its roof. The Midget's Club on Chicago's South Side once catered to the little person's needs. No Dwarf Tossing or Midget Bowling, just proportional barstools, chairs, and tables. But that's gone, too.

Still others have packed up and left town. The Bicycle Museum once housed in Chicago's North Pier moved to Ohio. The 1,500-piece holy relic collection at Peoria's St. Francis Monastery closed when its clerical order relocated to Indiana. Did Galena Wax Museum's 50-odd Civil War figures end up as candles in the town's knickknack shops after the museum shuttered its doors? Perhaps. And who even knows what happened to Evanston's Museum of Funeral Service Artifacts, the life-sized Bigfoot replica on display at a resort in Oilfield, or the World's Largest Black Velvet Elvis that once hung in Chicago's World Tattoo Gallery?

The first edition of *Oddball Illinois* had a photo of Berwyn's iconic *Spindle* on its cover, eight full-sized cars jammed on a spike in the Cermak Plaza parking lot. It was taken down in 2008 to make room for a Walgreens. A Walgreens. In suburban Chicago, where there's a Walgreens on every third corner. Smooth move.

Do you get the picture? Nothing lasts forever. I didn't write this book to have you sit on the couch and imagine what it would be like to visit these places. You have to see them for yourself. Fill up your gas tank and hit the road TODAY, while these weird wonders are still around.

ACKNOWLEDGMENTS

This book would not have been possible without the assistance, patience, and good humor of many individuals. My thanks go out to the following people for allowing me to interview them about their roadside attractions: Mrs. LaRae Ackerson (Rest Cottage), John Aranza (Horrorbles), Jack Barker (Sculpture Park), Carrie Brantley (Egyptian Theatre), Christen Carter (Busy Beaver Button Museum), Suzan Cook (Carlock Cemeteries), "Southside" Alton Craig (Untouchable Tours), Phyllis Danner (Sousa Library), Dave Dardis (Dave's Secret Garden), Gail Donze (Friendship Shoe Fence), David Douglass (Dave's Down to Earth Rock Shop), Sandy and Mike Dunphy (the Barn B&B), Ted Frankel (Uncle Fun), Jan Gallimore (Lake County Museum), Mike Gassmann (World's Largest Catsup Bottle), Denise Gibson (Busy Beaver Button Company), Deborah Gust (Curt Teich Postcard Archives), Rich Henry (Henry's Ra66it Ranch), Margery Hinrichs (Ida Public Library), Heather Holbus (Intuit), Richard Jenkins (Lincoln-Douglas Valentine Museum), Cynthia Kallile (Meatloaf Bakery), Jerzy Kenar (*Shit Fountain*), Wayne Lensing (Historic Auto Attractions), Tony Lupo (Pert's Antique Fabricare Museum), Scott Maruna (Mad Gasser of Mattoon), Callie McKenna (Evergreen Memorial Cemetery), Cookie Oppedisano (Hala Kahiki), Richard Pollard (Pollard's Collection), Robert Rea (Old Franklin County Jail Museum), Judy Robins and Patrick Sim (the Wood Library-Museum of Anesthesiology), Richard Sklenar (Theatre Historical Society of America), Spinach Can Collectibles (Popeye Town), Ed Stockey (Midwest Carver's Museum), Joe Swiatek (Imperial Hardware), Helen and Roy Tuttle (Moonshine Burgers), Jim Warfield (Raven's Grin Inn), Greg Warmack (Mr. Imagination's Grotto), and Mary Ann Warmack (Alton Museum of History and Art).

For research assistance, I am indebted to the librarians in the Illinois communities of Belvidere, East Dubuque, Highwood, Lincolnshire, New-

ton, Mt. Sterling, Sparta, and White Hall. Ken Little was kind enough to review my Chicago Fire material, and I would not have found him without the help of Chris Greve. Also, John Cieciel and the mysterious Tony Shaia have pointed me in the direction of more than a few interesting and out-of-the-way sites.

Friends, family members, and complete strangers willingly volunteered to act as models for the photographs in this book, oftentimes against their better judgment: Jenny Birmingham, John Birmingham, T. J. Birmingham, "Southside" Alton Craig, Tirza Ernst, Tony Fernandez, Ted Frankel, James Frost, Olga Granat, Tom Granat, Kyle Granat, Taylor Granat, Ann Grusdis, Stephanie Herbek, Eugene Marceron, Mike Musick, Pat O'Brien, Joe Pohlen, Pam Pohlen, Joey Pohlen, Zak Pohlen, Samantha Pohlen, Michael "Shifty" Rubin, Mary Ann Schultz, Tess Shea, Karen Soll, Ed Stockey, Lorraine Swanson, Jim Warfield, and John Wiener. Jim Pohlen, Teresa Pohlen, Matthew Pohlen, Eric Pohlen, and Daniel Pohlen would have gladly confronted the Devil Baby of Hull House had they not been buried by the New Year's Blizzard of 1999. On my travels, I appreciated the hospitality of Curt and Amy Himstedt and Dave Michalak and Elizabeth Wangler.

Without the early support I received for *Cool Spots*, this book would not have been written. Steven Svymberky, Patience Allen, Lee Azus, Mark Maynard, Chuck Shepherd, Lorraine Swanson, Liz Clayton, and R. Seth Friedman gave me that encouragement.

To those at Chicago Review Press who made this edition a reality—Kelly Wilson, Jon Hahn, Allison Felus, and Mary Kravenas—my great thanks. To all those at CRP who have built and supported the Oddball series over the years—Lisa Rosenthal, Lisa Reardon, Gerilee Hundt, Curt Matthews, Linda Matthews, Rita Baladad, Kathy Mirkin, Drew Hamrick, and Mel Kupfer—I can't thank you enough. But most especially, I want to thank my longtime editor, Cynthia Sherry, who has championed my books from the beginning. You are the patron saint of oddballs everywhere.

To my WBEZ doppelganger, Gianofer Fields, who helped bring *Cool Spots* to air, I enjoyed our road trips more than you can imagine. To Cate Cahan and Steve Edwards, my thanks as well. And to Danielle Montana and John Terendy, who knows, it may happen yet!

Finally, I wish to thank Robert Johnson, Gordon Wells, Bonnie Papke, Kathy Royer, and my parents, Joseph and Barbara Pohlen.

RECOMMENDED SOUrCES

*I*f you'd like to learn more about the places and individuals in this book, the following are excellent sources.

Introduction

General Illinois Guides: *Chicago on Foot*, fifth edition, by Ira J. Bach and Susan Wolfson (Chicago Review Press, 1994); *Awesome Almanac: Illinois* by Jean F. Blashfield (B&B Publishing, 1993); *Illinois Curiosities* by Richard Moreno (Globe Pequot, 2011); *The Illinois Road Guide to Haunted Locations* by Chad Lewis and Terry Fisk (Unexplained Research, 2007); *The I-Files* by Jay Rath (Trails Books, 1999); *Daytrip Illinois* by Lee N. Godley and Patricia M. O'Rourke (Aphelion Publishing, 2000); *Illinois Historical Tour Guide* by D. Ray Wilson (Crossroads Communications, 1991); *Great Little Museums of the Midwest* by Christine Des Garrenes (Trails Books, 2002).

1. Chicago! Chicago!

General Chicago Guides: *City of the Century* by Donald L. Miller (Touchstone, 1996); *Metro Chicago Almanac* by Don Hayner and Tom McNamee (Bonus Books, 1993); *Wild Chicago* by Will Clinger, Mindy Bell, and Harvey Moshman (Globe Pequot, 2005); *Illinois Off the Beaten Path*, seventh edition, by Bob Puhala (Globe Pequot, 2003); *Hands-On Chicago* by Kenan Heise and Mark Frazel (Bonus Books, 1987); *Greater Chicago Historical Tour Guide* by D. Ray Wilson (Crossroads Communications, 1989).

Chicago Architecture: *Chicago's Famous Buildings* by Franz Schulze and Kevin Harrington (University of Chicago, 2003); *Pocket Guide to Chicago Architecture* by Judith Paine McBrien (Norton, 1997).

The *Raisin in the Sun* House: *To Be Young, Gifted, and Black* by Lorraine Hansberry (Signet Classics, 2011).

The Playboy Mansion: *Inside the Playboy Mansion* by Gretchen Edgren (General Publishing Group, 1998).

Banksy: *Wall and Piece* by Banksy (Random House, 2007).

The Chicago Historical Society: *What George Wore and Sally Didn't* by Rosemary K. Adams (Chicago Historical Society, 1998).

The Field Museum: *The Lions of Tsavo* by Bruce Patterson (McGraw-Hill, 2004); *The Man-eaters of Tsavo* by J. H. Patterson (St. Martin's, 1986; first published in London in 1907 by Macmillan).

Willie Dixon: *I Am the Blues* by Willie Dixon (Da Capo, 1990).

The Union Stock Yards: *The Jungle, Complete and Unabridged* by Upton Sinclair (Wilder, 2010; first published in 1906 by Doubleday, Page); *Chicago's Pride* by Louise Carroll Wade (University of Illinois, 2002).

Adolph Luetgert: *Alchemy of Bones* by Robert Loerzel (University of Illinois, 2003).

Oscar Meyer Wienermobile: *Dog Days* by Dave Ehlenfeld (Sterling, 2011).

Chicago and Hollywood: *Hollywood on Lake Michigan* by Arnie Berenstein (Lake Claremont, 1998).

Essanay Studios: *Broncho Billy and the Essanay Film Company* by David Kiehn (Farwell Books, 2003).

Bob Newhart: *Hi Bob!* by Joey Green (St. Martin's, 1996).

The Chicago Fire: *The Great Chicago Fire* by Ross Miller (University of Illinois, 1990); *The Great Chicago Fire and the Myth of Mrs. O'Leary's Cow* by Richard Bales (McFarland, 2002); *The Great Chicago Fire* by David Lowe (Dover, 1979); *Smoldering City* by Karen Sawislak (University of Chicago, 1995); *Mrs. O'Leary's Comet!* by Mel Waskin (Academy Chicago, 1985).

Iroquois Theater Fire: *Chicago Death Trap* by Nat Brandt (Southern Illinois University, 2006); *Tinder Box* by Anthony Hatch (Academy Chicago, 2003).

Our Lady of the Angels Fire: *To Sleep with the Angels* by David Cowan and John Kuenster (Ivan R. Dee, 1996); *The Fire That Will Not Die* by Michelle McBride (ETC, 1979).

Heat Wave of 1995: *Heat Wave* by Eric Klineberg (University of Chicago, 2003).

The Haymarket Riot: *Haymarket Revisited* by William J. Adelman (Illinois Labor History Society, 1986); *Death in the Haymarket* by James Green (Anchor, 2007).

Herman Mudgett and the Murder Castle: *Devil in the White City* by Erik Larson (Crown, 2003); *Depraved* by Harold Schechter (Pocket Books, 1994); *The Torture Doctor* by David Franke (Avon, 1975).

Eastland Disaster: *The Sinking of the Eastland* by Jay Bonansinga (Citadel Press, 2004).

U-505 Submarine: *Twenty Million Tons Under the Sea* by Daniel Gallery (Bluejacket Books, 2001); *U-505* by James Wise Jr. (US Naval Institute, 2005).

Opus Dei: *Opus Dei* by John Allen (Image, 2007); *Opus Dei* by Michael Walsh (Harper-One, 2004).

Chicago Ghosts: *Chicago Haunts*, revised edition, by Ursula Bielski (Lake Claremont, 1998); *Chicagoland Ghosts* by Dylan Clearfield (Thunder Bay, 1997).

Chris Farley: *The Chris Farley Show* by Tom Farley and Tanner Colby (Viking Adult, 2008).

Clarence Darrow: *Clarence Darrow* by John Farrell (Doubleday, 2011); *Clarence Darrow* by Andrew Kersten (Hill and Wang, 2011).

Chicago Cemeteries (General): *Graveyards of Chicago* by Matt Hucke and Ursula Bielski (Lake Claremont, 1999).

Camp Douglas: *To Die in Chicago* by George Levy (Pelican, 1999).

Graceland Cemetery: *A Walk Through Graceland Cemetery* by Barbara Lanctot (Chicago Architecture Foundation, 1988).

Birth of the Bomb: *The Manhattan Project* by Cynthia Kelly and Richard Rhodes (Black Dog and Leventhal, 2009).

2. Chicago Suburbs

McDonald's: *Grinding It Out* by Ray Kroc (St. Martin's, 1992); *McDonald's: Behind the Arches* by John Love (Bantam, 1995).

Frances Willard and the WCTU: *Frances Willard* by Ruth Bordin (University of North Carolina, 1986); *How I Learned to Ride the Bicycle* by Frances E. Willard (Fair Oaks, 1991).

Emma Goldman's Grave and the Haymarket Monument: *Nature's Choicest Spot* by the Historical Society of Oak Park and River Forest (Historical Society of Oak Park and River Forest, 1998); *Living My Life* by Emma Goldman (CreateSpace, 2011).

Resurrection Mary: *Resurrection Mary* by Kenan Heise (Chicago Historical Bookworks, 1990); *Resurrection Mary* by Troy Taylor (Whitechapel Productions, 2007).

Ernest Hemingway in Oak Park: *Ernest Hemingway: The Oak Park Legacy* edited by James Nagel (University of Alabama, 1996).

Frank Lloyd Wright: *Guide to Frank Lloyd Wright and Prairie School Architecture in Oak Park* by Paul Sprague (Chicago Review Press, 1986).

Bahá'í House of Worship: *An Earthly Paradise* by Julie Badiee (George Ronald, 1992).

3. Northern Illinois

Mary Todd Lincoln: *The Insanity File* by Mark E. Neeley Jr. and R. Gerald McMurtry (Southern Illinois University, 1986); *The Madness of Mary Lincoln* by Jason Emerson (Southern Illinois University, 2007); *Mary Todd Lincoln: A Biography* by Jean H. Baker (Norton, 1987).

Ronald Reagan: *Innocents at Home* by Garry Wills (Doubleday, 1987).

Woodland Palace: *Fred Francis and Woodland Palace* by Rosemary Kuster (M&D Printing, 1975).

W. D. Boyce and the Boy Scouts: *Boyce of Ottawa* by John F. Sullivan (Sigma, 1985).

Billy Graham: *Just As I Am* by Billy Graham (HarperSanFrancisco, 1997).

Zion: *Zion City, Illinois* by Philip L. Cook (Syracuse University, 1996).

4. Central Illinois

Rockome Gardens: *Rockome Sayings . . . and a Collection of Amusing Amish Dutch Expressions* by Elvan Yoder (Fahrenkrug Studios, 1970).

John Philip Sousa: *John Philip Sousa* by Paul Bierley (Warner Brothers Publications, 2001).

Greenwood Cemetery: *Where the Dead Walk* by Troy Taylor (Whitechapel Productions, 1997).

Lincoln Tourism: *In Lincoln's Footsteps* by Don Davenport (Prairie Oak, 1991); *Following in Lincoln's Footsteps* by Ralph Gary (Carroll and Graf, 2001).

The Mad Gasser of Mattoon: *The Mad Gasser of Mattoon* by Scott Maruna (Swamp Gas Books, 2003); *Rumor, Fear, and the Madness of Crowds* by J. P. Chaplin (Ballantine Books, 1959).

Wyatt Earp: *Wyatt Earp* by Casey Tefertiller (Wiley, 1999).

Route 66 in Illinois: *Traveling the New, Historic Route 66 of Illinois* by John Weiss (A. O. Motivation Programs, 1997).

Abraham Lincoln's Tomb: *The Tomb of Abraham Lincoln* by Bess Martin (Lincoln Souvenir and Gift Shop, 1941); *Stealing Lincoln's Body* by Thomas Craughwell (Belknap, 2008); *The Great Abraham Lincoln Hijack* by Bonnie Stahlman Speer (Reliance, 1997).

General Santa Anna: *A Glorious Defeat* by Timothy J. Henderson (Hill and Wang, 2008).

5. Southern Illinois

Cleopatra's Tomb: *The Mystery Cave of Many Faces* by Russell Burrows and Fred Rydholm (Superior Heartland, 1991).

Reverend Elijah Lovejoy: *Freedom's Champion, Elijah Lovejoy* by Paul Simon (Southern Illinois University, 1994).

The Piasa Bird: *The Curious Person's Guide to the History and Mystery of the Piasa Bird* by Scott Maruna (Swamp Gas Books, 2008); *The Piasa* by Ruth Means (Alton Council, date unknown).

Our Lady of the Snows: *National Shrine of Our Lady of the Snows* by the Missionary Oblates of Mary Immaculate (National Shrine of Our Lady of the Snows); *Messages from Our Heavenly Mother to Her Children* by Ray Doiron (People's Prayer Group, 1997).

Charlie Birger: *A Knight of Another Sort* by Gary DeNeal (Southern Illinois University, 1998).

R. Buckminster Fuller: *Buckminster Fuller's Universe* by Lloyd Sieden (Basic Books, 2000).

Popeye: *Popeye* by Fred Grandinetti (McFarland, 1994).

Cahokia Mounds: *Cahokia* by Timothy Pauketat (Penguin, 2010); *The Ancient Splendor of Prehistoric Cahokia* by Sidney Denny, Ernest Schusky, and John Adkins Richardson (Arressico, 1992).

6. Theme Tours

Sideshow Folk (General): *Very Special People* by Frederick Drimmer (Citadel, 1991).

Robert Wadlow: *Boy Giant* by Dan Brannan (Alton Museum of History and Art, 2003); *Looking Back and Up* by Sandra Hamilton (Alton Museum of History and Art, 1996).

Deaf Bill: *Modern Mummies* by Christine Quigley (McFarland, 1998).

Museum of Science and Industry: *Inventive Genius* by Jay Pridmore (Museum of Science and Industry, 1996).

Devil Baby of Hull House: *Twenty Years at Hull House* by Jane Addams (MacMillan, 1910).

Robert Earl Hughes: *Robert Earl Hughes* by Scott Maruna (Swamp Gas Books, 2008).

Chicago Crime and the Mob: *The Outfit* by Gus Russo (Bloomsbury, 2001); *Murder City* by Michael Lesy (Norton, 2008); *Return to the Scene of the Crime* by Richard Lindberg (Cumberland House, 1999); *Murder and Mayhem on Chicago's South Side* by Troy Taylor (History Press, 2009); *The Wicked City* by Curt Johnson (Da Capo, 1998), *Chicago by Gaslight* by Richard Lindberg (Academy Chicago, 1996).

Al Capone: *Capone* by John Kobler (Da Capo, 2003); *Mr. Capone* by Robert J. Schoenberg (Quill, 1992); *Al Capone* by Rick Hornung (Park Lane, 1998).

St. Valentine's Day Massacre: *St. Valentine's Day Massacre* by William Helmer and Arthur Bilek (Cumberland House, 2006); *Chicago Valentines* by Jeffrey Gusfield (Chicago Review Press, 2012).

John Dillinger: *John Dillinger* by Dary Matera (Da Capo, 2005); *Dillinger* by G. Russell Girardin (Indiana University, 1994); *Dillinger: A Short and Violent Life* by Robert Cromie and Joseph Pinkston (Chicago Historical Bookworks, 1990).

Baby Face Nelson: *Baby Face Nelson* by Steve Nickel and William Helmer (Cumberland House, 2002).

INDEX BY City Name

Woodstock

    Elvira in Seat DD 113, 178

    Groundhog Day, 179

    Royal Victorian Manor, 179

    Woodstock Opera House, 178

Yale

    Mug Tree, 257

Zion

    Flat Earth Town, 179–81

    Shiloh House, 179–81

    Zion Historical Society, 179–81

INDEX BY Site Name